DIFFUSION OF INNOVATIVE ENERGY SERVICES

DIFFUSION OF INNOVATIVE ENERGY SERVICES

Consumers' Acceptance and Willingness to Pay

ANNA KOWALSKA-PYZALSKA

Department of Operations Research and Business Intelligence
Wrocław University of Science and Technology
Wrocław, Poland

ELSEVIER

ACADEMIC PRESS
An imprint of Elsevier

Academic Press is an imprint of Elsevier
125 London Wall, London EC2Y 5AS, United Kingdom
525 B Street, Suite 1650, San Diego, CA 92101, United States
50 Hampshire Street, 5th Floor, Cambridge, MA 02139, United States
The Boulevard, Langford Lane, Kidlington, Oxford OX5 1GB, United Kingdom

ISBN: 978-0-12-822882-1

For information on all Academic Press publications
visit our website at https://www.elsevier.com/books-and-journals

Publisher: Mica H. Haley
Acquisitions Editor: Kathryn Eryilmaz
Editorial Project Manager: Naomi Robertson
Production Project Manager: Selvaraj Raviraj
Cover Designer: Christian J. Bilbow

Typeset by VTeX

Contents

Biography

Anna Kowalska-Pyzalska—With an MSc in Management (2001), a PhD in Electrical Power Systems (2006), four years spent in the power industry (2006–2010), and a habilitation in Management Science (2019), she possesses unique expertise on the interface of energy markets and economics. Her most recent research interests include investigation of social acceptance of innovative energy services, such as smart meters or small-scale renewable generation, as well as of alternative fuel vehicles, such as battery electric ones. In addition to empirical studies, she is keen on the modeling of adoption rates and diffusion of innovation by means of agent-based simulation. She has published in top-tier journals (most notably in Renewable and Sustainable Energy Reviews, Energy Policy, Energy Reports, Information Processing & Management, Physica A, Energies, Telematics and Informatics) and is an ad-hoc reviewer for a number of journals listed in the Journal Citation Reports (JCR). She was an investigator on national and EU-funded projects and principal investigator of NCN (National Science Centre, Poland) grants.

Preface

Energy markets are currently evolving due to technological development, the growing amount of renewables at the lower voltage level, and the rapid digitization of processes. As consumers are becoming more central actors in energy markets through demand elasticity and new types of services, it is critical and inevitable to design solutions in a user-centered manner.

At the same time, contemporary trends in innovation management, such as open innovation or user-driven innovation approaches, make it clear that the customer is a vital component of any innovation—from the conception of a new product or service to its implementation in the market. As the researchers emphasize, the consumer should be treated as a key resource of any organization and as a co-creator of innovations. The consumer also appears in most models of innovation, because, as their creators argue, both observation of consumer attitudes and analysis of their behavior and its changes over time can become sources of innovation. Finally, the essence of the effectiveness of an innovation is its market validation, which is acceptance by demand. Lack of demand for new products not only is a barrier related to the implementation of innovations, but also can discourage a company from seeking new solutions and improvements.

These observations are particularly true for the energy market, which, due to its characteristics and the dynamics of change observed in recent decades, offers many innovations aimed at energy end-users. However, here the challenges are much greater than in markets for ordinary consumer goods, because of the specifics of this market, significantly differentiating it from markets for food, household goods, or cosmetics, for example. The energy market is technically, economically, and legally very complex. The ultimate consumers of it are consumers who only recently have been able to play an active role rather than just a passive one. Socio-economic changes, increased awareness of the need to protect the environment and climate, and the very strict requirements placed on the industry to increase efficiency and energy efficiency are forcing companies to make many changes in the ways in which they communicate with consumers, and in the design of the goods that they offer.

Among the most common innovations in the energy market, there are modern energy generators based on renewable energy sources and installed at the low-voltage level at end-users, smart meters and smart metering platforms together with a plenty of enabling technologies that make energy monitoring easier, demand-side management and demand response tools, including, for example, dynamic electricity tariffs, and many others. Hence, companies who want to offer such goods and services in the energy market must learn about their consumers' attributes and preferences in order to design the offers in an appropriate way.

The topic of innovation diffusion in the energy market is very broad, but within this book we will focus especially on the analysis of:

- the determinants of successful diffusion and adoption of innovation;
- the impact of socio-economic factors, as well as norms and values on adopting innovations (willingness to accept, buy, and pay for a new good, consumer preferences and expectations);
- models of consumer acceptance of innovations (external and internal factors favoring the acquisition of innovation or causing resistance and opposition to them); and
- practical marketing recommendations for companies present in the energy market that want to design and launch an innovative energy service.

Learning about consumers' needs and characterizing their socio-economic factors and their willingness to pay for a given good can help properly target innovations to increase their marketability, and thus positively influence consumer buying behavior. Information on consumer behavior is important for companies for two reasons. Firstly, consumer behaviors are an excellent source of information on the effectiveness of converting potential demand into effective demand, which translates into the company's sales and revenue performance, as well as its position in the market. Secondly, on the basis of consumer preferences, a company can create innovations and the structure of its components. There is no doubt that by implementing innovations (such as product or marketing innovations), a company can increase its competitive advantage in the market.

Despite the rich literature in the field of diffusion of innovation, as well as factors affecting the acceptance of new solutions on the energy market, I found it necessary to fill the research gap related to the identification and assessment of factors affecting the adoption of product, process of marketing innovations offered by enterprises on the energy market, and undertaking research that would answer the following questions:

- What causes a new, innovative product or a service in the energy market to be embraced and accepted by customers?
- How can one create innovations in the energy market so that customers are interested in buying and implementing them?

- What are the barriers to the diffusion of innovative products and services in general and in a specific energy market like in Poland, where traditional, coal-based energy production methods dominate?
- How can one overcome the abovementioned barriers to innovative diffusion, or what marketing strategies can be helpful in spreading innovation in the energy market?

This book is structured as follows. In the first chapter, an introduction to the innovative energy services (IES) in transitioning energy markets is provided. The political background of the smart grid approach is discussed, together with the motivation to activate residential households in the energy market. Next, consumers' role and opportunities in the contemporary energy markets are discussed. In this chapter, the innovative energy services included in this book are presented. Then, the third chapter contains the introduction to the theoretical background of innovation diffusion theory, and the fourth chapter provides the comparison between most common behavioral theories explaining humans' decision-making and adoption, as well as readiness for behavioral change. The next chapter presents and discusses the research findings from field experiments, pilot programs, and simulation studies devoted to consumers' acceptance, engagement of IES, and their willingness to accept, adopt, and pay for these innovations. Finally, in the last chapter, behavioral strategies and marketing interventions are provided, together with a discussion regarding marketing mix tools, referring to both commercial and social marketing approaches. This chapter ends with a set of recommendations regarding the enhancement of further diffusion of IES in future energy systems.

Anna Kowalska-Pyzalska
Wrocław, Poland

Introduction to innovative energy services (IES) in transitioning energy markets

1.1 Introduction

The energy sector is undergoing changes around the world due to long-lasting liberalization and unbundling processes, increased demand for electricity, with the rising amount of distributed generation sources, and fulfillment of ambitious climate goals. There are many different reasons for this reform, but one of its key objectives is to improve efficiency in order to lower prices for electricity consumers and reduce the negative impact of the sector on the climate. To achieve the ambitious aims of energy transition, more competitive electricity markets are needed on one side, and ensuring the security of supply is a necessity on the other.

The process of energy market liberalization in Europe started in the 1990s and was intended to reduce state interference in the functioning of the market and to introduce transparent and competitive market rules. It also aimed to create a common European market for electricity that leads to market integration and ensures energy security and lower, acceptable prices for end-users (Bolton, 2022; Belyaev, 2010). The liberalization process has created competition in the buying and selling of energy and brought an advantage to consumers, who are now able to choose freely their supplier. The transport and distribution areas have remained a natural monopoly due to high investments costs, but they are at least unbundled from the production and supply part.

The energy transition, which is an ongoing process, additionally provides new challenges to the sector by opening it up to even more competition and uncertainty in the area of energy generation (apart from centralized power plants, a large number of distributed energy generators are installed at a low- or medium-voltage level) and energy selling. The concept of smart grid has become an unprecedented opportunity to move the power industry into a new era of a modernized grid in which electricity generation, transmission, and distribution are intelligently, responsively,

Diffusion of Innovative Energy Services. https://doi.org/10.1016/B978-0-12-822882-1.00007-X

and cooperatively managed through a bidirectional automation system (Alotaibi et al., 2020). Although the domains of smart grid applications and technologies differ in function and form, in general, they share common potentials, such as smart energy curtailment, effective integration of demand response, distributed renewable generation, energy storage, and the activation of electricity end-users (Verbong et al., 2013; Schweiger et al., 2020; Siano, 2014).

We also cannot forget the recent challenges experienced by industries, including the energy sector, such as the recovery after the COVID-19 pandemic, as well as ongoing demand and supply shocks as a result of the war in Ukraine. The International Energy Agency (IEA) emphasizes that in these turbulent times, reliable and efficient energy systems become even more important. Hence, clean and efficient energy transition should be at the center of economic recovery and stimulus plans (Jiang et al., 2021). Last but not least, recent historical events have shown electricity consumers how important it is to achieve higher levels of energy-efficiency, energy conservation, and energy independence.

As a result, both the deregulation of the energy market and the recent global climate and geopolitical challenges have completely changed the position of end-users of electricity. Now residential consumers not only can make choices by themselves regarding the energy seller and their role in the power system, but also can offer ancillary services to the energy system operators and/or become the owners of electricity generators (Ellabban and Abu-Rub, 2016; Shaukat et al., 2018). The solutions currently present in the markets are not fully satisfying for various market players. There are still many barriers and obstacles regarding the way in which electricity consumers can participate in the energy market. However, before examining the possibilities that consumers have, in this chapter we will present the background of the energy transition in terms of climate policy and the transformation of the traditional power grid into a smart one. We will show why end-users of electricity, such as households, may have a tremendous effect on achieving the ambitious goals of sustainable development in the energy field.

1.2 Energy system: past, present, and future

Traditionally, energy was generated in one place and consumed in another. Hence, the structure of the power system was simplistic and linear. First, electrical energy was produced from fossil fuels, such as coal, lignite, or gas, in large, centralized power plants. Next, distribution system operators (DSOs) and transmission system operators (TSOs) were responsible for the energy distribution from producers to electricity end-users. Lastly, consumers such as firms, municipalities, or households consumed the electricity for their needs. The flow of power in the energy system was unidirectional and the role of electricity end-users was a completely passive one, limited to consumption of electricity supplied and paying electricity bills.

Due to numerous innovations, the supply chain of electrical energy has already changed a lot, and in the future will alter even more. New opportunities and threats (flexibilities and constraints) driven by digitalization, decentralization, and decarbonization have emerged. The evolved supply chain has become bidirectional, combining producers and consumers much more than before. Bidirectional power flow has proven to be a challenge from a technical point of view, but has also created new opportunities for next innovations. We have already experienced some innovations, such as roll-out of smart meters, rapid development of energy storage, and extensive diffusion of distributed renewable energy resources appearing in a low-voltage network. Recently, the development of battery electric vehicles (BEVs) has increased the demand for electricity, but has also provided some new opportunities for energy storage in batteries. The rapid development of innovations in the energy sector, supported by internet-based advanced technology, has led to the deployment of innovations such as vehicle-to-everything (V2X, communication between a vehicle and any entity), Internet-of-Things (IoT) applications, or omnipresent smart home devices (Sovacool and Furszyfer Der Rio, 2020).

However, innovation and technological progress are not the only reasons for the energy transition. They are facilitators of the change rather than its main cause. As Fig. 1.1 shows, the power system had to evolve due to many different circumstances, such as:

- slow but inevitable depletion of fossil fuels;
- social and political aversion to nuclear power plants;
- outdated technical infrastructure, not adapted to receive energy produced at low voltage;
- transformation of the energy markets from centralized into decentralized ones, with a large number of dispersed local energy generators;
- unbundling process in the production and supply chain;
- constant increase of the demand for electricity; and
- negative impact of the energy sector on the climate of the Earth.

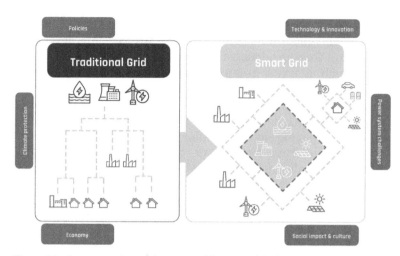

Figure 1.1. Power systems of the past and future and their political, technological, economic, and social environments (image source: Li et al., 2017).

In the EU itself, energy use accounts for a huge share of European GHG emissions, achieving 91% in 2020.[1] In addition, in the US the largest source of greenhouse gas emissions from human activities comes from burning fossil fuels for electricity, heat, and transportation.[2] Hence, for a few decades there has been a strong pressure to protect the natural environment of our planet, among others, by means of sustainable development in the energy market. The main challenges in this area relate to pollution of the environment due to the generation of energy from fossil fuels and excessive energy consumption. That is why sustainable development in the field of energy is based on three main pillars:

- increase of energy efficiency (and thus lower energy consumption and reduced losses in energy transmission and distribution);
- decreased emissions of greenhouse gases, such as CO_2; and
- increased share of renewable energy sources (RES) in the energy mix.

All the abovementioned reasons have led to the so-called **energy transition**, supported by many strategic and legislative regulations, such as the Paris Climate Agreement, EU Directives, national acts and regulations describing various ways to achieve CO_2 reduction, growth of RES, and increase of energy efficiency.

[1]https://www.eea.europa.eu/signals/signals-2017/articles/energy-and-climate-change (accessed November 12, 2021).
[2]https://www.epa.gov/ghgemissions/sources-greenhouse-gas-emissions (accessed July 19, 2022).

Apart from political and economic incentives, the energy transition is motivated by environmental and social incentives. Within this chapter, we will present the background and motivation for the changes being made in energy markets. We will pay special attention to the smart grid approach, which summarizes the general idea of how a modern electricity grid and energy market should be organized to activate all market participants, including consumers of electricity, such as households.

1.3 Energy transition: overview

The power system of today is experiencing vital challenges. Firstly, the current electricity system is demand driven, so that production can be increased and decreased while following changes in electricity demand (Umpfenbach et al., 2022). However, the future electricity system will be supply driven mainly because of the rising role of renewable energy sources in the energy mix. The level of energy production from solar or wind depends not only on the time of day, but also on the season, and the general weather conditions. Hence, production fluctuates and is not fully regulated, even though various technologies, such as assistance of energy storage, are implemented. In result, demand has to be matched with supply, rather than the other way round, as we have all been accustomed to previously (European Commission, 2020; Umpfenbach et al., 2022). Constant increase of RES in the future energy systems will make the matching between the supply and demand of energy even more difficult.

Secondly, in the past and still today in many of the current energy systems, electricity production is centralized fully or partly. The majority of electricity is produced in a small handful of massive power plants that generate enormous amounts of energy. However, gradually we are witnessing a process of emergence of multiple distributed energy sources located by the end-users of electricity. In future energy systems, electricity production will become even more decentralized than at present, with a large number of distributed generators producing small amounts of electricity and heat (Umpfenbach et al., 2022; European Commission, 2020). It should be emphasized at this point that the process of decentralization should not be seen only through the lens of potential technical issues that it may cause. At the same time it provides opportunities for a large number of parties to become stakeholders in the energy market (Hall et al., 2019). Furthermore, unlike centralized ownership by large energy companies, local ownership may lead to many social benefits for individuals and whole communities (Umpfenbach et al., 2022).

Thirdly, the electricity demand at households is expected to double by 2050 due to more use of air conditioning, heat pumps and electric vehicles (Hall et al., 2019). Current energy supply systems are often outdated, based on old, insufficient infrastructure, and not flexible enough to deal with the rising demand. The need for increased electricity supply and demand necessitates strengthening the power system and better interconnections (Umpfenbach et al., 2022). At the beginning of the COVID-19 pandemic, the Global Energy Review 2020 revealed a general decline in the energy demand between 18–25% dependent on the lockdown restrictions. But at the same time energy consumption among residential consumers has risen significantly, due to lockdowns and various restrictions, and changes in daily routines (e.g. working and learning from home). As a result, the average electricity bills of residential consumers have increased due to greater use of electricity for lighting, cooking, and heating, while spending less on communication and transportation (Cheshmehzgani, 2020).

The issues outlined above do not cover all of the events and processes taking place in the energy markets in recent years. However, we are keen to show that the changes that have already taken place and those to come in future should not be considered a negative factor. History teaches us that changes and challenges can and should be treated as opportunities to create many socially and economically useful innovations. For example, to overcome the challenge of real-time matching of electricity supply and demand, the following instruments or solutions can already be used: (1) demand-side management tools that affect the elasticity of demand by making sure that demand matches supply; (2) short-term energy storage, such as batteries, can be used to resolve differences between supply and demand during the day or week, and some of the energy produced can be stored in batteries or thermal storage systems to meet energy demand at night; and (3) long-term (and seasonal) energy storage can be proposed to address seasonal imbalances between supply and demand, or to manage long periods of low production or higher energy consumption due to certain weather patterns (Umpfenbach et al., 2022; Hall et al., 2019; Good et al., 2017). The future will undoubtedly bring further solutions, probably based on data science, artificial intelligence, and advanced information and communication technology (ICT).

The overview of contemporary power system starts with a brief description of the global and EU climate policy with regard to the sustainable development of energy markets.

1.3.1 Climate policy

According to the European Energy Agency (EEA), the generation and usage of energy has represented the largest source of greenhouse gas (GHG) emissions from human activities in recent years. About two-thirds of GHG emissions are linked to burning fossil fuels (mostly coal and natural gas) for energy to be used for heating, electricity, transport, and industry. According to the U.S. Environmental Protection Agency (EPA), in 2020 electricity production generated the second largest share of greenhouse gas emissions, just after transportation.[3] In Europe, too, the energy processes are the largest emitter of greenhouse gases, being responsible for 78% of total EU emissions in 2015, and 91% in 2020 (EEA, 2020).

There are two main ways in which GHG emissions related to energy can be cut: first by replacing fossil fuels with noncombustible renewable sources, and second by reducing the overall consumption of energy through energy savings and energy efficiency gains, for example, by improving home insulation or using greener transport modes (Umpfenbach et al., 2022; Vitiello et al., 2022). That is why the global political, economic, technological, and social efforts to mitigate climate change with regard to energy refer to these specific actions, such as an increase of RES in the energy mix, an increase of the energy efficiency, and reduction of CO_2 emissions.

Global efforts to mitigate climate change culminated in the **Paris Agreement** in 2015. Through this agreement, 195 countries adopted the first ever universal and legally binding, global climate deal. The target of the agreement—limiting the global average temperature rise to well below 2 °C, while aiming to limit the increase to 1.5 °C—is ambitious and cannot be achieved without a major overhaul of global energy production and consumption.[4]

In the EU, the European Commission (EC) supports the global climate agenda by various political actions. In 2015, the EC introduced the **Climate and Energy Package 3x20%**, including a 20% cut in greenhouse gas emissions (compared with 1990 levels), 20% of energy consumption coming from RES, and a 20% improvement in energy efficiency. Then, in 2021 the EU delivered a package of proposals called the **European Green Deal**, with a view to reducing net greenhouse gas emissions by at least 55% by 2030

[3]https://www.epa.gov/ghgemissions/sources-greenhouse-gas-emissions (accessed July 19, 2022).
[4]https://unfccc.int/process-and-meetings/the-paris-agreement/the-paris-agreement (accessed July 19, 2022).

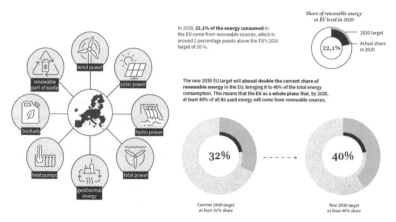

Figure 1.2. EU targets for the development of renewable energy sources (source: https://www.consilium.europa.eu/en/policies/green-deal/fit-for-55-the-eu-plan-for-a-green-transition/).

and the ultimate objective of becoming climate neutral by 2050.[5] It interlinks with a number of other proposals, notably the revised Renewable Energy Directive, the Emissions Trading System (ETS), the new Social Climate Fund, and the revision of the Effort Sharing Regulation, being part of the so-called **"Fit for 55 package"** that aims to align current laws with the 2030 and 2050 ambitions.[6]

The transition to cleaner forms of energy is necessary to achieve climate neutrality. Here mainly **renewable energy sources** are included, as they emit less carbon than fossil fuels. By 2050, most of the energy consumed in the EU will need to come from renewable sources. With its Fit for 55 package, the EU plans to boost its share of renewable energy by 2030 beyond the current target agreed in 2018. In 2020, 22.1% of energy consumed in the EU came from renewable energy sources. As shown in Fig. 1.2, the new EU 2030 target will almost double the current share of RES, bringing it to 40% of the total energy consumption. To meet the EU's energy and climate targets for 2030, EU countries need to establish a 10-year integrated national energy and climate plan (NECP) for the period from 2021 to 2030, indicating among other things how to reach the new 2030 renewable energy target.

Next, the rise of **energy efficiency** is the main principle of EU energy policy (European Commission, 2022). In late 2022, in line with the Climate Target Plan, the EU introduced a higher target

[5]https://ec.europa.eu/info/strategy/priorities-2019-2024/european-green-deal_en (accessed July 19, 2022).

[6]https://www.consilium.europa.eu/en/policies/green-deal/fit-for-55-the-eu-plan-for-a-green-transition/ (accessed July 19, 2022).

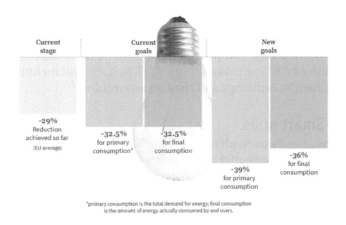

Current stage

Current goals

New goals

-29% Reduction achieved so far (EU average)

-32.5% for primary consumption*

-32.5% for final consumption

-39% for primary consumption

-36% for final consumption

*primary consumption is the total demand for energy; final consumption is the amount of energy actually consumed by end users.

The target is binding at EU level. Member states will define their indicative national targets reflecting their national specificities.

Figure 1.3. Increased efficiency target in EU (source: https://www.consilium. europa.eu/en/infographics/fit-for-55-how-the-eu-will-become-more-energy-efficient/ (accessed October 25, 2022)).

for reducing primary (39%) and final (36%) energy consumption by 2030, in comparison to the current, binding target of 32.5% (for both primary and final consumption), see Fig. 1.3. Moreover, it has introduced a benchmarking system for Member States to set their national indicative contributions to the binding EU target. The revised energy efficiency directive (European Commission, 2022) also proposes to nearly double Member State annual energy savings obligations in end use. In order to encourage this acceleration, the proposal concentrates on sectors with high energy-savings potential, including heating and cooling, industry, and energy services, and places special attention on the public sector for the role it can play in driving the transition.

Apart from the discussed regulations and strategies, due to the COVID-19 pandemic and its negative impact on industries, the EU has proposed the **Renovation Wave strategy**. The idea contains methods to enhance refurbishment while also benefiting society by tackling energy poverty and increasing consumer empowerment. The proposal also outlines a number of changes that should increase the uptake of energy efficiency investments in light of the potential for renovation to act as a springboard for economic recovery in the wake of the pandemic and the emphasis placed on the building sector in the EU's Recovery and Resilience Facility.

Finally, the EU Emissions Trading System (EU ETS) is the EU's key tool for reducing greenhouse gas emissions. Since 2005, EU emissions have been cut by 41% in the sectors covered, which are electricity and heat generation, energy-intensive industry sectors, and commercial aviation. The reform of the system is a part of the "Fit for 55" package and plans, among others, to increase annual reduction of GHG emissions from 2.2% to 4.2% and include new sectors such as buildings and road transportation.[7]

1.3.2 Smart grids

It has already been identified that climate change can alter energy generation potential and people's energy needs. For example, changes to the water cycle may have an impact on hydropower, and warmer temperatures increase the energy demand for cooling in the summer, while decreasing the demand for heating in the winter (Kumar, 2019). At the same time, the political, economic, and environmental incentives of energy transition lead to the creation and development of new goods and solutions directed at private and industrial electricity consumers.

Nowadays, many products and services, as well as concepts and ideas, must be "smart" to catch consumers' attention. This is also true for the energy market. The word "smart" means intelligent, user friendly, and that a product or a service can be used automatically and remotely without the customer's assistance.

In the case of energy markets, a general concept of **smart grids (SGs)** has been developed and implemented in various parts of the electricity network (Ellabban and Abu-Rub, 2016; Verbong et al., 2013; Crispim et al., 2014; Ponce-Jara et al., 2017; Shaukat et al., 2018; Lobaccaro et al., 2016). The general definition of an SG says that it is an electrical grid with automation, communication, and IT systems that can monitor power flows from points of generation to points of consumption (even down to appliances level) and control the power flow or restrict the load to match generation in real time or near real time. This concept is based on the broad usage of modern communication technologies to exchange information between market participants, such as energy generators, energy suppliers and sellers, market operators, and end-users (Avancini et al., 2019). It aims to increase energy efficiency in production, transmission, and consumption. Fig. 1.4 illustrates the bidirectional process in the modern power system. Special attention is given to indicate the participation of the demand-side of the energy market in generation and consumption (i.e., the presence of not only dispersed energy generators but also energy storage, charging of electric vehicles, and active network management).

---

[7]https://www.consilium.europa.eu/en/infographics/fit-for-55-eu-emissions-trading-system/ (accessed October 18, 2022).

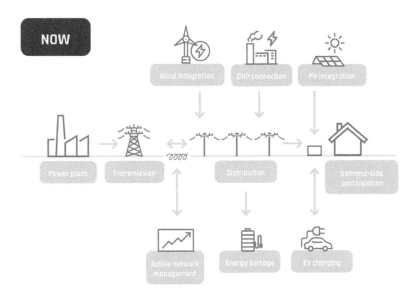

Figure 1.4. Bidirectional energy flow in smart grids.

SGs are supposed to provide high-quality power that meets 21st-century demand. By making use of all generation and storage options, SGs meet customers' needs, while taking into account changes and challenges (Acharjee, 2013). In particular, SGs integrate all grid users, especially renewable energy sources and high-efficiency local generation with no or low carbon emissions (Acharjee, 2013; Kumar, 2019; Ponce-Jara et al., 2017). By means of advanced ICT, artificial intelligence, and combination of many smart devices, SGs improve the security and reliability of supply in line with the requirements of the fourth and fifth industrial revolutions (Dogaru, 2020). The change in thinking about the power system and the energy market enables the creation of new products, services, and markets to optimize asset utilization and operational efficiency (Acharjee, 2013).

As Kumar (2019) states, the purposes behind developing smart grids are inherently social and financial, involving ensuring financial security for electricity utilities, and reconciling consumer and producer interests. According to Crispim et al. (2014) there are three main drivers that are responsible for the development of SG:

1. integration of renewable energy sources (RES) and distributed generation (DG);
2. growing role of demand response (DR); and
3. optimization of new end-uses of electricity.

Smart grids are electricity networks that deliver electricity in a controlled way, offering multiple benefits such as growth and ef-

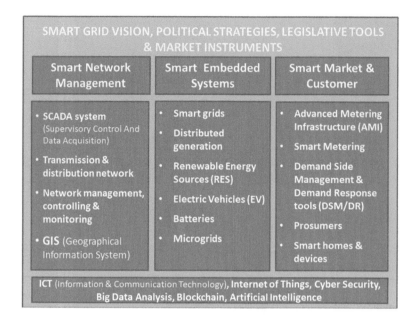

Figure 1.5. Smart grid structure and elements (EMI, 2014).

fective management of renewable energy sources (Lamnatou et al., 2022).

Smart grids can be presented by three main pillars: smart network management, smart embedded systems, and smart market and customers, as proposed by EMI (2014) (see Fig. 1.5). Firstly, distribution businesses' diverse operations, including network management, business process management, and IT systems, are included in smart network management. Advanced distribution management systems, supervisory control and data acquisition (SCADA), advanced network monitoring management and control systems, and other systems are also included. Geographical data and resource management systems are two other crucial technical components of this pillar (Lamnatou et al., 2022).

Secondly, smart embedded systems, located in medium-voltage or low-voltage networks, are vital in achieving low-carbon goals and energy efficiency (Procter, 2013). Smart embedded systems, in this context, include distributed energy resources (DER) at various scales, based mainly on renewable energy sources, energy storage systems, and electric vehicles. They may also consist of microgrids; these are small networks of electricity users with a local sources of supply and storage systems that are usually attached to a centralized national grid, but are able to function independently (Lamnatou et al., 2022).

Thirdly, the smart markets and smart customer pillar includes all of the components that can be directly associated with consumers/end-users of the smart grid. It consists of some basic elements, such as smart meter infrastructure, meter data management systems, demand management and energy trading. Components included in this pillar, such as advanced metering infrastructure (AMI) or smart metering (SM) infrastructure, are very costly and require huge investments. But they allow end-users of electricity (i.e., households) not only to monitor their energy consumption on a real-time basis, but also to provide energy or demand-side response services to balance the grid (Verbong et al., 2013; Shaukat et al., 2018; Papachristos, 2017).

The framework's bottom section describes additional technological challenges classified as common smart components. Big data analysis, communication infrastructures, cyber security, and other topics are covered (Hua et al., 2022; Lobaccaro et al., 2016; Pagani and Aiello, 2016). The advanced information and control infrastructures of smart grids allow interoperability among various stakeholders (Hua et al., 2022; Papachristos, 2017). Under this circumstance, increasing numbers of consumers produce, store, and consume energy, giving them a new role as prosumers. Two essential components—flexible energy market structures and intelligent power system operations—are necessary for the integration of prosumers and accommodation of costly bidirectional energy and information flows. Innovative technologies such as blockchain and artificial intelligence (AI) are being used to address these two issues; blockchain offers decentralized trading platforms for the energy markets, and AI helps power systems operate at their best (Hua et al., 2022; Lobaccaro et al., 2016). The whole concept is shaped by the smart grid vision and some political strategies, legislative tools, and market instruments.

In Schweiger et al. (2020) the authors recapitulate that "smart energy systems are a complex puzzle of very different elements," including individual consumers and their social environment, and together with physical environment, digital realities, and economic and legislative conditions must be considered and integrated to allow successful operation. Bearing in mind the complex environment of the energy markets, within this book we will focus on the smart market and customers' pillar, and explain firstly what opportunities consumers have in the modern energy market, and secondly what makes consumers accept these new, innovative products and services.

1.3.3 Impact of recent geopolitical challenges on residential consumers

In recent years, markets, including the energy one, have experienced demand and supply shocks due to the COVID-19 pandemic and then the war in Ukraine. The impact of the pandemic on electricity prices and residential consumers has been complex and multifaceted, varying from country to country and region to region. There are some common key impacts, however, and these include the following:

- Changes in electricity demand: As lockdowns and social distancing measures were implemented to control the spread of the virus, electricity demand patterns changed significantly. Many commercial and industrial activities were curtailed or shut down altogether, leading to a drop in overall electricity demand. At the same time, residential electricity consumption increased as people spent more time at home. These changes had a mixed effect on electricity prices, depending on the specific circumstances of each market (Cheshmehzgani, 2020).
- Changes in energy mix: The pandemic also had an impact on the energy mix used to generate electricity. In some cases, there was an increase in the use of renewable energy sources such as wind and solar, as demand for fossil fuels dropped. This led to a reduction in carbon emissions in some countries. However, in other cases, the pandemic disrupted supply chains and led to a temporary increase in the use of fossil fuels (Zhong et al., 2020; Shen et al., 2022).
- Changes in electricity supply: The pandemic also disrupted electricity supply chains, particularly in the early stages of the crisis. In some regions, there were concerns about the availability of fuel and other inputs required for electricity generation. This led to price spikes in some markets, particularly in areas that relied heavily on natural gas or other fossil fuels (Li et al., 2022; Jiang et al., 2021; Navon et al., 2021).
- Government interventions: In some countries, governments took steps to stabilize electricity prices and protect consumers during the pandemic. This included measures such as temporarily suspending disconnections for nonpayment, providing financial assistance to households struggling to pay their bills, and implementing price caps or other regulatory measures.

One example of the impact of COVID-19 on electricity prices can be seen in the United States. During the pandemic, many businesses and industries were shut down or significantly reduced their operations, which led to a decrease in the demand for electricity. At the same time, many people were working from home, which increased residential electricity consumption. This shift in demand caused electricity prices to become more volatile and less predictable.

In some areas, particularly those with high levels of renewable energy, wholesale electricity prices plummeted as a result of reduced demand. For example, in California, the state's aggressive renewable energy goals, combined with decreased demand during the pandemic, caused negative electricity prices in some instances. This meant that producers had to pay grid operators to take their excess electricity. On the other hand, in some regions, electricity prices increased due to increased demand for residential electricity and decreased supply from coal- and natural gas-fired power plants. This was particularly evident during the winter storm in Texas in February 2021, where power outages led to a surge in demand for backup power sources, such as natural gas and diesel generators. Overall, the impact of the pandemic on electricity prices and residential consumers has been complex and varied. While there have been some temporary price spikes and supply chain disruptions in some markets, in other cases, the pandemic has accelerated the shift toward cleaner, renewable energy sources. Governments have also taken steps to protect consumers and stabilize prices during this challenging time.

In addition, the outbreak of the war in Ukraine in February 2022 had a huge impact on residential consumers, especially in Europe. Some of the key impacts include the following:

- Energy prices: The conflict has led to disruptions in the supply of natural gas from Russia, which is a major supplier to the EU. This has led to increased energy prices, particularly in countries that rely heavily on Russian gas, such as Bulgaria, Hungary, and Slovakia.
- Economic impact: The conflict has had a negative impact on the economies of both Ukraine and the EU. This has resulted in job losses and reduced economic growth, which has had an indirect impact on residential consumers.
- Security concerns: The conflict has created security concerns for many EU residents, particularly those who live in countries that share a border with Ukraine. This has led to increased security measures and border controls, which can be inconvenient and time-consuming for residents.
- Humanitarian concerns: The conflict has led to a significant humanitarian crisis, with many people being displaced from their homes and suffering from shortages of food, water, and medical supplies. Some EU countries have provided aid and assistance to those affected by the conflict, but this has also placed a strain on resources.

Overall, the war in Ukraine has had a range of negative impacts on residential consumers in the EU, particularly in terms of energy prices and security concerns. However, the full extent of the impact will depend on a number of factors, including the duration of the conflict and any future developments.

1.4 Summary

In summary, today's energy markets must adapt to the challenges of climate protection and the depletion of fossil fuels. At the same time, the enormous technological progress, the development of ICT, and artificial intelligence allow for the transformation of traditional power systems into smart grids. In addition, political pressure forces the direction of change of the energy transformation of the traditional power systems into smart ones, making usage of the rapid development of ICT to monitor, forecast, and share data about energy production and consumption in real time.

The energy transition, in which fossil fuels are being replaced by renewable energy sources such as wind and solar, the increased role of local power generation, and the emphasis on energy efficiency and environmental protection has brought a revolution in thinking about the role and place of the energy consumer. Historically, the consumer has always been at the end of the supply chain, playing a passive role in it. However, the transformations experienced by electricity systems and energy markets give consumers an active role, shifting part of the responsibility to them to achieve the ambitious political and strategic goals of increasing the share of RES, energy efficiency, and reducing CO_2 emissions. In addition, the recent challenges due to the global pandemic and then outbreak of war in a neuralgic region of the world in terms of the supply of fossil fuels may have an impact on electricity consumers, leading to increases in awareness, interest, and willingness to become more energy-efficient and energy-independent. However, it is not clear if these experiences will lead to long-lasting behavioral changes in the area of monitoring and control over households' energy consumption and overall reduction of the energy demand among consumers (Sheth, 2020).

According to the IEA, the pandemic may have a positive impact on consumers, by drawing them toward more energy-efficient solutions available in the energy market. Such an increase of consumers' interest and engagement would be of course desired, as currently it is still limited (Kowalska-Pyzalska and Byrka, 2019; Gans et al., 2013; Batalla-Bejerano et al., 2020; Shaukat et al., 2018; Chawla et al., 2020b). Taking all of the above into account, we must admit that the energy markets need adjusted solutions, new business models, and marketing strategies that will allow all market players, including electricity consumers, to adapt to the new market circumstances. These new market circumstances should be used by the energy suppliers and authorities to offer innovative solutions which will not only motivate consumers to increase efficiency of their energy consumption, but at the same time will enhance the gross domestic product (GDP) growth rate. In the next chapter, we will explain what opportunities consumers have in the modern power systems, and what their new role is in the energy transition.

1.5 References and additional reading proposals

Liberalization of the energy markets:
- Belyaev (2010) Electricity Market Reforms: Economics and Policy Challenges, Springer-Verlag New York Inc.
- Bolton (2022) Making Energy Markets, Springer Nature Switzerland AG (Bolton, 2022)

Impact of COVID-19 pandemic on the electricity market:
- Cheshmehzgani, A. (2020) COVID-19 and household energy implications: what are the main impacts on energy use? Heliyon 6(10), e05202 (Cheshmehzgani, 2020)
- Jiang et al. (2021) Impacts of COVID-19 on energy demand and consumption: challenges, lessons and emerging opportunities. Appl. Energy 285, 116441 (Jiang et al., 2021)
- Li et al. (2022) Impact of COVID-19 on electricity energy consumption: a quantitative analysis on electricity. International Journal of Electrical Power & Energy Systems 140, 108084 (Li et al., 2022)
- Sheth, J. (2020) Impact of Covid-19 on consumer behavior: will the old habits return or die? Journal of Business Research 117, 280–283 (Sheth, 2020)

Consumers' empowerment and engagement:
- Ellabban and Abu-Rub (2016) Smart grid customers' acceptance and engagement: An overview, Renewable and Sustainable Energy Reviews 65, 1285–1298 (Ellabban and Abu-Rub, 2016)
- Hall et al. (2019) Prosumers for the Energy Union: mainstreaming active participation of citizens in the energy transition. In: Business models for prosumers in Europe, Deliverable 4.1 of the Horizon 2020 PROSEU project (H2020-LCE-2017) (Hall et al., 2019)

- Schweiger et al. (2020) Active consumer participation in smart energy systems. Energy and Buildings 227, 110359 (Schweiger et al., 2020)
- Shaukat, et al. (2018) A survey on consumers empowerment, communication technologies, and renewable generation penetration within Smart Grid, Renewable and Sustainable Energy Reviews 81, 1453–1475 (Shaukat et al., 2018)
- Umpfenbach et al. (2022) Energy prosumers in Europe Citizen participation in the energy transition. In: European Environment Agency (ed.); EEA Report No 01/2022. Luxembourg: Publications Office of the European Union (Umpfenbach et al., 2022)
- Verbong et al. (2013) Smart grids or smart users? Involving users in developing a low carbon electricity economy. Energy Policy 52, 117–125 (Verbong et al., 2013)

Smart grids: concept, technologies, regulation, and challenges:
- Acharjee et al. (2013) Strategy and implementation of smart grids in India. Energy Strategy Reviews 1(3), 193–204 (Acharjee, 2013)
- Alotaibi et al. (2020) A comprehensive review of recent advances in smart grids: A sustainable future with renewable energy resources. Energies 13, 6269 (Alotaibi et al., 2020)
- Avancini et al. (2019) Energy meters evolution in smart grids: A review. Journal of Cleaner Production 217, 702–715 (Avancini et al., 2019)
- Crispim et al. (2014) Smart grids in the EU with smart regulation: Experiences from the UK, Italy and Portugal. Utilities Policy 31, 85–93 (Crispim et al., 2014)
- Hua, et al. (2022) Applications of blockchain and artificial intelligence technologies for enabling prosumers in smart grids: a review. Renewable and Sustainable Energy Reviews 161, 112308 (Hua et al., 2022)
- Kumar, A. (2019) Beyond technical smartness: rethinking the development and implementation of sociotechnical smart grids in India. Energy Research & Social Science 49, 158–168 (Kumar, 2019)
- Lamnatou, et al. (2022) Smart grids and smart technologies in relation to photovoltaics, storage systems, buildings and the environment, Renewable Energy 1376–1391 (Lamnatou et al., 2022)
- Lobaccaro, et al. (2016) A review of systems and technologies for smart homes and smart grids. Energies 9(5), 1–33 (Lobaccaro et al., 2016)

- Pagani and Aiello (2016) From the grid to the smart grid, topologically. Physica A: Statistical Mechanics and its Applications 449, 160–175 (Pagani and Aiello, 2016)
- Papachristos (2017) Diversity in technology competition: the link between platforms and sociotechnical transitions. Renewable and Sustainable Energy Reviews 73, 291–306 (Papachristos, 2017)
- Peters, et al. (2018) The role of environmental framing in socio-political acceptance of smart grid: the case of British Columbia, Canada. Renewable and Sustainable Energy Reviews 82, 1939–1951 (Peters et al., 2018)
- Ponce-Jara, et al. (2017) Smart grid: assessment of the past and present in developed and developing countries. Energy Strategy Reviews 18, 38–52 (Ponce-Jara et al., 2017)
- Siano (2014) Demand response and smart grids—a survey. Renewable and Sustainable Energy Reviews 30, 461–478 (Siano, 2014)
- Sovacool and Furszyfer Der Rio (2020) Smart home technologies in Europe: a critical review of concepts, benefits, risks and policies. Renewable and Sustainable Energy Reviews 120, 109663 (Sovacool and Furszyfer Der Rio, 2020)
- Vitiello et al. (2022) Smart metering roll-out in Europe: where do we stand? Cost benefit analyses in the clean energy package and research trends in the Green Deal. Energies 15, 2340 (Vitiello et al., 2022)

Legislation:
- Accelerating Clean Energy Innovation: COM(2016) 763 final: Winter Package, European Commission, Brussels (European Commission, 2016)
- Clean energy for all Europeans, European Commission, Directorate-General for Energy. Publications Office https://data.europa.eu/doi/10.2833/9937 (European Commission, 2019).
- Communication from the Commission to the European Parliament, the European Council, the Council, the European Economic and Social Committee and the Committee of the Regions "REPowerEU Plan", (COM(2022) 230 final of 18 May 2022) (European Commission, 2022)
- Directive 2012/27/EU of the European Parliament and of the Council of 25 October 2012 on energy efficiency, amending directives 2009/125/EC and 2010/30/EC and repealing directives 2004/8/EC and 2006/32/EC (European Commission, 2012)
- Clean energy for all Europeans, European Commission, Directorate-General for Energy. Publications Office https://data.europa.eu/doi/10.2833/9937 (European Commission, 2019).

Consumers' roles and opportunities in the energy market

2.1 Introduction

Currently, global energy markets are experiencing fundamental changes related to the implementation of ambitious targets for mandatory increase of the share of renewable energy sources (RES) in energy production, increasing energy efficiency (on the part not only of the producer or energy suppliers, but also of the end-user: household or company), as well as reducing greenhouse gas emissions. Increasing energy efficiency and increased use of renewable energy is postulated by, among others, the European Commission, which in the so-called climate package has recognized these actions as the basic pillars of a sustainable energy policy (Winter Package 2016, Climate Package 3x20 and others). Undoubtedly, the diffusion of many innovative services and products on the energy market may positively affect the improvement of social well-being through the protection of the natural environment, reduction of carbon dioxide and other pollutants, as well as the creation of new jobs.

This chapter starts by elaborating how the traditional role of passive electricity consumers has changed in recent years. Understanding the potential role of consumers in the energy market is important for further discussion of the determinants of consumers' acceptance and engagement. Future energy systems' design and operation must take into account the rising challenges, such as predicted rise of the total energy demand in general, and consumer energy demand in particular, integration of large shares of volatile renewable energy while improving overall system efficiency, and balancing the demand and supply of energy in a flexible way.

To better comprehend the scope and potential presence of active customers' participation in future energy systems, we will discuss a variety of innovative energy services (IES) dedicated to households and individual customers.

Diffusion of Innovative Energy Services. https://doi.org/10.1016/B978-0-12-822882-1.00008-1

2.2 Active role of consumers in future energy systems

In the past, the consumer has often been portrayed as a "passive, uninformed individual striving to maximize egoistic, material gains" (Schweiger et al., 2020). Their role was limited to consuming electricity when needed, and paying the electricity bills. Households were usually offered an electricity flat tariff, meaning a fixed price of electricity, without any pricing signals to adjust the demand to the current situation in the power grid. The installation of self-generation at the household level was uncommon. From the energy utilities and system operators' point of view, efforts to optimize the energy system have often been aimed at bypassing any kind of active consumer involvement to avoid potential problems from this side. This essentially negative understanding of the role of the consumer seems to be outdated nowadays, as the power system experiences a technical and organizational revolution (Schot et al., 2016).

The transformation of the role of consumers in the energy market from a passive into an active one is shown in Fig. 2.1. We can see that now the empowerment of electricity end-users has changed the whole process by adding a loop between the consumers and retailers—including energy suppliers, that is, distribution system operators (DSOs), energy sellers and traders, and energy market aggregators. The power flow has changed from unidirectional (from a generator via transmission and distribution electricity networks to the final consumers, where the electricity is consumed) to bidirectional, where the electricity generated by the consumer (i.e., prosumer) transferring to the distribution network is feasible.

The observed current change of the position and role of consumers in the energy market is still gradual, and in different parts of the world it is at different stages. Nevertheless, this ongoing process takes place all over the world due to several external factors, including the following:

1. Transformation of the energy markets caused by cleaner and more cost-efficient energy is driving electrification from the centralized generation and distribution of electricity into decentralized and dispersed generation often by means of volatile, renewable energy sources, at the low (end-user) voltage level.

2. Legislative support such as strategic packages, directives, and national laws, leading to a change of the former paradigm of a passive consumer role into an active one, including energy market liberalization and unbundling referring to legal

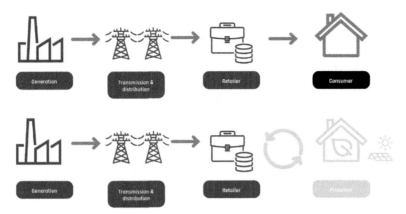

Figure 2.1. The transformation from passive consumers to active prosumers (Yavuz et al., 2019).

separation of different components of electricity production and supply, such as generation, transmission, distribution, and retail supply or sale of electricity, third-party access (TPA) principle—giving suppliers and consumers the right to access the electricity network system that belongs to other companies for transportation, delivery, and trade.

3. Social change, including rising awareness of climate change in society, and the digitization of individual skills lead to, among other things, monitoring of personal energy consumption and production of own electricity at the household level.

4. Technological advance and the Internet of Things (IoT), which refers to the network of physical devices, vehicles, and other objects embedded with sensors, software, and connection, allowing these devices to collect and exchange data, resulting in embedded connectivity and computing in devices and building automation systems. Additionally, the IoT makes it possible to regulate dispersed energy resources in real-time, including heating, ventilation, and air-conditioning systems (HVAC), freezers, refrigerators, water boilers, and battery electric vehicle (BEV) charging stations. By utilizing IoT technologies, innovative energy services can be optimized and delivered in a more efficient and effective way.

Due to aforementioned circumstances including energy transition from the traditional power system into the smart grid, market decentralization, implementation of information and communication technology in generation, transmission, distribution, and sale of electricity, and the rising presence of renewable energy sources (RES) on the lower voltage levels, **new possibilities have arisen for consumers** (Kowalska-Pyzalska, 2015; Siano, 2014;

Moreno-Munoz et al., 2016). They are no longer perceived as passive end-users of electricity. Instead, they can now play an active role in various dimensions of the power system. The revolution in thinking about electricity consumers started some time ago, but with each passing year consumers have more legislative, technical, and economic solutions, allowing them to engage significantly in the energy market. For example, the Third Party Access policy, as a result of a broader market liberalization,[1] has allowed firstly companies, and since 2007 also individual households, to change their energy supplier and to choose a specific pricing program (Belyaev, 2010; Bolton, 2022). Moreover, residential consumers can now start generating energy relatively easily and use it for their own needs or sell the surplus to the distribution system operators. In this way they can become prosumers, i.e., consumers who consume and produce energy at the same time. Electricity users are also being involved in active management of the electricity demand by means of demand-side management and demand response tools, which usually involves some need of the behavioral change or adjustment at the consumer side.

The role of the active customers of tomorrow's electricity market design is also realized by the power grid experts (Schweiger et al., 2020; Shaukat et al., 2018). With the fast emergence of technical advancement, in solar and storage systems, for example, customers are empowered to change their behavioral patterns and make active choices, not only for their own benefit (energy savings, sustainable heating and mobility) but also for the benefit of the community and the whole electricity system. By optimizing their renewable generation, they release the pressure and challenges on the electricity grid connected with the integration of dispersed generation sources, and also offer a vast flexibility potential to support the integration of high shares of renewables (frequency regulation, congestion management).

2.2.1 Definitions of active consumers

The literature presents different definitions of active consumers. First, in the Directive on Common Rules for the Internal Market in Electricity (Art. 2, paragraph 6) with its further amendments (Directive (EU) 2019/944), an **active consumer** means "a customer or a group of jointly acting customers who consume, store or sell electricity generated on their premises, including through aggregators, or participate in demand response or energy

---

[1] https://www.europarl.europa.eu/ftu/pdf/en/FTU_2.1.9.pdf (accessed January 10, 2023).

efficiency schemes provided that these activities do not constitute their primary commercial or professional activity" (European Commission, 2012).

Then, the **Winter Package** from 2016 states that "Consumers are active and central players on the energy markets of the future. Consumers across the EU will in the future have a better choice of supply, access to reliable energy price comparison tools and the possibility to produce and sell their own electricity" (European Commission, 2016). The Winter Package specifies also that member states should ensure that consumers are entitled to "generate, store, consume and sell self-generated electricity in all organized markets either individually or through aggregators without being subject to discriminatory or disproportionately burdensome technical and administrative requirements, procedures and charges that are not cost reflective" (European Commission, 2016). Taking all of this into account, one may easily state that active involvement of the individual customers in the energy systems are welcome and supported, at least from the regulation side (Verbong et al., 2013; Olmos et al., 2011).

Next, the **Clean Energy Packaging (CEP) framework**, adopted in 2019, makes the consumer the key element of the EU energy policies even more (European Commission, 2019). Customers are encouraged to participate actively and decide about the management of their consumption in order to achieve greater efficiency and therefore obtain economic benefits in terms of their energy bills. This legislative framework is supposed to accelerate the clean energy transition. The package includes eight legislative files, of which four are collectively known as the electricity market design. In terms of consumers' involvement, these new rules outlines a comprehensive framework for consumer protection, information, and empowerment in the EU electricity sector (European Commission, 2019). In particular, the CEP promises that:

- information in energy bills will be improved to become clearer and easier to understand to help consumers better control their costs;
- customers will get a summary of key contractual conditions to help them better understand sometimes complex terms and conditions; and
- providers should give free-of-charge access to at least one energy comparison tool, allowing consumers to find the best deal in the market.[2]

The studies of Immonen et al. (2020), Coy et al. (2021), Lennon et al. (2019), Lammers and Hoppe (2019), Coenen and Hoppe

---

[2]https://energy.ec.europa.eu/topics/markets-and-consumers/energy-consumer-rights/protecting-energy-consumers_en (accessed October 25, 2022).

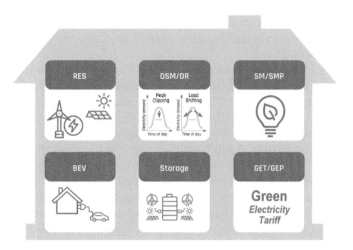

Figure 2.2. Innovative energy services, from a household point of view.

(2022) and Fouad et al. (2022) reveal that the revolution in the way consumers think and act in the energy market has already started, especially in countries where the energy transition takes place dynamically, such as in Germany, Sweden, Finland, or Holland. Immonen et al. (2020) state that "consumers have already been active as prosumers and are becoming increasingly energy-aware, knowing the effects of their own behavior on energy consumption." In the coming years, the active role of electricity end-users can only increase, making the power system more elastic and flexible.

2.3 Market opportunities for households' electricity users

2.3.1 Innovative energy services (IES)

The recent changes in the energy markets, involving a transition from traditional power systems into smart ones, have led to the development of a number of innovative energy services (IES), offered to electricity end-users by energy utilities (i.e., demand-side management, DSM/DR tools, smart meters, and smart meters platforms), energy sellers (i.e., green or dynamic electricity tariffs), or various companies (i.e., small-scale generators using RES, enabling technologies, and others).

The most popular innovative energy services (IES) are presented in Fig. 2.2 and include:

- small-scale generation based on renewable energy sources (RES): used for local production of electricity and heat; some of them, such as photovoltaic (PV) panels or small wind generators, can be installed in consumers' households, allowing them to produce electricity or heat for their own needs;

- green electricity tariffs and programs: voluntary or mandatory electricity tariffs that include some share of green energy and are usually more expensive than a typical tariff including only conventional power;
- smart metering and smart metering information systems (SM platforms): including smart meters (SMs), internet widgets and platforms, smartphone applications, and in-home displays designed to share the information about the current electricity prices and its consumption between the household and the energy supplier;
- demand-side management and demand response tools (DSM/ DR), including incentive and price-based programs, such as dynamic tariffs (time-of-use, real-time-price tariff, etc.), and others. Their aim is to flatten the demand curve by shifting electricity consumption from on-peak to off-peak hours;
- enabling technologies: examples include smart plugs, smart appliances, or home area networks (HANs) that optimize and automate electricity consumption according to its market price and consumers' requirements; and
- others, including electricity storage systems and battery electric vehicles (BEVs) strongly influencing the flexibility of consumers' demand.

Although IES have different attributes and roles, they still have a lot in common with each other (Kowalska-Pyzalska, 2018b). As mentioned by Kowalska-Pyzalska (2018b), all of these IES belong to a portfolio of possible solutions, which, if used in a wise and reasonable way, can lead to increases of social welfare and economic growth. A holistic approach to various energy innovations proposed by Kowalska-Pyzalska (2018b) is supposed to improve the effectiveness of marketing tools and pricing policies applied not only at the level of individual suppliers of these products and services, but also at the regulator and governmental level, and to increase the acceptance and popularity of these solutions among consumers. IES are often interdependent and can be used jointly to activate consumers, by giving them incentives and possibilities to increase energy efficiency at the household level. In this way, a substantial behavioral change can be achieved. All of these IES should be offered and promoted concurrently in order to meet the political goals of high energy efficiency. This is particularly true for complementary services, or products that may be used or consumed simultaneously, such smart metering information systems including enabling technologies and dynamic pricing. Last but not least, these IES have comparable difficulties and barriers during the adoption process (Kowalska-Pyzalska, 2018b).

Below we discuss the possible ways of consumers' engagement in the current and future energy systems and markets. The discussion will include the most common innovative energy services, in which individual electricity consumer—namely households—can participate.

2.3.2 Small-scale renewable generation

The discussion will start with a description of small-scale generators, based on renewables, that allow consumers to become partly or fully energy-independent and are usually the first, and most popular, way of achieving consumer engagement in the power system. The majority of these small-scale generators are based on renewable energy sources (RES), such as wind, solar, water, and biomass.

On the macroscopic level, among large producers of energy, RES are perceived as a green, sustainable alternative to fossil fuels. Even though RES have some significant disadvantages (i.e., unstable production of electricity), the amount of energy produced from those sources systematically increase, due to the inevitable advantages that these sources offer (fewer or no CO_2 emissions, lack of dependence on imported fuels, faster time of installation in comparison to the conventional power plants, etc.).

According to Eurostat, in 2022 renewables accounted for 22% of the total energy demand in the EU (Umpfenbach et al., 2022), so there is still further potential for growth. Fig. 2.3 shows the increase of the share of electricity production from renewables in 27 member states of the European Union between 2010 and 2020 in comparison to the production from fossil fuels. In 2020, renewable energy sources made up 37% of gross electricity consumption in the EU, up from 34% in 2019 (Umpfenbach et al., 2022). Wind and hydropower accounted for more than two-thirds of the total electricity generated from renewable sources (36% and 33%, respectively). The remaining one-third of electricity came from solar power (14%), solid biofuels (8%), and other renewable sources (8%). Solar power is the fastest-growing source: in 2008, it only accounted for 1% of the electricity consumed in the EU (Umpfenbach et al., 2022).

Eurostat reveals that among EU member states, more than 70% of electricity consumed in 2020 was generated from renewable sources in Austria (78%) and Sweden (75%). The generation of electricity from renewable sources was also high, and accounted for more than half of the electricity consumed in Denmark (65%),

Renewables overtake fossil fuels
% share is electricity production in EU-27

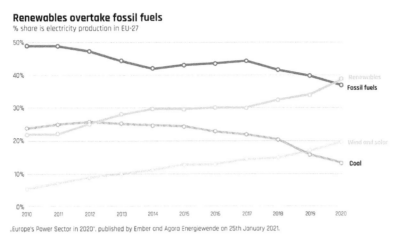

„Europe's Power Sector in 2020", published by Ember and Agora Energiewende on 25th January 2021.

Figure 2.3. Comparison of share of electricity production in EU-27 between renewables and fossil fuels (source: Agora Energiewende and Ember (2021)).

Portugal (58%), and Croatia and Latvia (both 53%). At the other end of the scale, the share of electricity from renewable sources was 15% or less in Malta (10%), Hungary and Cyprus (both 12%), Luxembourg (14%), and the Czech Republic (15%).

2.3.3 Prosumers

RES are present in the energy mix not only on a macro-scale, by means of large wind or PV farms, but also on a micro scale among individual consumers. RES has already become an interesting and attractive option for households, which may install microgeneration at their homes, and hence become so-called prosumers of electricity, meaning they simultaneously produce and consume electricity (Kowalska-Pyzalska, 2018b).

Active customers get actively engaged and invest their own resources into a personalized renewable energy solution. There are various options available for households, depending on the geographical location, technical infrastructure (e.g., the shape of the roof, access to the electricity network), and of course financial liability. For example, if a house is located close to a lake or a river, a small hydroelectric system may be suitable for it. Small wind generators as free-standing poles or installations on the building comprise another solution. Most residential households, however, decide on photovoltaic (PV) solar power generation, as this is currently the most common technology used by prosumers in Europe (Hall et al., 2019). Other technologies suitable for prosumers include energy storage (such as batteries or heat storage), electric

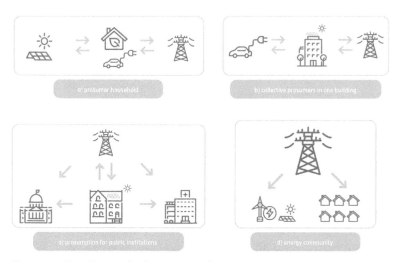

Figure 2.4. Four different business models for prosumers (Umpfenbach et al., 2022).

vehicles, heat pumps, biomass systems or electricity, and district heating networks.[3]

Apart from prosumers, recently the term **flexumers** also appeared (Köppl et al., 2022; Jee et al., 2022). The idea of flexumers comes from a combination of flexibility and consumer, and refers to consumers who provide flexibility to the power system (Jee et al., 2022). In other words, flexumers are those who not only generate energy (so are self-supplying prosumers) but also are able to respond to signals from the system operator according to the situation of energy supply and demand, often by owning energy storage and smart home energy systems (Jee et al., 2022). Flexumers can be distinguished from consumers by a technical feasibility to react on signals from the system operator. The most common signal is price; flexumers respond to price incentives by changing their electricity consumption level. Power system operators, mainly distribution ones (DSOs), assess the impact of the consumer on the power system in terms of quantity and time. Dependent on the quantity of demand that can be changed if required and time needed for the change, flexumers can be distinguished from regular consumers. Hence, price responsiveness, consistency, flexible amount, and response time are determined to be the defining characteristics of flexumers (Jee et al., 2022).

[3]https://www.eonenergy.com/spark/ways-to-power-your-home-with-renewable-energy.html (accessed August 14, 2022).

2.3.4 Types and forms of prosumption

Prosumption exists in numerous types and forms, and can be characterized by several attributes, such as entity, technology, or a business model. As shown in Fig. 2.4 there are four most popular business models for prosumers:

- prosumer household;
- collective prosumers in one building;
- prosumption for public institutions; and
- energy community.

In most cases, prosumers are individuals or groups, including households, small and medium-sized enterprises (SMEs), public institutions (e.g., hospitals, schools, or town halls) that both produce RES-based energy and self-consume, and sometimes also offer energy services to the system, such as flexibility or storage or by owning and operating grid infrastructure (Umpfenbach et al., 2022). Unlike utility companies, selling energy or providing energy system services are not prosumers' main commercial activities.

Next, there are owners' associations that own a PV plant on the roof of an apartment complex. The apartment owners form an owners' association and contribute to the investment. Depending on the regulations in place, they may also be able to consume directly the power delivered by the plant. It is also possible that an SME or a public institution, such as a government office or a school, may own a PV plant installed on the roof of its building (Umpfenbach et al., 2022).

Another common business model for prosumption is based on energy communities and energy cooperatives that are groups of citizens that jointly invest in renewable energy production or energy system services. Energy communities are entities with a local, regional, or even national focus. In many situations, however, they invest in RES products close to the residences of the community's members or stockholders (Hall et al., 2019; Neska and Kowalska-Pyzalska, 2022).

Prosumer initiatives must be lucrative (or at the very least cost-neutral), even though prosumption cannot be considered a business activity. Otherwise, the majority of citizens would not think to interact with them. The prosumer business model outlines the roles and relationships between the various stakeholders, such as the prosumer and the relevant grid operators and energy companies, as well as possibly a service provider that supports the project, in addition to who will bear the costs and risks and decide who will benefit from the savings (Umpfenbach et al., 2022).

2.3.5 Pros and cons of prosumption

It should be highlighted that prosumption, can be advantageous to both the participants and society at large. These advantages could be economic, social, and environmental, but they are highly dependent on the project's details and the legal framework that the government has established (Horstink et al., 2020). Most stakeholders will need a strong business case before they will commit to a project, (Hall et al., 2019). A desire for autarchy or a desire to aid in the energy transition, are two further conceivable causes. The type of equity, which involves various types of funding, voting rights, information rights, obligations, and risks, as well as the purpose of the organization, such as societal benefits and profit maximization, are some important legal problems that must be taken into account (Umpfenbach et al., 2022; Lowitzsch, 2019).

Prosumerism brings benefits but also costs to those involved (Sung and Park, 2018). According to the European Environment Agency (EEA), with high energy prices and energy insecurity currently affecting Europe, small-scale prosumption provides a pathway for citizens to increase their energy independence. According to the recent REPowerEU proposal and its Solar Rooftop initiative, prosumers are the key element and in future, all EU citizens can potentially become energy prosumers.[4] Social benefits, including a sense of community and empowerment, are other significant values of prosumption. At the same time, prosumers face many challenges, including costs, regulatory barriers, and lack of knowledge and expertise in many different areas, including technology, policies, regulations, and financing. However, opportunities for prosumers are growing with technological development and, importantly, an increasingly supportive EU policy framework (Umpfenbach et al., 2022).

The most significant benefits and barriers of prosumerizm are summarized in Tables 2.1 and 2.2.

Effective policies and support mechanisms can help to decrease the aforementioned barriers (Umpfenbach et al., 2022). Government policies are an important enabler of prosumption. Prosumption can only grow where government regulations enable it to, and if effective and stable policies that promote these developments are in place (Umpfenbach et al., 2022). The EU provides a broad policy framework and objectives, with a recent emphasis on consumption as part of the REPowerEU plan (European Commission, 2022). As seen in Table 2.3, national governments apply and implement distinct policies adapted to their requirements and specific conditions (Umpfenbach et al., 2022).

---

[4]https://www.eea.europa.eu/highlights/citizens-can-contribute-to-europes-energy-transition (accessed October 20, 2022).

Table 2.1 A summary of the advantages of various sorts of prosumers (Umpfenbach et al., 2022).

Benefits for:	Individual prosumers	Collective prosumers	Public institutions
Environmental			
GHG emission reduction	All types of prosumer models contribute to reduction of GHG emissions in comparison to fossil-fuel generation systems.		
Reduction in usage of land	Rooftop PVs reduce the amount of land used for RES. Local consumption of electricity produced on-site reduces the need for new transmission lines.		
Social			
Public support for RES	All types of prosumer models contribute to public support of RES.		
Empowerment	Engaged citizens in all models are responsible to some extent for their own energy supply. Collective prosumption models give an opportunity for engagement even for consumers who would not invest in RES because of high investment cost.		
Sense of community	Limited, as individual households produce and consume the electricity for their own needs	High, as prosumers in a community share the benefits with their neighbors	Usually limited to employees of an organization involved
Fairness of distribution of benefits	Only owners of the building can participate and benefit	All community members can benefit from RES	Public institution may become a part of the energy community and hence share the benefits with its members
Financial			
Benefits and revenues for prosumers	Depends on various factors such as type of a business model, cost of technology and legislation framework		
Access to financial support	All prosumer models create access to funds for investment in RES projects		

Table 2.2 A summary of the barriers and challenges faced by various sorts of prosumers (Umpfenbach et al., 2022).

Barriers for:	Individual prosumers	Collective prosumers	Public institutions
Legislative			
Legislative setting	Regulation for individual prosumers is usually well developed, whereas for energy communities it is much more complex and less clear.		Rules are less clear when an public institution act as a part of a collective.
Financial			
Investment cost	Most of prosumers have to bear high investment cost which can be lowered dependent on the country-specific regulations and support systems.		
Access to financial support	It may be difficult for individual prosumers to cope with a high initial investment cost.	It is usually easier for collective prosumers to get financing, since investment cost splits between all community members.	It is usually easier for public institutions to get access to funds than households.
Technical			
Required infrastructure	Self-consumption usually does not require additional energy infrastructure.	Usually power grid reinforcement is needed for new collective projects.	Self-consumption usually does not require additional energy infrastructure
Lack of knowledge			
Deficit of knowledge about legislative framework, policies and RES technologies	Households often do not have specific knowledge about RES	Usually some members of the community have some knowledge, but the legislation for collectives is usually much more complex than for the individual prosumers.	Some institutions have enough knowledge, whereas the others do not. Generation of energy is not the core business here and therefore it may be often neglected.

Table 2.3 Solutions to barriers and challenges for prosumers (Umpfenbach et al., 2022).

Barriers	Prosumer model	Solution	Responsible stakeholder
Uncertain legislative framework	Mainly collective prosumers	● Define properly legal forms of prosumer models ● Define prosumers property rights	EU; national governments
High investment cost	All prosumer models	● Support financial schemes or grants	EU; national & local governments
Access to finance	Mainly individual prosumers	● Support financial schemes or loans	national & local governments
Missing required energy infrastructure	Mainly collective prosumers	● Provide necessary grid reinforcements	national & local governments Banks & financial institutions
Lack of knowledge of legislation and polices	All prosumer models	● Provide information campaigns by professional facilitators and service providers	national & local governments
Lack of knowledge of RES technologies	All prosumer models	● Provide information campaigns by professional facilitators and service providers	national & local governments associations and NGOs

2.3.6 Green electricity programs and tariffs

The second option for consumers' engagement includes green electricity tariffs or programs offered by energy sellers or governments in various countries. Such tariffs are offered by the energy suppliers, who guarantee that some or all of the electricity delivered by them has been generated from RES (Bird et al., 2002).

In the literature there are many different definitions of green electricity tariffs (GETs); see, for example, the studies of Bird et al. (2002), MacDonald and Eyre (2018), Hast et al. (2015), Diaz-Rainey and Tzavara (2012), or Mendonca et al. (2009). In most cases, however, green electricity tariffs describe:

- either a consumption based tariff where the consumer pays for the electricity produced in renewables; or

- paying a certain amount, proportional to electricity usage, in order to offset the carbon emissions including in the purchase of energy from an usual supplier.

As Diaz-Rainey and Tzavara (2012) state, green electricity tariffs are product innovations whereby the electricity supply company guarantees that the quantity of electricity delivered to the end consumer is matched by an equivalent amount of renewable energy generation. The tariffs thus provide additional investment incentives for the deployment of renewable energy sources (RES).

Green electricity tariffs are not a new phenomenon; Germany has had green electricity tariffs since the mid-1990s, while other countries such as Latvia have only just introduced systems. The existing literature on green electricity tariffs suggests that many factors can explain the differences in enrollment levels observed around the world. As the price of renewable electricity generation falls, the price differential between green electricity and conventional electricity will narrow. This process is already underway in many countries, prompting governments to eliminate subsidies such as feed-in tariffs. The voluntary sale of green power, as well as the accompanying market for renewable energy certificates, have had little effect on decisions to invest in renewable energy or the economic feasibility of such installations.

Green tariffs are also generally more expensive than standard electricity tariffs (MacDonald and Eyre, 2018). Energy markets are not designed to deal efficiently with sources such as renewables, which cost a lot to build but much less to operate than fossil fuels.[5] Governments offer producers long-term, fixed-price contracts for the renewable energy they produce. This is the biggest driver of investment, and competitive auctions of these contracts for companies wanting to build renewable power plants have reduced construction costs the most. On the other hand, households and other small consumers can rarely buy fixed-price contracts more than a year or two in advance, due to the uncertainty of wholesale prices and governments' encouragement of competitive switching. Electricity generated under renewable energy contracts is fed into the rest of the system, which offsets variable generation from renewables by generating more or less from conventional sources. This adds about $1.3 per kWh to the cost of renewable electricity in the UK and Europe. Even taking this into account, the difference between cheap renewables and expensive electricity becomes unimaginable.

As explained in the work of Schleich et al. (2022) and Danne et al. (2021), green electricity tariffs and programs offered by elec-

[5]https://www.ucl.ac.uk/news/2022/jan/opinion-renewables-are-cheaper-ever-so-why-are-household-energy-bills-only-going.

tricity companies are mostly certified via **green electricity labels**, such as in the case of Germany: "Grüner Strom Label," "ok-power," and "TÜV-Süd," "Eesti Energy Estonia" in Estonia, "Blue Energy Slovenia" in Slovenia, "Green-e" in the USA, or "EKOenergy label" in the UK, which are supposed to signal that the green electricity products have real environmental benefits (MacDonald and Eyre, 2018). There are also countries such as Norway, Iceland, or Austria where no consumer participation is involved in the decision to purchase green energy. It is caused by the fact that most, if not all, electricity produced in these countries come from RES.

2.3.7 Benefits and limitations of green electricity programs

Green electricity programs may provide significant benefits for electricity consumers.[6] First of all, correctly designed GETs may provide some cost protection or even a reduction in the electricity bill, while acting as a hedge on brown power costs, minimizing the impact of fluctuating power prices. Secondly, GETs have a positive impact on buyers' reputations, which is more important in the case of businesses than household electricity users. However, the literature still provides evidence of a neighboring effect, meaning that individuals living in the same area start to compete with each other in terms of eco-friendly behaviors, including energy savings and investments in renewable energy sources and programs Nolan et al. (2008); Allcott (2011); Ayers et al. (2013).

At the same time, green tariff programs have some limitations. Market adoption of these commodities is difficult because power is an abstract commodity and consumers rarely conserve it unless they are driven by financial, environmental, or social incentives. Dependent on the offer provided by the electrical utility, sometimes the buyers have to cope with the cost burden connected with the generation of electricity from RES. The tariffs are subjected to the regulatory processes, which may impact the design of the tariff in both positive and negative way, leading to the lack of stable solutions and contracts. Finally, some green electricity tariffs programs are inconsistently designed. Green tariffs are designed differently across utility service territories, which means that each green tariff needs a fresh assessment of benefits and risks by a customer willing to decide on it.[7]

---

[6]https://www.customerfirstrenewables.com/blog/greentariffs (accessed August 26, 2022).

[7]https://www.customerfirstrenewables.com/blog/greentariffs (accessed August 26, 2022).

Adoption of green electricity tariffs and programs require participation in switching processes from traditional electricity tariffs to green power tariffs, which often encounters resistance from consumers (Gerpott and Mahmudova, 2010; Clark et al., 2003). The condition for a consumer to switch to a green energy tariff is that the person is adequately informed about the process of migration to the other energy seller, and the impact of the change on the person's continuity of power supply (Gerpott and Mahmudova, 2010; Kowalska-Pyzalska, 2018b).

MacDonald and Eyre (2018) also observed a very important limitation for further spread of GETs. Electricity markets are projected to undergo significant change in the future years as technology such as smart meters and microgeneration become more widely available. These technologies have the potential to radically alter how customers interact with energy usage, and the tight division between retailer and consumer may no longer be valid in the future. This is already being seen in Australia, where consumer preferences are shifting away from paying green tariffs and toward more visible and local renewable energy assistance initiatives. This will be challenging for both green power marketers, who must compete with these new, more regional methods of supporting renewables, and regulators, who must decide how to integrate these new technology and activities into the grid and markets (MacDonald and Eyre, 2018).

2.3.8 Regulatory aspects of GETs

As MacDonald and Eyre (2018) pointed out, the number of countries where green electricity tariffs are available and the number of households purchasing tariffs have increased noticeably in recent decades. Markets that are well-established, including the Netherlands, Germany, and New Zealand, have had tremendous expansion. Recent market expansions in places like Eastern Europe have significantly increased the number of consumers who can choose to buy green electricity tariffs. Placement of green electricity pricing within the larger literature on support mechanisms for renewable electricity is also crucial (MacDonald and Eyre, 2018).

Research and development, prioritized grid access, product standards, and economic measures such as subsidies or obligations are only a few of the complicated policies used to support renewable energy sources. The final category of economic policies, which seek to narrow the price gap between green and gray electricity[8], is most relevant to this chapter. Many nations now decide to promote the growth of green electricity by raising the price that project developers are paid for the electricity they produce. Traditionally, this would be accomplished in one of two ways: either by a feed-in-tariff, which offers a fixed-price subsidy per generated unit (Mendonca et al., 2009), or through an obligation on suppliers to purchase a certain proportion of green electricity through a renewables portfolio standard.

The literature reveals that further adoption of green electricity tariffs requires:

- viewing green electricity products in their regulatory context;
- promoting GETs among consumers to increase their engagement in this field; and
- establishing of competitive retail electricity markets in enabling new innovative products to thrive.

Often the debate around energy market regulation focuses on delivering price reductions to consumers, perhaps ignoring other benefits in terms of innovative products which deliver other forms of value to customers (MacDonald and Eyre, 2018).

2.3.9 Smart metering and smart metering information systems

The widespread adoption of smart meters (SMs) among electricity end-users is one of the key milestones in the conversion of the conventional power system to smart grids (SG) (Bugden and Stedman, 2019; Ellabban and Abu-Rub, 2016; Verbong et al., 2013). SMs are intelligent, network-enabled measuring systems for resources such as water, gas, or electricity that use computer-aided measurement, determination, and control of consumption and supply for residential, commercial, and industrial buildings. SMs are opposed to traditional standalone analog-based meters, which do not have the ability to wireless send meter readings.

There are various kinds of smart meters, measuring electricity, water, or gas consumption. Dependent on the purpose, SMs require different mechanisms and offer different measurements. For example, smart electric meters record information about consumption of electric energy, voltage levels, current, and power factor.

A report published by Bonafide Research, "Global Smart Meter Market Outlook, 2027," revealed that all three kinds of smart meters (electricity, gas, and water) contributed to more than 55% of the market share in 2021 (Report, 2022). The report showed

---

[8]Gray electricity is a product's hidden energy, which is the entire energy utilized during the product's life cycle, from manufacture to disposal.

the replacement ratio between the traditional analog meters into the smart ones. The SM market in total reached approximately 20 billion in 2021. It is expected to expand at a compound annual growth rate (CAGR) of 8.7% from 2022 to 2027. Such a rapid growth rate is caused by the fact that many countries' governments have taken a step toward making SM mandates and regularly provide incentives for the installation of SMs, which drives their robust growth in the future.

The broad implementation of electricity SMs in Europe has been induced by, among others, the EU directives concerning common rules for the internal market for electricity and gas (2009/72/EC and 2009/73/EC) (European Commission, 2009) and the EU directive on energy efficiency (2012/27/EC) (European Commission, 2012). These regulations require EU member states to ensure the implementation of SMs in order to enable active participation of consumers in the energy market. From an energy system point of view, smart metering and smart grid rollout are expected to reduce EU emissions and annual household energy consumption by as much as 9%.[9] The EU had established for diffusion of electricity smart meters a very ambitious penetration target of 80% by 2020, but recently these expectations have been lowered to 72%, which is still a lot, as finally the rollout of SMs is implemented based on national regulations and agreements.

The current stage of SM deployment differs among countries. In the EU, there are countries that have already finalized their implementation of SMs, but in many others, billing is still performed on quarterly or even yearly forecasts rather than on the basis of real electricity consumption (Zhou and Brown, 2017; Avancini et al., 2019; Chawla et al., 2020b). For example, countries like Denmark, Sweden, Finland, Estonia, and Spain have already finalized the implementation of SMs. At the same time, countries such as Norway, Italy, and the UK are in an advanced stage (Sovacool et al., 2017; Zhou and Brown, 2017), and other countries, such as Germany, the Czech Republic, Greece, and Ireland, demonstrate a lower level of commitment toward the implementation of SMs (European Commission, 2018; Chawla et al., 2020b).

The European electrical industry, which sees significant benefits from smart meters, is in favor of increasing digitalization at the same time. Eurelectric estimates that by 2030, solar PV systems installed on rooftops will account for more than half of all electricity generated in Europe. By that time, the EU anticipates that more than 40 million electric vehicles will be driving on European roads. In the meantime, it's anticipated that the number of electric heat

---

[9]https://ec.europa.eu/energy/en/topics/markets-and-consumers/smart-grids-and-meters/overview (accessed September 6, 2019).

pumps, batteries, and other smart grid-connected devices would increase significantly. It is anticipated that smart meters will be necessary for all of this equipment to operate effectively.[10]

The deployment of electricity SMs is not limited to Europe. In contrast, the Asia Pacific SM market dominates globally with more than 38% market share in 2021, and is expected to continue its position due to government mandates, higher investments toward the digitization of grids, and public-private partnerships (Report, 2022). China and Japan are the largest markets, and India has the fastest-growing SM market. Market experts predict further growth rates for SMs due to the imposed governmental regulations in these countries (Chawla et al., 2020c; Kumar, 2019; Joseph, 2015; Thakur and Chakraborty, 2019; Acharjee, 2013; Rathi and Chunekar, 2015).

The North America region is a very mature market for smart electricity meters. The further deployment of SMs in the United States is overseen by individual states and territories rather than the federal government (Report, 2022). Providers are rapidly innovating to be on a par with smart meter technology. Moreover, the adoption of smart appliances, smart homes, shared mobility, and 3D printing is enabling the growth of smart electric meters (Report, 2022).

Recently, the highest growth rate of SM rollout has been observed among residential consumers. This is driven by the increased use of smart home appliances in residential buildings (Report, 2022). SMs help in integrating distributed energy resources, energy storage technologies, and EV charging facilities. Moreover, they allow consumers to learn about their current energy consumption and are a precondition to use demand-side management and demand response tools. On the other hand, commercial and industrial sectors have other motivations for meter replacement. As Report (2022) indicates, the commercial sector has started a rapid replacement of the meters from analog into smart ones, in order to increase the efficiency of electricity usage and enable better renewable energy integration into the grid. The industrial sector is hoping for effective load management and is forecasting a reduction of energy thefts due to smart meter installation.

2.3.10 Benefits of SMs

According to Biresselioglu et al. (2018), Zhou and Brown (2017), and Burchell et al. (2016), SMs may bring various benefits to

[10]https://www.euractiv.com/section/energy/news/smart-meter-woes-hold-back-digitalization-of-eu-power-sector (accessed September 10, 2019).

both consumers and suppliers. Consumers can take advantage of the advantages of progressive digitalization of the energy market through various different functionalities by:

- receiving much more accurate billing; and
- gaining an opportunity to control one's energy consumption in real time.

The information collected by SMs can provide consumers with **feedback on current energy consumption and energy efficiency** via a **smart metering information system platform (SMP)** and **enabling technologies** that include an internet platform or mobile apps, and are often combined with other smart appliances, such as in-home displays, home area networks (HANs), smart home appliances, and smart plugs (Foulds et al., 2017; Schleich et al., 2017; Buchanan et al., 2014; Kowalska-Pyzalska and Byrka, 2019; Krishnamutri et al., 2012; Nachreiner et al., 2015).

In the work of Chawla and Kowalska-Pyzalska (2019), the authors reviewed the literature and revealed that the access to the data from smart meters by means of SMP and enabling technologies helps consumers to make informed decisions about electricity consumption, thus resulting in average energy savings of 2–4% (Ofgem, 2011; Meijer et al., 2018). Customers who have access to data on their electricity consumption can also learn about the various electricity tariffs available based on the time and the spot electricity price (Faruqui and Sergici, 2010; Star et al., 2010), which may lead to lower electricity bills (Gans et al., 2013; Verbong et al., 2013; Burchell et al., 2016; Schleich et al., 2017; Krishnamutri et al., 2012). The adoption of innovative goods and services like smart appliances and home batteries may increase with the help of SMs. These can be controlled remotely or automatically based on information about energy tariff prices (Hinson et al., 2019; Aghaei and Alizadeh, 2013). SMs would also make it easier for consumers to change between suppliers, creating a more competitive market with lower tariffs.

Smart meters also offer certain benefits to the energy suppliers, including:

- better communication between producers, distributors, sellers, and consumers (Ellabban and Abu-Rub, 2016; Biresselioglu et al., 2018; Crispim et al., 2014; Zhou and Brown, 2017);
- elimination of manual monthly meter readings;
- enabled monitoring of load in real time;
- the possibility to introduce dynamic pricing (as part of demand-side management);
- encouraging more efficient use of electricity;

- providing responsive data for balancing electric loads in order to reduce blackouts; and
- elimination of energy thefts.

The exchange of current meters to SMs in the power system may also avoid the capital expense of building new power plants by optimizing the usage of existing resources (Avancini et al., 2019).

2.3.11 Demand-side management and demand response tools

The management of power systems is classified into two different types: supply-side management and demand-side management (DSM). Both strategies, as Jabir et al. (2018) have emphasized, are useful for mitigating contingencies, increasing network loading capacity, and reducing peak loads, but they have important differences.

The goal of supply-side management is to make the production, transmission, and distribution of electricity more productive. In order to maximize consumer value, supply-side management benefits include: (1) ensuring efficient energy production at the lowest possible cost; (2) meeting electricity demand without the need for additional infrastructure investments; and (3) reducing environmental impacts through the effective operation of power system assets (Jabir et al., 2018).

In contrast to supply-side management, DSM is concerned with electrical load levels and usage patterns and is therefore unaffected by external factors, such as volatility of fuel prices. Taking into account a forecasted growth of electricity demand expanding the expansion rate of the power system, DSM is perceived as a more beneficial strategy than supply-side management (Jabir et al., 2018). DSM is defined as "the planning, implementation, and monitoring of distribution network utility activities designed to influence customer use of electricity in ways that will produce desired changes in the load shape" (AlSkaif et al., 2018). In most cases, DSM instruments cover educational or marketing campaigns informing and encouraging consumers to conduct more energy-efficient behaviors while consuming electricity.

On the other side, demand response (DR) includes all the tools, mechanisms, and programs that send price incentives to the customers and make them adjust their electricity demand to the needs of the power system, as shown in Fig. 2.5. DR covers (Darby and McKenna, 2012; Faruqui and Sergici, 2010; Gerpott and Mahmudova, 2010; Strbac, 2008):

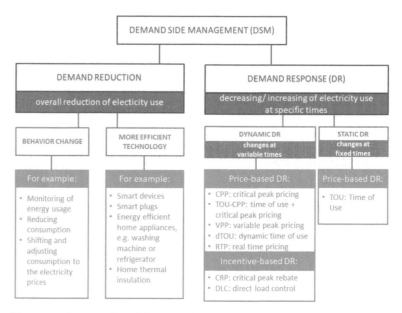

Figure 2.5. Classification of demand-side management techniques and demand response programs (Alotaibi et al., 2020).

- **time-based pricing**, including time-of-use rates, critical peak pricing, real-time pricing, and others; and
- **incentive-based demand response**, including direct load control, emergency demand response programs, capacity market programs, and others.

The typical division of DSM/DR tools is presented in Fig. 2.5.

DSM/DR tools are offered by energy suppliers to residential, commercial, and industrial customers in order to achieve three goals:

- peak-shaving by shifting the consumption from peak to off-peak times of the day;
- balance the demand and supply; and, ultimately,
- lower and flatten the demand by energy conservation behaviors (Batalla-Bejerano et al., 2020; Martin, 2020).

In practice, DSM/DR can be offered by energy suppliers to retail customers in the energy market in the form of (optional) programs with voluntary subscription. Implementation of these tools requires first the installation of an electricity smart meter at the household level. Thus, having a SM installed at the household is a precondition to adopt the majority of DSM/DR instruments.

2.3.12 Dynamic pricing as the most common DSM/DR tool for residential consumers

From the broad range of DSM/DR tools, individual consumers are mostly experienced with time-based pricing, often called **dynamic tariffs** or **dynamic pricing**. The main difference between dynamic pricing and flat, conventional tariffs is the dependence of the electricity price on the balance between supply and demand in the market in the case of dynamic tariffs. The initial idea of dynamic electricity tariffs is to transfer a signal to the customer (Freier and von Loessl, 2022). With such a tariff, the consumer may notice many shifts in price levels throughout the course of the day as a result of variations in supply and demand (Faruqui and Sergici, 2010; Strbac, 2008; Thorsens et al., 2012; Kowalska-Pyzalska et al., 2014).

Dynamic tariffs were developed to flatten the curve and move demand from peak to off-peak hours. On the one hand, the shift in load indicates a change in the habits and daily routines of consumers. However, it is sometimes associated with a reduction in overall energy consumption (Kowalska-Pyzalska et al., 2014). Dynamic tariffs can bring benefits for consumers (potential savings, satisfaction about being ecological) and for the electricity retailers, and even more for distribution system operators (lower investment and operational costs).

Supporting demand flexibility usually involves some kind of behavioral change, such as doing laundry or heating water at different times than normal, or otherwise modifying consumption behavior when necessary. Demand flexibility in more sophisticated solutions necessitates consumer consent for different actors to collect data from smart devices on the consumer's premises, as well as a signed agreement allowing a third party actor to control the consumer's devices as agreed, when necessary (Immonen et al., 2020). However, it should be noted that in most circumstances, consumers have limited options for transferring load, and even if they are willing to do so by modifying their own behavior and consuming patterns, this usually has no major effect on the prices they pay (Immonen et al., 2020).

Numerous pilot projects and studies carried out in recent years have demonstrated how challenging it is to persuade consumers to convert to a new tariff and engage them fully (Allcott, 2011; Faruqui and Sergici, 2010; Star et al., 2010; Thorsens et al., 2012; Duetschke and Paetz, 2013). This is due to the general indifference of people about energy and electricity tariffs in particular. Secondly, the savings that can be gained due to dynamic pricing are in many single cases not impressive enough to encourage more people to enroll in these pricing programs. Finally, switching to a new tariff is often connected with some discomfort, because of rescheduling of the energy consumption according to the price signals (ATKearney, 2012; Faruqui and Sergici, 2010; Thorsens et al., 2012; Kowalska-Pyzalska et al., 2014).

2.3.13 Grid services

The consumers' participation in DSM/DR can be a part of grid services, which should be separately billed and taxed to the electricity consumption. Energy storage, which may become very popular among prosumers, especially the owners of PVs, may allow them to store electricity from the grid for a short time to provide frequency control services. Such a service should be metered and charged separately. At the same time, consumption from the grid should be charged and taxed in an ordinary way.

The impact of individual consumers and their ability to offer grid services for the power system is usually limited because of three main reasons (Biegel et al., 2014). Firstly, flexible consumption devices in an individual household have a limited energy capacity and therefore cannot provide actual energy deliveries. Secondly, it is often difficult to make an accurate consumption baseline estimate for a portfolio of flexible consumption devices. Thirdly, the regulations for providing ancillary services do not always include individual electricity end-users. That is why sometimes grid services are offered jointly by a kind of market aggregator (Biegel et al., 2014).

Today, active customers often lose their benefits from renewable support schemes (Feed-in premium or tariff, guarantees of origins) when they provide flexibility services, for example, under the German renewable energy for tenants' scheme. Indeed, when an active customer uses their battery facility to provide services both with their self-generated renewable electricity and electricity from the grid, their stored "green" electrons lose their right to related financial incentives (Immonen et al., 2020).

This constitutes a significant barrier to providing ancillary services with renewable electricity, which is crucial to optimize renewable generation and adapt to the system's needs. In addition, it becomes more beneficial to restrict renewable energy compared to storing it and using it for flexibility. It is therefore crucial that active customers are guaranteed their access to financial incentives linked with their renewable self-generation, including when stored.[11]

[11] https://ec.europa.eu/info/funding-tenders/opportunities/portal/screen/opportunities/topic-details/horizon-cl5-2022-d3-01-08 (accessed January 20, 2023).

2.4 Summary

Around the world, smart and eco-friendly technologies are gaining popularity. The greater and quicker penetration of these products into the energy markets is due to a number of factors. It is sufficient to note the pressing need for social and energy transformation of energy systems from conventional—based on fossil fuels with passive consumers—to smart grids, in which contemporary information and communication technologies play a significant role, allowing real-time information exchange between all market participants: energy producers, sellers, distributors, and end electricity users, i.e., consumers.

Consumer participation in the energy market is now encouraged. By installing their own energy generators in their homes, consumers can turn into producers of heat and electricity under the smart or micro grid method.

The introduction of electric smart meters, combined with other enabling technologies such as DSM/DR tools or smart metering information platforms (SMPs), gives consumers access to and better control over their energy consumption (Chawla and Kowalska-Pyzalska, 2019; Biresselioglu et al., 2018; Bellido et al., 2018).

This market trend will continue in the years to come and indeed the role of energy users is predicted to increase further. In future scenarios of the energy domain actors, as emphasized by, among others, Immonen et al. (2020), the electricity consumer will have a key role. In these scenarios, homes and properties equipped with smart appliances will form a total package of flexible potential that is delivered to flexibility markets. To make this possible, electricity consumers agree to allow a third party to collect data from their home appliances on their electricity consumption behavior and to control their home appliances remotely. In addition, consumers become active market participants, aware of the consequences of their behavior in the market.

2.5 References and proposed additional reading

Renewables and prosumption:
- Coenen and Hoppe (2022) Renewable Energy Communities and the Low Carbon Energy Transition in Europe, Palgrae MacMillian, 1st edition (Coenen and Hoppe, 2022)
- Coy et al. (2021) Rethinking community empowerment in the energy transformation: a critical review of the definitions,

drivers and outcomes. Energy Res. Social Sci. 72, 101871 (Coy et al., 2021)

- Engelken et al. (2016) Comparing drivers, barriers and opportunities of business models for renewable energy: a review. Renewable and Sustainable Energy Reviews 60, 795–809 (Engelken et al., 2016)
- Hall et al. (2019) Prosumers for the Energy Union: mainstreaming active participation of citizens in the energy transition. In: Business Models for Prosumers in Europe, Deliverable 4.1 of the Horizon 2020 PROSEU project (H2020-LCE-2017) (Hall et al., 2019)
- Horstink et al. (2020) Collective renewable energy prosumers and the promises of the energy union: taking stock. Energies 13(2), 421 (Horstink et al., 2020)
- Jee et al. (2022) Data-analytic assessment for flexumers under demand diversification in power system. IEEE Access 10, 33313–33319 (Jee et al., 2022)
- Kardooni et al. (2016) Renewable energy technology acceptance in peninsular Malaysia. Energy Policy 88, 1–10 (Kardooni et al., 2016)
- Köppl et al. (2022) Enabling Business Models and Grid Stability: Case Studies from Germany, Energy Communities. Academic Press 229–243 (Köppl et al., 2022)
- Kumar et al. (2017) A review of multi criteria decision making (MCDM) towards sustainable renewable energy development. Renewable and Sustainable Energy Reviews 69, 596–609 (Kumar et al., 2017)
- Lennon et al. (2019) Community acceptability and the energy transition: a citizens' perspective. Energy Sustain. Soc. 9(1), 35 (Lennon et al., 2019)
- Lowitzsch (2019) Energy Transition—Financing Consumer Coownership in Renewables. Palgrave Macmillan, Cham, Switzerland (Lowitzsch, 2019)
- Martin (2020) Making sense of renewable energy: practical knowledge, sensory feedback and household understandings in a Scottish island microgrid. Energy Research and Social Science 66, 101501 (Martin, 2020)
- Milciuviene et al. (2019) The role of renewable energy prosumers in implementing energy justice theory. Sustainability 11, 5286 (Milciuviene et al., 2019)
- Neska and Kowalska-Pyzalska (2022) Conceptual design of energy market topologies for communities and their practical applications in EU: a comparison of three case studies. Renewable and Sustainable Energy Reviews 169, 112921 (Neska and Kowalska-Pyzalska, 2022)

- Sung and Park (2018) Who drives the transition to a renewable-energy economy? Multi-actor perspective on social innovation. Sustainability 10, 448–480 (Sung and Park, 2018)
- Strantzali and Aravossis (2015) Decision making in renewable energy investments: a review. Renewable and Sustainable Energy Reviews 55, 885–889 (Strantzali and Aravossis, 2015)
- Radl et al. (2020) Comparison of profitability of PV electricity sharing in renewable energy communities in selected European countries. Energies, 13(19), 5007 (Radl et al., 2020)
- REN21, Renewables 2021 Global Status Report; Renewable Energy Policy Network for the 21st Century: Paris, France, ISBN 978-3-948393-03-8 (REN21, 2021)
- Thakur and Chakraborty (2019) Impact of compensation mechanisms for PV generation on residential consumers and shared net metering model for developing nations: a case study of India. Journal of Cleaner Production 218, 696–707 (Thakur and Chakraborty, 2019)
- Umpfenbach et al. (2022) Energy prosumers in Europe—citizen participation in the energy transition. In: European Environment Agency (ed.); EEA Report No 01/2022. Luxembourg: Publications Office of the European Union (Umpfenbach et al., 2022)
- Wicki et al. (2022) Factors determining the development of prosumer photovoltaic installations in Poland. Energies 15, 5897 (Wicki et al., 2022)

Green electricity tariffs and programs:
- Clark et al. (2003) Internal and external influences on pro-environmental behavior: participation in a green electricity program. Journal of Environmental Psychology 23, 237–246 (Clark et al., 2003)
- Bird et al. (2002) A review of international green power markets: recent experience, trends, and market drivers. Renewable and Sustainable Energy Reviews 6, 513–536 (Bird et al., 2002)
- Danne et al. (2021) Analyzing German consumers' willingness to pay for green electricity tariff attributes: a discrete choice experiment. Energ. Sustain. Soc. 11(15) (Danne et al., 2021)
- Diaz-Rainey and Tzavara (2012) Financing the decarbonized energy system through green electricity tariffs: a diffusion model of an induced consumer environmental market. Technological Forecasting & Social Change 79, 1693–1704 (Diaz-Rainey and Tzavara, 2012)
- Diaz-Rainey and Ashton (2011) Profiling potential green electricity tariff adopters: green consumerism as an environmental policy tool? Business Strategy and The Environment 20(7), 456–470 (Diaz-Rainey and Ashton, 2011)

- Gerpott and Mahmudova (2010) Determinants of green electricity adoption among residential customers in Germany. International Journal of Consumers Studies 34, 464–473 (Gerpott and Mahmudova, 2010)
- Hast et al. (2015) Review of green electricity products in the United Kingdom, Germany and Finland. Renewable and Sustainable Energy Reviews 42, 1370–1384 (Hast et al., 2015)
- Kowalska-Pyzalska (2015) Social acceptance of green energy and dynamic electricity tariffs—a short review. In: International Conference on Modern Electric Power Systems (MEPS'15), 6–9 July 2015, Wroclaw, Poland (Kowalska-Pyzalska, 2015)
- Kowalska-Pyzalska (2018) An empirical analysis of green electricity adoption among residential consumers in Poland. Sustainability 10, 2281 (Kowalska-Pyzalska, 2018a)
- MacDonald and Eyre (2018) An international review of markets for voluntary green electricity tariffs. Renewable and Sustainable Energy Reviews 91, 180–192 (MacDonald and Eyre, 2018)
- MacPherson and Lange (2013) Determinants of green electricity tariff uptake in the UK. Energy Policy 62, 920–933 (MacPherson and Lange, 2013)
- Mendonca et al. (2009) Powering the Green Economy: The Feed-in Tariff Handbook. Routledge, 1st edition (Mendonca et al., 2009)
- Schleich et al. (2022) Do green electricity tariffs increase household electricity consumption? Applied Economics, https://doi.org/10.1080/00036846.2022.2102574
- Thorsens et al. (2012) Consumer responses to time varying prices for electricity. Energy Policy 49, 552–561 (Thorsens et al., 2012)

DSM/DR and enabling technologies:
- Aghaei and Alizadeh (2013) Demand response in smart electricity grids equipped with renewable energy sources: a review. Renewable and Sustainable Energy Reviews 18, 64–72 (Aghaei and Alizadeh, 2013)
- Chen et al. (2021) Electricity demand response schemes in China: pilot study and future outlook. Energy 224, 120042 (Chen et al., 2021)
- Darby and McKenna (2012) Social implications of residential demand response in cool temperature climates. Energy Policy 49, 759–769
- D'hulst (2015) Demand response flexibility and flexibility potential of residential smart appliances: experiences from large pilot test in Belgium. Applied Energy 155, 79–90 (D'hulst et al., 2015)

- Faruqui and Sergici (2010) Household response to dynamic pricing of electricity—a survey of the experimental evidence. Journal of Regulatory Economics 28, 193–220 (Faruqui and Sergici, 2010)
- Freier von Loessl (2022) Dynamic electricity tariffs: designing reasonable pricing schemes for private households. Energy Economics 112, 106146 (Freier and von Loessl, 2022)
- Jabir et al. (2018) Impacts of demand-side management on electrical power systems: a review. Energies 11, 1050 (Jabir et al., 2018)
- Kowalska-Pyzalska et al. (2014) Turning green: agent-based modeling of the adoption of dynamic electricity tariffs. Energy Policy 71, 164–174 (Kowalska-Pyzalska et al., 2014)
- O'Connell et al. (2014) Benefits and challenges of electricity demand response: a critical review. Renewable and Sustainable Energy Reviews 39, 686–699 (O'Connell et al., 2014)
- Procter, R.J. (2013) Integrating time-differentiated rates, demand response, and smart grids to manage power system costs. The Electricity Journal 36(3) 50–59 (Procter, 2013)
- Pratt and Erickson (2020) Defeat the peak: behavioral insights for electricity demand response program design. Energy Res. Soc. Sci. 61, 101352 (Pratt and Erickson, 2020)
- Siano (2014) Demand response and smart grids—a survey. Renewable and Sustainable Energy Reviews 30, 461–478 (Siano, 2014)
- Strbac (2008) Demand-side management: benefits and challenges. Energy Policy 36(12), 4419–4426
- Tahir et al. (2020) Significance of demand response in light of current pilot projects in China and devising a problem solution for future advancements. Technology in Society 63, 101374 (Tahir et al., 2020)

Smart meters and smart metering platforms:
- Avancini et al. (2019) Energy meters evolution in smart grids: a review. Journal of Cleaner Production 217, 702–715 (Avancini et al., 2019)
- Batalla-Bejerano (2020) Smart meters and consumer behaviour: insights from the empirical literature. Energy Policy 144, 111610 (Batalla-Bejerano et al., 2020)
- Bugden and Stedman (2019) A synthetic view of acceptance and engagement with smart meters in the United States. Energy Research and Social Science 47, 137–145 (Bugden and Stedman, 2019)
- Burchell et al. (2016) Householder engagement with energy consumption feedback: the role of community action and

communications. Energy Policy 88, 178–186 (Burchell et al., 2016)

- Chawla and Kowalska-Pyzalska (2019) Public awareness and consumer acceptance of smart meters among Polish social media users. Energies 12, 2759 (Chawla and Kowalska-Pyzalska, 2019)
- Chawla et al. (2020) Marketing and communications channels for diffusion of electricity smart meters in Portugal. Telematics and Informatics 50, 101385 (Chawla et al., 2020b)
- Foulds et al. (2017) Energy monitoring as a practice: investigating use of the iMeasure online energy feedback tool. Energy Policy 104, 194–402 (Foulds et al., 2017)
- Gans et al. (2013) Smart meter devices and the effect of feedback on residential electricity consumption: evidence from a natural experiment in Northern Ireland. Energy Economics 36, 729–743 (Gangale et al., 2013)
- Hinson et al. (2019) Energy smart meters. Commons Library Briefing, April 3, 2019; No. 8119 (Hinson et al., 2019)
- Kowalska-Pyzalska and Byrka (2019) Determinants of the willingness to energy monitoring by residential consumers: a case study in the city of Wroclaw in Poland. Energies 12, 907 (Kowalska-Pyzalska and Byrka, 2019)
- Olmos et al. (2011) Energy efficiency actions related to the rollout of smart meters for small consumers: application to the Austrian system. Energy 36, 4396–4409 (Olmos et al., 2011)
- Meijer et al. (2018) Impact of Home Energy Monitoring and Management Systems (HEMS): Triple-Λ: Stimulating the Adoption of Low-Carbon Technologies by Homeowners through Increased Awareness and Easy Access. Report on Impact of HEMS; Interreg: Lille, France (Meijer et al., 2018)
- Moreno-Munoz et al. (2016) Mobile social media for smart grids customer engagement: emerging trends and challenges. Renewable and Sustainable Energy Reviews 53, 1611–1616 (Moreno-Munoz et al., 2016)
- Nachreiner et al. (2015) An analysis of smart metering information systems: a psychological model of self-regulated behavioral change. Energy Research & Social Science 9, 85–97 (Nachreiner et al., 2015)
- Sovacool et al. (2017) Vulnerability and resistance in the United Kingdom's smart meter transition. Energy Policy 109, 767–781 (Sovacool et al., 2017)
- Schleich et al. (2017) Persistence of the effects of providing feedback alongside smart metering devices on household electricity demand. Energy Policy 107, 225–233 (Schleich et al., 2017)

- Zhou and Brown (2017) Smart meter deployment in Europe: a comparative case study on the impacts of national policy schemes. Journal of Cleaner Production 144, 22–32 (Zhou and Brown, 2017)

Consumers' empowerment:
- Biresselioglu et al. (2018) Examining the barriers and motivators affecting European decision makers in the development of smart and green energy technologies. Journal of Cleaner Production 198, 417–429 (Biresselioglu et al., 2018)
- Ellabban and Abu-Rub (2016) Smart grid customers' acceptance and engagement: an overview. Renewable and Sustainable Energy Reviews 65, 1285–1298 (Ellabban and Abu-Rub, 2016)
- Schweiger et al. (2020) Active consumer participation in smart energy systems. Energy and Buildings 227, 110359 (Schweiger et al., 2020)
- Shaukat et al. (2018) A survey on consumers empowerment, communication technologies, and renewable generation penetration within smart grid. Renewable and Sustainable Energy Reviews 81, 1453–1475 (Shaukat et al., 2018)
- Verbong et al. (2013) Smart grids or smart users? Involving users in developing a low carbon electricity economy. Energy Policy 52, 117–125 (Verbong et al., 2013)

Others:
- Acharjee (2013) Strategy and implementation of smart grids in India. Energy Strategy Reviews 1(3), 193–204 (Acharjee, 2013)
- Allcott (2011) Social norms and energy conservation. Journal of Public Economics 95, 1082–1095 (Allcott, 2011)
- Ayers et al. (2013) Evidence from two large field experiments that peer comparison feedback can reduce residential energy usage. The Journal of Law, Economics and Organization 29(5), 992–1022 (Ayers et al., 2013)
- Fouad et al. (2022) Perceptions of consumers towards smart and sustainable energy market services: the role of early adopters. Renewable Energy 187, 14–33 (Fouad et al., 2022)
- Immonen et al. (2020) Consumer viewpoint on a new kind of energy market. Electric Power Systems Research 180, 106153 (Immonen et al., 2020)
- Joseph (2015) Smart grid and retail competition in India: a review on technological and managerial initiatives and challenges. Procedia Technology 21, 155–162 (Joseph, 2015)
- Kumar (2019) Beyond technical smartness: rethinking the development and implementation of sociotechnical smart grids in India. Energy Research & Social Science 49, 158–168 (Kumar, 2019)

- Kowalska-Pyzalska (2018) What makes consumers adopt to innovative energy services in the energy market? A review of incentives and barriers. Renewable and Sustainable Energy Reviews 82(3) 3570–3581 (Kowalska-Pyzalska, 2018b)
- Lammers and Hoppe (2019) Watt rules? Assessing decision-making practices on smart energy systems in Dutch city districts. Energy Research & Social Science, 47, 233–246 (Lammers and Hoppe, 2019)
- Nicholson (2015) RECIPE for meaningful gamification. In: Gamification in Education and Business. Springer International Publishing, Cham, 1–20 (Nicholson, 2015)
- Schot et al. (2016) The roles of users in shaping transitions to new energy systems. Nature Energy 1(5), 1–7 (Schot et al., 2016).

3

Theoretical background of innovation diffusion in the context of the energy market

3.1 Introduction

In this chapter, we introduce the theoretical background of innovation diffusion models. In particular, we will present the main assumptions of Rogers' innovation diffusion model (Rogers, 2003), comparing it with the Bass and percolation models. We explain the elements and steps of the adoption process and show how it works in the case of innovative energy services in the energy market.

Not all of the innovations succeed in the market. In fact, there is a high rate of failure of innovations (Claudy et al., 2015). The process of designing and launching an innovation consumes time, money, and effort. Hence, it is essential to understand why and under what circumstances consumers adopt innovations (Valor et al., 2022). Traditionally, researchers have focused on the rational factors or motives for adopting innovations, such as financial and nonfinancial costs and benefits, and socio-economic and psychological attributes of adopters (Marikyan et al., 2019; Arts et al., 2011). For example, the meta-analysis of Arts et al. (2011) has shown that consumers are found actually to adopt innovations with less complexity and higher relative advantages. Recently, the study of Valor et al. (2022) paid additionally attention to the role of emotions on the innovation adoption.

The innovation diffusion literature differentiates two stages in adoption process:

- intention adoption—forming an opinion toward an innovation; and
- behavior adoption—deciding on a given innovation and making a purchase/starting using it or behaving in a new way.

These will be briefly discussed in the sections below.

Diffusion of Innovative Energy Services. https://doi.org/10.1016/B978-0-12-822882-1.00009-3

3.2 The process and determinants of innovation diffusion

3.2.1 Innovation diffusion

As mentioned in earlier chapters (see Chapters 1 and 2), to ensure a reliable, sustainable, and efficient power system in the future, successful diffusion of innovative energy services is needed. Moglia et al. (2017) explained that in physics, **diffusion** is a process in which:

- particles intermingle; and
- the heat is transferred between objects that are in contact with each other.

Rogers (2003) already in 1962 introduced the term **technology diffusion**, or **innovation diffusion**; this is a metaphor that refers to the process by which technology spreads and is adopted in a social system.

The theory of innovation diffusion is supposed to help understand how and why some innovations—products, services, or ideas, perceived by individuals as new—are spread (diffused) successfully among consumers in the market. **Diffusion** itself is a process in a **social system** where an innovative idea, concept or a good is spread by members of the social group through certain communication channels within a certain period of time (Rogers, 2003). In general, diffusion research seeks to understand the spread of innovations by modeling their entire life cycle from the perspective of communications and consumer interactions (Peres et al., 2010). Although the beginning of the innovation diffusion theory dates to the early years of the 20th century, the main assumptions involved in this theory were formulated by Rogers (2003) in the first edition of his book, published in 1962. Rogers' diffusion of innovations (DoI) model seeks to explain how, why, and at what rate new ideas and technology spread in the entire life cycle from the perspective of communications and consumer interactions (Peres et al., 2010). According to Rogers, diffusion is the process through which invention spreads over time among members of a social network. The DoI model states that four key factors affect the growth of a new good, service, or concept: a social network (system), time, the innovation itself, and a communication channel.

Communication channels include traditional mass media (TV, radio, newspapers) and social media (Facebook, Twitter, Instagram, etc.) as well as interpersonal communication (i.e., word of mouth, WOM). Diffusion of innovation needs some amount of **time**, which is necessary for an individual to follow the steps of the adoption process (explained below). Rogers emphasizes that the innovation must be widely adopted in society in order to self-sustain and spread. That is why this model pays great attention to human capital. There is a point, within a certain rate of adoption, at which innovation reaches "critical mass," which allows the innovation to spread further in the market (Kowalska-Pyzalska et al., 2014). In other words, successful implementation of innovative solutions require high consumer **adoption rates**, which refers to the number of members of a society who start using a new technology or innovation during a specific period of time (Kowalska-Pyzalska, 2018b). This indicates that consumers play a crucial role in the innovation adoption process (Zhang and Nuttall, 2011; Bollinger and Gillingham, 2012; Frank et al., 2015; Jager, 2006).

The definition of innovation provided by Peres et al. (2010) emphasizes the role of social interactions. According to the authors, "innovation diffusion is the process of the market penetration of new products and services that is driven by social influences, which include all interdependencies among consumers that affect various market players with or without their explicit knowledge" (Peres et al., 2010). Rogers describes an innovation as a product, service, or idea that has the following features (Rogers, 2003):

- relative advantage of an innovation in comparison to the conventional products, services, or ideas;
- compatibility with existing values, past experiences and needs of potential adopters;
- complexity (or simplicity) of an innovation, meaning the skills and effort needed to adopt an innovation;
- trialability of the innovation, meaning whether the innovation can be tested prior to adoption; and
- observability of the innovation in the market, i.e., peer discussion about the innovation in the market.

In other words, to treat something as an innovation, it must offer some new quality or usefulness to customers. Its design or concept should satisfy some individual or societal need. People should be able to observe or try the innovation before they decide to adopt it.

Let us take an example of the innovative solar PV technology to analyze its attributes in the context of adoption decisions (similarly to the comparison provided by Wilson and Downlatabadi, 2007). Firstly, cost savings in terms of electricity bills or household energy safety can provide a relative advantage over the incumbent technology or practice and can be responsible for its compatibility with the consumers' needs. At the same time some perceived barriers to adoption of solar PV such as high investment cost or technical requirements of the household can be responsible for the complexity of the innovation. Peer experience or social feedback may reduce uncertainty about the innovation, making it easier to adopt. Finally, solar PV technologies have greater normative appeal to people, being responsible for its higher observability in comparison to another less visible innovative home installation.

According to Arts et al. (2011), **innovation characteristics** have a strong but different effect on both stages in the adoption process: intention and behavior adoption. The same drivers of innovation adoption to a large extent affect intention and behavior differently. For example, benefits from adoption may affect both intention and behavior, with compatibility being a stronger driver of intention and relative advantage of behavior. Next, complexity has a positive effect on intention, but negatively affects adoption behavior. Perceived uncertainty shows a stronger effect on intention than on adoption behavior. **Consumer demographics** does not influence innovation adoption much. In contrast, consumers' **psychological attributes** are powerful drivers of innovation adoption, with respect to both intention and behavior. Therefore, it is very important to take a dynamic perspective of innovation adoption.

3.2.2 Division of innovations in the IES context

Innovations can be divided into different types dependent on the criterion included. From the point of view of innovative energy services, two types of innovations are relevant: social innovations and eco-innovations. Following Franz et al. (2012), **social innovation** is intented to improve anything in what individuals accomplish alone or jointly, at least as they view it. Hochgerner (2012) wrote that social innovations move through a "4i" process consisting of an idea, intervention, implementation, and finally impact stage. Completing the last stage—impact—makes the innovation socially significant, because social innovations should benefit people by leading to a more equitable, just, and empowered society (Sung and Park, 2018; Hubert, 2011; Pol and Ville, 2009). Social innovations have recently been broadly investigated in the context of the energy transition in the works of Wittmayer et al. (2022), Matschoss et al. (2021), Dall-Orsoletta et al. (2022), and many others.

Eco-innovations were defined by OECD (2009) as those that "include the creation, implementation of new or significantly improved products, processes, marketing methods, organizational structures and institutional arrangements which lead to the environmental improvements compared to relevant alternatives." In the case of IES, eco-innovations include renewable energy sources, such as wind farms, PV installations, or other green energy products, like green electricity tariffs or programs (Karakaya et al., 2014; Mahmood et al., 2022; Huang et al., 2022).

A consumer-centered approach, especially in modern innovation management, has created the terms **open innovation** or **user-driven innovation** (UDI). The UDI approach clearly indicates that the customer is an essential element of any innovation—from the moment a new product or service concept is created until its implementation into the market. In other words, UDI can be defined as the process of drawing on users' knowledge to develop new products, services, and concepts, which are based on a genuine understanding of users' needs and systematically engage users in the process of the development of an enterprise. This approach is often observed among energy communities and includes not only new technologies and services, but also the introduction of new, adjusted business models (de Vries et al., 2016).

As researchers in user-driven innovation emphasize, the consumer should be treated as a key resource of every organization and a cocreator of innovation (Smith, 2006). This is one of the reasons why the consumer appears in most of the innovation models because, as their creators claim, both the observation of consumers' attitudes and analysis of their behavior and its change over time can become sources of innovation (Bass, 1969; Rogers, 2003).

3.2.3 Innovation adoption process

Following the general concept of Rogers (2003), a typical innovation adoption process follows five regular, sequential steps:

- knowledge stage—gaining knowledge of an innovation;
- persuasion stage—forming an opinion (attitude) toward it;
- decision stage—deciding to adopt or reject it;
- implementation stage—implementing it; and finally
- confirmation stage—confirming the decision.

The innovation adoption process always starts with gaining knowledge about the innovation. This stage is essential, as consumers must be aware that the innovative product or a service exists (Pongiglione, 2011; Rogers, 2003; Kowalska-Pyzalska, 2015). As Claudy et al. (2010) noted, most of the surveys and researches assume that consumers are aware of the existence of the innovative products, such as green energy or dynamic tariffs. However, as the authors emphasize, it does not always have to be true. These green innovations may not have received much consumer consideration, or perhaps more crucially, many consumers may not even be aware that they exist. Consumer awareness varies according to the consumers' origins, market segments, and the particular technology in question (Pongiglione, 2011; Rogers, 2003; Kowalska-Pyzalska, 2015). The levels of knowledge that consumers have depend strongly on prior conditions including previous practice, needs and perceived problems, being risk-averse or risk-seeking and hence being more or less willing to adopt an innovation, and sensitivity to the norms of the social system (Claudy et al., 2010). In addition, access to the information about the innovation is fundamental. The most essential sources of information include other people (family, friends, neighbors, and the whole social network) and mass media and social media (TV, radio, the internet, Facebook, Twitter, etc.).

After getting to know about an innovative good, product or idea, a person forms an opinion toward it. The opinion does not have to be constant. As Kowalska-Pyzalska et al. (2014) explained, the opinion may fluctuate due to conflicting information that people receive. For example, one day they may be in favor of a given good because of some positive, informative signals obtained, but the next day they are against it due to new, negative information that they collect. This effect is even stronger when people are indifferent toward a given good, meaning that they do not find it interesting and worth their attention, which is true in the case of many innovative energy services (Kowalska-Pyzalska et al., 2014).

In the third step, people make their first decision, which is whether to buy a given good or not. If this decision is fixed, in the next step people implement it by some real actions (e.g., signing a contract, buying a good, starting to perform a new behavior). Switching to the new product or behavior is often connected with some discomfort of changing the habits and routine, and transaction cost (i.e., cost of collecting the information and making a decision). For example, in the case of switching to dynamic electricity tariffs, the results of pilot studies have shown the magnitude of consumers' opinion about an electricity tariff, mainly due to the rescheduling of the energy consumption according to price signals (ATKearney, 2012; Thorsens et al., 2012; Faruqui and Sergici, 2010). Consumers' opinions and final decisions are also influenced by social impact of the neighbors (people want to have the same opinion as the majority of the group) and external influence (e.g., advertising of new pricing programs by some electricity retailers) (Kowalska-Pyzalska et al., 2014).

Finally, in the last stage, if the consumer confirms their willingness to continue using a certain good, the adoption process is completed. Such a customer can then be a further source of information about the good (by word of mouth, WOM) (Kowalska-Pyzalska et al., 2014; Sznajd-Weron et al., 2014a,b). Through a per-

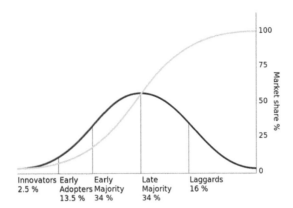

Figure 3.1. The typical shape of innovation diffusion curve and its correlation with the types of innovation adopters (source: Wikipedia).

son's social network, he or she may spread the news about the product, and hence influence the diffusion speed. In this stage, a person can also reject the innovation, if he or she is dissatisfied with it. In this case, negative WOM may spread and hinder further diffusion of a good (Kowalska-Pyzalska et al., 2016).

3.2.4 S-shape of the diffusion curve

Typical innovation spreads in time following the shape of an S-curve, as shown in Fig. 3.1. The slow start of the diffusion is followed by a rapid growth. This is caused by an increase in the number of adopters and rising presence of the innovation in the market. Finally, after reaching the peak, the spreading of innovation slows down. The shape of the curve can be explained analytically by equations-based models, such as the classical Bass model (Bass, 1969), epidemic model (Zeppini et al., 2013; Gupta and Jain, 2012), or a logistics model (Gruber and Verboven, 2001); see Moglia et al. (2017) for more details. At the same time, the shape of the S-curve is correlated with the types of customers interested in adopting the innovation at a given stage of its diffusion. As innovations are adopted by subsequent categories of adopters, the consolidated share of users in the social system grows until it reaches the saturation level. On the other hand, the number of new users of a given innovation initially increases to reach the maximum level, and then decreases (which may be tantamount to the fact that a given product or service has become popular on the market and the level of market penetration by a given product is close to 100%).

The works of Peres et al. (2010) and Kiesling et al. (2012) provide the division of the innovation adopters into innovators, early adopters, early majority, late majority, and laggards (see Fig. 3.1). Innovators are usually seen as a risk-seeking group who like to experiment with new products or goods. The second group—early adopters—embrace new goods before most other people do. They tend to buy or try out new products or services sooner than most of their peers. In the case of innovative technologies, both innovators and early adopters are the enthusiasts who appreciate technology for its own sake and are likely to take all the risks initially connected with a new good. Then, the early majority is the largest group of customers who buy a given good after it has been tried and positively evaluated by early adopters and innovators. The late majority defines people who adopt a good after its position in the market has already been established. Finally, laggards decide on a given good much later, after the product or a service has become well-known and appreciated by other customers. A study by Negro et al. (2012) pointed out that even among a group of innovators and early adopters, different segments of consumers can be identified. These groups are characterized by different sets of motivating factors, including environmental concern, interest in technology, economic profit, self-sufficiency, willingness to utilize excess material, promotion of innovations, and image reasons (Negro et al., 2012). They have also encountered different kinds of barriers to their actions, such as lack of relevant information, poor product quality, and lack of economic and institutional support. Getting to know the differences between the consumers is especially important when designing a product and preparing it for its launch into the market.

3.2.5 Other models of innovation diffusion

Although the DoI model gives a clear definition, explanation, and analysis of determinants of the diffusion phenomena in society, it lacks the analytical apparatus to investigate thoroughly the course of diffusion. The first concepts to mathematically model a new product's spread in a marketplace were rooted in analogies in the models of epidemics, or biology and ecology (Kiesling et al., 2012). The most influential contribution to date was made by Bass (1969), who introduced a differential equation growth model for consumer durable goods and provided a closed-form solution.

The **Bass model** followed the fundamental assumptions of Rogers' DoI theory (Bass, 1969). He has characterized the diffusion of an innovation as a contagious process driven by **external influence** (e.g., advertising, mass media, and other communications initiated by a company) and **internal influence** (e.g., word of mouth and other interactions among adopters and potential adopters in the social system) (Kiesling et al., 2012). At each point in time, new adopters join the market as a result of these types of influences. The Bass model specifies that an individual's probability of adopting a new product at time t, given that he or she has not adopted it yet, depends linearly on these two influences (Goldenberg et al., 2001). The social network into which the innovation diffuses is assumed to be fully connected and homogeneous (Peres et al., 2010). The main aspect of the Bass model is the "spreading" process, which analyzes word-of-mouth marketing. The theoretical model of diffusion of innovation, according to Bass, defines the way in which the producer or supplier tries to reach the customer and convince him or her of the benefits of accepting the innovation. Such measures are aimed at reducing the risk of diffusion failure. As a result, the Bass model states that the probability that an individual will adopt the innovation—given that the individual has not yet adopted it—is linear with respect to the number of previous adopters.

The review of usage of Bass model in the analysis of IES diffusion is presented in the work by Moglia et al. (2017). While showing some examples of successful usage of the Bass model in the case of, for example, the analysis of solar panels and electric vehicles to estimate the adoption of these technology options spatially across the landscape of heterogeneous consumers in Higgins et al. (2012) or the investigation about heating, ventilating and air-conditioning (HVAC) energy-efficient technology to simulate the adoption of energy efficient HVAC technology in Noonan et al. (2013), the authors stated that traditional analytical models can be supported by agent-based modeling and simulations (Moglia et al., 2017).

Apart from an already mentioned model of innovation diffusion, there is also the **percolation model** (Zeppini et al., 2013). In this model, the process of diffusion of innovation consists of informing consumers about the appearance of something completely new: a phenomenon/product. This moment is defined as exceeding the percolation threshold. This model assumes that consumers do not support the product from the very beginning. They learn about its existence from its current users. In this way, new buyers of innovations are won. The main element of the theoretical percolation model is the **percolation threshold**. It may be equal, for example, to the limit price (the maximum price that the customer is willing to pay for the product). Only if the price of the innovation is lower than the threshold will the customer consider adoption of the innovation. Percolation models are used to analyze social systems, in which individual nodes represent con-

Table 3.1 The overview of the studies examining the diffusion of particular innovative energy services.

Category	Rogers' DoI model	Bass model	Percolation model
Components:	innovation, communication channel, time, social system	current and potential users of an innovation	innovation and the percolation threshold
Type of adopters:	innovators, early adopters, early and late majorities, laggards	current users: innovators and potential users: followers	current users: innovators and potential users: followers
The diffusion process	5 steps including: knowledge, persuasion, decision, implementation, and confirmation.	impact of word of mouth (WOM)	the process of reaching the percolation threshold

sumers, households, or, for example, members of a given community. The links between them correspond to realistic social ties (the social network).

Finally, there are epidemic models that compare the manner of innovation diffusion to the spread of infectious disease in a population. The model is based on a random encounter and information sharing between adopters (infected) and nonadopters (exposed), which may lead to innovation adoption by the nonadopter. In other words, information diffusion drives the innovation diffusion (Geroski, 2000; Cantono and Silverberg, 2009).

Table 3.1 compares Rogers' DoI model with the Bass and percolation models, showing what they have in common.

3.3 Agent-based modeling

One of the simulation methodologies is agent-based modeling (ABM). The definition of simulation is the replication of a process or system's behavior over time in the real world. It entails creating a system model that can forecast the system's behavior across time. In order to improve the design or explore the results of various actions, simulation is frequently used to test and examine the performance of a system under various scenarios.

Through the use of agent-based modeling and simulation, it is possible to explore how interactions between individual agents result in emergent behavior at the system level (Kiesling et al., 2012). Each agent in an agent-based simulation is represented as a distinct entity with unique traits and behavior, and interactions between these agents are guided by rules that outline how they should act in certain circumstances. They are especially helpful for analyzing nonlinear systems, where little changes can have significant effects on the system as a whole.

ABM is a common tool to verify which factors affect the rate and extent of diffusion. ABM has been used to analyze, for example, dynamic eclectic tariffs (Kowalska-Pyzalska et al., 2014), green electricity (Kowalska-Pyzalska, 2017; Palmer et al., 2015; Guenther et al., 2011), smart meters (Zhang and Nuttall, 2011; Chou et al., 2015; Ringler et al., 2016), and smart metering information systems (Weron et al., 2018; Kowalska-Pyzalska, 2016). Agent-based modeling allows relations and behavioral patterns to be linked with individual market participants and the effect of introducing additional incentives, such as subsidies, education and training, advertising, or social impact, can be checked on the spread of the analyzed products and services on the market.

Some ABMs used for examining the energy market, have their origins in the statistical physics (Kowalska-Pyzalska et al., 2014; Byrka et al., 2016). What distinguishes these models from others is a focus on the network topology and the social influence (in particular, word of mouth) among neighbors. Moreover, agents responsiveness to the social influence (conformity, independence, or anticonformity) plays a major role (Przybyła et al., 2014; Sznajd-Weron et al., 2014b; Kowalska-Pyzalska et al., 2016). Even though these models are quite simple in comparison to, e.g., the ABM used in Zhang and Nuttall (2011) and Sopha et al. (2017), they still allow important conclusions to be drawn. Below we provide some interesting examples.

3.3.1 Impact of social influence on ABM

Social influence in general and word of mouth (WOM) in particular are crucial elements of each ABM (Deffuant et al., 2005; Przybyła et al., 2014). In works by Kowalska-Pyzalska et al. (2016) and Maciejowska et al. (2016), the authors sought to answer the question of how WOM influences demand curves for product innovations and strategic business decisions.

A literature review leaves no illusions that the impact of WOM on the diffusion of innovation is enormous (Cambell, 2013; East et al., 2008). However, there is no agreement among researchers on how WOM (positive and negative) affects the demand curve for a given good (Deffuant et al., 2005). In order to indicate what significance WOM may have for the participation of a given innovation in the market, an agent-based model was built from the point of view of a company that, operating in an imperfectly competitive market, provides an innovative product or service by manipulating the price to achieve the maximum level of sales (Kowalska-Pyzalska et al., 2016; Maciejowska et al., 2016).

Using Monte Carlo simulations (for real social networks) and the mean-field analytical treatment method, the influences were noted of three parameters on the market demand curve:

1. social impact (WOM);
2. advertising; and
3. individual assessment of adaptation difficulties.

An important element of the model is the introduction of marginal price of P_i (reservation price), which is the equivalent of the willingness to pay of consumers (WTP) for a given good, depending on how much they value it. The difference between P_i and the market price of a given good (parameter P) defines the level of consumer benefit, called the consumer surplus.

The dependence of acceptance of a given innovation by the consumer (equivalent to the decision to purchase a given innovation), from fulfilling the condition that $P_i > P$, allows demand curves to be obtained and important conclusions and recommendations to be made for producers and suppliers of innovations on the market. The model assumes that each consumer behaves independently with a certain probability p and form an opinion based on an individual, subjective assessment of difficulty. At the same time, with probability $(1 - p)$ the consumer's opinion is shaped by social influence (if all his or her neighbors have the same opinion) and by advertisement h.

The last parameter, denoted as f, describes the effect of the analysis of nonfinancial benefits and costs related to the adoption of a given innovation (e.g., feeling of discomfort, the need to change habits or the costs of seeking information).

As shown by the results of the simulation in Fig. 3.2, strong WOM combined with high prices negatively affects the diffusion of innovation, reducing the positive impact of advertising, and at the same time strengthening the effect of perceived difficulties. In turn, at low price levels, WOM can strengthen diffusion, positively affecting advertising, and lowering the importance of the perceived difficulty in adopting a given innovation (Kowalska-Pyzalska et al., 2016; Maciejowska et al., 2016).

This means that depending on the pricing strategy chosen by a company, and thus what the market share is, the company should strengthen or weaken the effect of word of mouth (WOM). If the

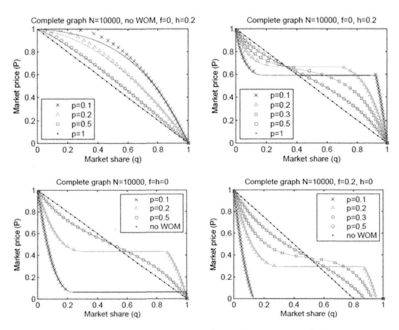

Figure 3.2. Comparison of demand curves depending on the level of parameters: p, h, and f and with reference to the market price P (Maciejowska et al., 2016; Kowalska-Pyzalska et al., 2016).

company wants to maintain a high price of the product with a low amount of product delivered (as in the case of a monopoly), it seems right to reduce the importance of WOM by building an information campaign aimed at strengthening individual consumer decisions. Such action should increase the company's demand and revenues.

On the other hand, if the company prefers to offer a lower price and to have a larger market share, it should strengthen the WOM effect, and thus its revenues. Such a strategy can be achieved by strengthening collective activities and encouraging discussion about a given innovative product and service, e.g., on social media (Kowalska-Pyzalska et al., 2016; Maciejowska et al., 2016).

3.3.2 ABM for the analysis of diffusion of smart metering platforms

Based on the agent-based model proposed in Kowalska-Pyzalska et al. (2016) and Maciejowska et al. (2016), another ABM explores the diffusion of smart metering information systems (SMPs), which can be included in product and process innovations and serve as an element of an innovative energy management system Kowalska-Pyzalska (2017). The aim of the study was to show what internal and external factors strengthen the diffusion of SMP. Using the marginal price mechanism (as in the work by Kowalska-Pyzalska et al., 2016), it was shown how an individual assessment of the difficulty of receiving SMP combined with positive or negative social impact and advertising can affect the spread of SMP on the market. It was crucial to perform analysis from the perspective of suppliers of these services because SMP and other technologies connected to smart meters are still in the early stages of diffusion and consumer interest is low. Based on data gathered from pilot programs and a literature research, the model was calibrated.

The analysis of the findings revealed that SMP suppliers need to be mindful of the influence of WOM on consumer demand reports, both good and bad. Consumers' perceived adaptation challenges (such decreased comfort or the need to adjust behaviors, for example) should also be taken into consideration. Producers could encourage customers to use a free trial of a specific gadget or service within a set time frame in an effort to lessen the perceived difficulty of adopting a given innovation. In order to lessen the need for consumer price control, they can also automate energy consumption based on market prices. It could also be beneficial to run educational initiatives and spread favorable information about SMP in the media.

Investigation on SMP diffusion was also the subject of the paper by Weron et al. (2018). When designing an ABM, it was understood that the first requirement for successful SMP distribution is awareness of its presence. This is influenced mostly by advertising, societal impact, and education and training. Furthermore, to use SMP, a certain level of internet skills are required. This ABM incorporates components of the SSCB model (see Chapter 4) as well as the impact of training and educational campaigns on: (1) the transition from the predecision to the action phase; and (2) the effective diffusion of innovative SMP tools.

The acquired results provide significant advice for smart metering information system suppliers. They specifically state that providers of these services who want to attract customers should use training and educational programs geared to specific categories of customers rather than general education and marketing campaigns. It has also been demonstrated that manipulating the time required for the client to make a decision (e.g., by promoting in a specific time interval) influences the rate of diffusion. It is also critical that businesses take steps to ensure that customers retain the necessary level of knowledge and skills learned during training, such as reminding them about SMP through text messages, emails, or information booklets.

3.3.3 ABM for the analysis of diffusion of dynamic electricity tariffs

The aim of the work by Kowalska-Pyzalska et al. (2014) was to show how consumers' personal characteristics (especially the level of their conformism or indifference to social impact), as well as the level of advertising and financial incentives, encourages consumers to form positive opinions about dynamic electricity tariffs (innovative product and an important element of innovative energy management systems), and finally also to make decisions about switching to these tariffs (from, for example, traditional tariffs characterized by a fixed amount of electricity fee).

In the developed agent-based simulation model, two blocks were distinguished: a block of opinions and a block of decisions. It was assumed that the condition for making a decision is to have a stable opinion on a given product (in this case, a dynamic electricity tariff) for a certain period of time. This assumption is followed by the Rogers' DOI model and the findings from the literature.

Similarly to the work of other authors (Nyczka and Sznajd-Weron, 2013; Przybyła et al., 2014), based on the decision rules regulating agents' (i.e., households or firms) behavior in the system introduced in the model, by averaging the Monte Carlo simulation results (MCS), the following outcomes were obtained. Firstly, it was shown that with the currently high level of consumer indifference regarding dynamic electric tariffs, it is very difficult to achieve a satisfactory level of innovation diffusion and adoption rate. Indifference (meaning: lack of interest, lack of care, disengagement) among consumers lead to a general instability of positive opinions regarding a potential switch to dynamic electricity tariffs, and hence to general reluctance about changing the electricity supplier and signing a new contract. Fig. 3.3 indicates that only if indifference is lower (left-hand side of the graph) will the adoption rate increase significantly. This is due to the fact that when consumers start to care, they become more sensitive to the social influence and to the strength of marketing efforts, such as advertising. In Fig. 3.3, the impact of advertisement is shown by means of the parameter h. With the current high indifference level, the impact of advertisement on the adoption rate is limited (Kowalska-Pyzalska et al., 2014).

3.3.4 ABM for the analysis of willingness to pay for green electricity

In work by Kowalska-Pyzalska (2017), in turn, the research goal was to show, using the ABM and simulations, how the average

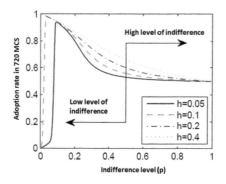

Figure 3.3. The comparison of impact of high and low indifference among electricity consumers and influence of the marketing efforts on the adoption rates of dynamic electricity tariffs (Kowalska-Pyzalska et al., 2014).

willingness to pay for green electricity may change dependent on some internal and external factors, such as advertising, subsidy schemes, and social impact stimulated by an educational campaign. The model was calibrated based on data from the pilot empirical study. In the agent-based model, it was assumed that each agent (i.e., household paying electricity bills) has a certain level of initial marginal price (as in Kowalska-Pyzalska, 2016, Kowalska-Pyzalska et al., 2014, and Maciejowska et al., 2016), which may change over time depending on social impact, advertising, or additional payment system. At the same time, each agent has a certain constant value (Ri_min), which is the result of the agent's opinion on renewable energy, taking into account the perceived difficulties with adopting a given innovation. It was assumed that for the agent to decide to support renewable energy, its marginal price must be higher than the constant Ri_min.

The results of the conducted research show that in countries such as Poland, where the popularity of renewable energy among consumers was relatively low, and the discrepancy between the fixed Ri_min and the individual marginal price (i.e., willingness to accept and pay) is high, to increase the adoption rate, it is necessary to introduce external factors, such as, subsidy schemes or advertising. Significant influence, as already shown by Kowalska-Pyzalska (2016), Kowalska-Pyzalska et al. (2014), and Maciejowska et al. (2016), also has the effect of word of mouth (WOM). If negative perceptions and opinions about RES in the society prevail, then it will be difficult to achieve a satisfactory level of market share of these products.

Thus, from the point of view of enterprises, to encourage consumers to buy an installation based on renewable energy or to choose a green electricity tariff, one should either seek to reduce the value of Ri_{min} through, among other things, emphasizing the benefits of renewable energy, by improving their efficiency and efficiency through the further development of technology, and/or raising the individual marginal price through, for example, investment subsidies and advertising spreading positive information about RES, and thus the use of a positive marketing effect.

3.4 Summary: insights regarding IES diffusion

There are no doubts that spreading of IES in the energy market can be analyzed from the perspective of the innovation diffusion models and theories. It is due to the fact that the acceptance and use of various IES, such as monitoring energy by means of SM platforms or switching to green electricity tariffs or adoption to RES, is a phased, staggered process (Ozaki, 2011; Weron et al., 2018; Kowalska-Pyzalska and Byrka, 2019).

Table 3.2 provides examples of studies in which diffusion of a chosen IES have been analyzed and explored.

Analysis of the aims and research questions of the papers dealing with diffusion of IES clearly indicates that the authors try to reveal the main incentives and barriers of adoption, and then to

Table 3.2 Overview of studies examining various aspects of diffusion of particular innovative energy services.

Object of the analysis	Research question	Reference
Impact of policies and marketing activities		
Patterns of induced diffusion in the case of wind energy in 25 OECD countries	Do patterns of induced diffusion differ from the conventional patterns observed when diffusion is unaffected by policy interventions?	(Diaz-Rainey and Ashton, 2011)
Evaluation of policy options for inducing SM adoption by simulation analysis	How effective and efficient are regulatory interventions to induce the diffusion of SM in Germany, if demand and supply evolve endogenously?	(Rixen and Weigand, 2014)

continued on next page

Table 3.2 continued

Object of the analysis	Research question	Reference
Framework to analyze technology diffusion from a sociotechnical systems perspective for PV installations and wind park in Sweden	Which drivers and barriers to diffusion could be addressed through policy or business strategy?	(Palm, 2022)
Marketing activities and strategies to enhance the diffusion of biomass fuel	What is the influence of various marketing activities and policies on the adoption behavior of consumers who have individual preferences and are embedded in a social network?	(Guenther et al., 2011)
Simulation of the future diffusion of small residential PV systems under different conditions	How will changes to the Italian support scheme affect the diffusion of PV systems among single- or two-family homes?	(Palmer et al., 2015)
Small-scale renewable energy technologies in Finland	Which channels dominate in diffusion and adoption process: commercial routes or among peers?	(Hyysalo et al., 2017)
Consumers' attributes		
Reasons of the nonuse of smart energy service	Is there a relationship between the nonuse of IES and consumer attitudes, social background and housing conditions?	(Kahma and Matschoss, 2017)
How the innovators and early adopters enhance diffusion of small-scale sustainable energy solutions	Which experiences, motivations and obstacles inhibit the diffusion of energy innovations?	(Nygren et al., 2015)
Social determinants for green technology adoption	How are beliefs about green technology (i.e., intelligent thermostats) influenced by personal environmental norms and innovativeness?	(Girod et al., 2017a)

continued on next page

Table 3.2 continued

Object of the analysis	Research question	Reference
Small-scale energy innovation	What is the impact of belonging to a certain segment of the innovator's on their experiences with similar projects, motivations for behavior, and obstacles that inhibit diffusion?	(Negro et al., 2012)
Social influence		
Solar PV diffusion	What is the impact of peer effects on diffusion of solar photovoltaic panels in California?	(Bollinger and Gillingham, 2012)
Energy efficient home innovations	What is the influence of social capital on information diffusion regarding the adoption of household energy-efficiency measures?	(McMichael and Shipworth, 2013)
Microscopic model of consumer behavior	Which factors are important in word of mouth marketing?	(Kowalska-Styczeń and Sznajd-Weron, 2012)
Reasons for slow or rejected diffusion		
Determinants of the slow diffusion of wood pellet technology for home heating in Norway	Which factors contribute to the under-utilization and lack of adoption of wood pellet?	(Sopha and Kloeckner, 2016)
Determinants of slow diffusion of RES technologies	What are the main barriers and obstacles for successful diffusion of RES?	(Negro et al., 2012)
Determinants of slow diffusion of smart energy services	What are the reasons of the innovation rejection?	(Kahma and Matschoss, 2017)

propose appropriate and adequate marketing strategies or policies that may help to enhance the deployment of IES in the energy market. An up-to-date literature review investigating IES diffusion, based on one of the diffusion models, reveals that there are several reasons for slow or limited diffusion. They include:

- the invisibility of the electricity as a good and the discrepancy between costs and benefits that customers encounter;

- inelastic demand for electricity, meaning that consumers' demand does not rapidly change due to the price signals;
- confusion of choice meaning that consumers are often lost and are not able to compare various options they can get;
- lack of advice makes it even harder to decide for a certain option;
- discomfort of usage connecting with some of IES discourages consumers;
- unstable opinions among consumers cannot translate into positive decisions; and
- free riding meaning participating in benefits of certain innovative energy services without financial or nonfinancial contribution to its distribution.

3.5 References and proposed additional reading

Diffusion of innovation:

- Arts et al. (2011) Generalizations on consumer innovation adoption: a meta-analysis on drivers of intention and behavior. Int. J. Res. Market. 28(2), 134–144 (Arts et al., 2011)
- Chandrasekaran and Tellis (2007) A critical review of marketing research on diffusion of new products. In: Review of Marketing Research, (Ed) Naresh K. Malhotra, Emerald Group Publishing Ltd., 3, 39–80 (Chandrasekaran and Tellis, 2007)
- Deffuant et al. (2005) An individual-based model of innovation diffusion mixing social Value and individual benefit. American Journal of Sociology 110(4) 1041–1069 (Deffuant et al., 2005)
- Hyysalo et al. (2017) The diffusion of consumer innovation in sustainable energy technologies. Journal of Cleaner Production 162, S70–S82 (Hyysalo et al., 2017)
- Kahma and Matschoss (2017) The rejection of innovations? Rethinking technology diffusion and the non-use of smart energy services in Finland. Energy Resources & Social Science 34, 27–36 (Kahma and Matschoss, 2017)
- Karakaya et al. (2014) Diffusion of eco-innovations: a review. Renewable and Sustainable Energy Reviews 33, 1935–1943 (Karakaya et al., 2014)
- Nygren et al. (2015) Early adopters boosting the diffusion of sustainable small-scale energy solutions. Renewable and Sustainable Energy Reviews 46, 79–87 (Nygren et al., 2015)
- Peres et al. (2010) Innovation diffusion and new product growth models: a critical review and research directions. International Journal of Research in Marketing 27, 91–106 (Peres et al., 2010)

- Rogers (2003) Diffusion of innovations. 5th Ed. Free Press, New York (Rogers, 2003)

Agent-based modeling for innovation diffusion:
- Guenther et al. (2011) An agent-based simulation approach for the new product diffusion of a novel biomass fuel. J. Oper. Res. Soc. 62, 12–20 (Guenther et al., 2011)
- Kiesling et al. (2012) Agent-based simulation of innovation diffusion: a review. Central European Journal of Operations Research 20(2) 183–230 (Kiesling et al., 2012)
- Kowalska-Pyzalska et al. (2016) Linking consumer opinions with reservation prices in an agent-based model of innovation diffusion. Acta Physica Polonica A 129(5) 1055–1059 (Kowalska-Pyzalska et al., 2016)
- Laciana et al. (2013) Exploring associations between micro-level models of innovation diffusion and emerging macro-level adoption patterns. Physica A: Statistical Mechanics and its Applications 392(8), 1873–1884 (Laciana et al., 2013)
- Moglia et al. (2017) A review of agent-based modelling of technology diffusion with special reference to residential energy efficiency. Sustainable Cities and Society 31, 173–182 (Moglia et al., 2017)
- Palm (2022) Innovation systems for technology diffusion: an analytical framework and two case studies. Technological Forecasting and Social Change 182, 121821 (Palm, 2022)
- Palmer et al. (2015) Modeling the diffusion of residential photovoltaic systems in Italy: an agent-based simulations. Technological Forecasting and Social Change 99, 106–131 (Palmer et al., 2015)
- Przybyła et al. (2014) Diffusion of innovation within an agent-based model: Spinsons, independence and advertising. Advances in Complex Systems 17(1), 1450004 (Przybyła et al., 2014)
- Rixen and Weigand (2014) Agent-based simulation of policy induced diffusion of smart meters. Technological Forecasting and Social Change 85, 153–167 (Rixen and Weigand, 2014)

Percolation and Bass models:
- Cantono and Silverberg (2009) A percolation model of eco-innovation diffusion: the relationship between diffusion, learning economies and subsidies. Technological Forecasting & Social Change 76(4), 487–496 (Cantono and Silverberg, 2009)
- Diaz-Rainey and Ashton (2011) Profiling potential green electricity tariff adopters: green consumerism as an environmental policy tool? Business Strategy and The Environment 20(7), 456–470 (Diaz-Rainey and Ashton, 2011)

- Diaz-Rainey and Tzavara (2012) Financing the decarbonized energy system through green electricity tariffs: a diffusion model of an induced consumer environmental market. Technological Forecasting & Social Change 79, 1693–1704 (Diaz-Rainey and Tzavara, 2012)
- Hohnisch et al. (2008) A percolation-based model explaining delayed takeoff in new-product diffusion. Industrial and Corporate Change 17(5) 1001–1017 (Hohnisch et al., 2008)
- Krishnan et al. (1999) Optimal pricing strategy for new products. Management Science 45(12), 1650–1663 (Krishnan et al., 1999)

Word of mouth and impact of social network on diffusion:
- Bollinger and Gillingham (2012) Peer effects in the diffusion of solar photovoltaic panels. Market Science 31, 900–912 (Bollinger and Gillingham, 2012)
- Byrka et al. (2016) Difficulty is critical: the importance of social factors in modeling diffusion of green products and practices. Renewable and Sustainable Energy Reviews 62, 723–735 (Byrka et al., 2016)
- Cambell (2013) Word of mouth and percolation in social networks. American Economic Review 103(6) 2466-2498 (Cambell, 2013)
- Chawla et al. (2020) Marketing and communications channels for diffusion of electricity smart meters in Portugal. Telematics and Informatics 50, 101385 (Chawla et al., 2020b)
- East et al. (2008) Measuring the impact of positive and negative word of mouth on brand purchase probability. International Journal of Research in Marketing 25, 215–224 (East et al., 2008)
- Kowalska-Styczeń and Sznajd-Weron (2012) Access to information in word of mouth marketing within a cellular automata model. Advances in Complex Systems 15(8) 1250080 (Kowalska-Styczeń and Sznajd-Weron, 2012)
- Maciejowska et al. (2016) Impact of social interactions on demand curves for innovative products. Acta Physica Polonica A 129(5), 1045–1049 (Maciejowska et al., 2016)
- McMichael and Shipworth (2013) The value of social networks in the diffusion of energy-efficiency innovations in UK households. Energy Policy 53, 159–168 (McMichael and Shipworth, 2013).

4

Individual behavioral theories

4.1 Introduction

Consumer behavior, especially the choice to purchase a particular good over another, is often argued to be complex and not very well-represented by a rational choice model of human behavior (Moglia et al., 2017; Frederiks et al., 2015). The rational choice model of human behavior assumes that a person objectively weighs up the benefits and costs of different options and chooses the option that maximizes their net benefits. In fact however, people are rarely fully rational in their decision-making process. Behavioral economics has demonstrated through rigorous experiments that people's economic decision-making is frequently based on well-known heuristics, mental shortcuts, and rules of thumb rather than on a logical evaluation of the advantages and disadvantages of the options.

The analysis of innovation diffusion would not be possible without understanding how people make decisions. There are several theoretical models, in both behavioral economics and social psychology, that reveal the background of humans' process of decision-making.

Within this chapter, we present the most popular individual behavioral theories, explaining how consumers make decisions, especially in the context of adopting technology or behavioral innovation in the energy market.

4.1.1 Consumers' energy behavior decisions

Consumer engagement is key to the success of smart energy systems. Smart products and services must be accepted, installed, and used by consumers. They must supply information and modify their behavior. Even fully automated solutions need some user interaction, and in the absence of automation, active customer involvement is crucial. Analysis of the literature clearly indicates that for a sustainable energy transition, it is important to embrace consumers as active contributors in energy systems (Vázquez-Canteli and Nagy, 2019; Schuitema et al., 2017; Moreno-Munoz

Diffusion of Innovative Energy Services. https://doi.org/10.1016/B978-0-12-822882-1.00010-X

et al., 2016; Gangale et al., 2013). In order to create a smart energy system, it is necessary to comprehend not only the economic aspects of the market and the technology opportunities and limitations, but also the consumer as a person and the dynamics that influence human behavior and behavioral change.

There are plenty of economic and psychological models and theories shedding light on the ways in which people make their decisions. It is especially important and useful to learn from such models in the case of products, services, or behaviors involving electricity, which is an invisible common good, where the benefits from a purchase or conducting a new behavior are often postponed to the financial and behavioral cost connected with a decision to adopt an innovation.

Because of the attributes of the innovative product, service or behavior—especially its complexity—its design has to be adjusted to lead to the specific target behavior. For example a service that requires consumers to interact with the interface repeatedly needs a different design than a service that only needs consumer input once (Schweiger et al., 2020). Installing smart home features to enable demand response is different to accepting a dynamic electricity tariff and adjusting behavior manually. In the first scenario, the chance to exhibit the desired behavior only infrequently arises (for example, when building a new home), and significant resources are required (for example, costs could be considerable) (Schweiger et al., 2020). Furthermore, motivation to adopt a given innovation might be decreased or even completely diminished by fear of losing control or by concerns about data privacy (Zabkowski and Gajowniczek, 2013; Kahma and Matschoss, 2017; Nachreiner et al., 2015; Hinson et al., 2019). That is especially true in the case of the consumer's interaction with smart meters and DSM/DR tools (Kowalska-Pyzalska, 2018b).

Adoption of an innovation, no matter whether it is a product, service, or a new behavior, requires some level of knowledge and awareness about the opportunities that an individual has. Many authors, including Claudy et al. (2010), Pongiglione (2011), and Schweiger et al. (2020), have emphasized that because consumers might not be aware of existing opportunities, they have to be reminded or prompted by those who are interested in launching an innovation or promoting a new behavior (Schweiger et al., 2020). What is even more important, to overcome habits, is strong motivation—it is arguably crucial. Many studies have shown that potential cost reductions in the electricity bill might not be substantial enough to encourage such a behavioral change (Nolan et al., 2008; Allcott, 2011). Therefore, the content of the service or the product has to fit to the desired behavior.

The behavioral models can help to identify the significant aspects of the decision-making process, determinants of acceptance and adoption of an innovation, and appropriate methods to enhance the adoption.

4.2 Comparison of the chosen behavioral models

Investigation and modeling of consumers' energy decisions with reference to innovative energy services (IES) adoption is a topic of many scientific publications (Pongiglione, 2011; Gadenne et al., 2011; Ozaki, 2011; Kowalska-Pyzalska et al., 2014; Peters et al., 2018). No matter which IES is particularly taken into account, the empirical surveys and behavioral models rely on one of the social or economic theory or model originating from:

- models grounded in conventional and behavioral economics:
  (a) consumer's demand model dependent on the price and income elasticity,
  (b) utility-based models (Wilson and Downlatabadi, 2007), and
  (c) behavioral models of residential energy use;
- technology adoption theory:
  (a) innovation diffusion theory (Rogers, 2003) (see Chapter 3 for more details),
  (b) technology acceptance model (Davis, 1989), and
  (c) the unified theory of acceptance of technology (UTAUT) Venkatesh et al. (2012);
- attitude-based models:
  (a) theory of planned behavior (Ajzen, 1991), and
  (b) attitude-belief-context model;
- stage-change models:
  (a) transtheoretical model (Ai He et al., 2010),
  (b) model of self-regulated behavioral change (Bamberg, 2013a),
  (c) behavior change wheel (Michie et al., 2014), and
  (d) behavior change model (Fogg, 2009);
- normative models from social and environmental psychology:
  (a) new environmental paradigm (Dunlap et al., 2000),
  (b) values-belief-norm model (Stern, 2000),
  (c) norm activation model (Abrahamse and Steg, 2009), and
  (d) cultural model of household energy consumption (Lutzenhiser, 1991).

Of course the aforementioned theories and models are not limited to the energy field. They present general observations regarding human decision-making. However, as the empirical research proves, these models are perfectly suited to investigation of consumers' intentions and behaviors toward IES in the energy market.

The aim to explain how individuals make decisions and how their attitudes, beliefs, norms, and values effect their behavior is what all of these behavioral models and frameworks have in common. Many scientists concur that it is essential to comprehend customer behavior in order to create an innovation's ideal attributes in a way that will encourage consumers to accept it (Gyamfi et al., 2013; Kowalska-Pyzalska, 2015; Lopes et al., 2012; Faires et al., 2007; Sidiras and Koukios, 2004; Jager, 2006).

Most of these models and theories contend that consumers' intentions to adopt innovations are a function of their cognitive assessments of three key factors:

- the innovation's perceived usefulness, with most studies focusing on technology as the innovation;
- social norms and adoption pressure; and
- an individual's capacity or opportunity to adopt an innovation.

Below, we will present the most commonly used models in energy research, explaining their main assumptions and elements. We will present what the individual decision-making process looks like, while choosing a certain innovation product, service, or a new behavior. We will also provide some examples of research studies related to IES, in which the theoretical or empirical setup of a survey is based on a given model.

4.2.1 Utility-based models

Most of the models originating from the conventional and behavioral economics assume some level of **rationality of consumers**. This is especially true in utility-based models of consumers' decision making (Krantz and Tversky, 1971). Microeconomic theories of consumer choice are based on the assumption that individuals seek to maximize utility—understood as person's satisfaction, or well-being—given consumers' budget constraints. A decision outcome with higher utility will be consistently preferred to an alternative outcome with lower utility (Wilson and Downlatabadi, 2007).

According to utility theory, a customer's overall utility of a specific good or service is determined by the total of the utilities of its parts. Additionally, it is anticipated that consumers choose options that will maximize their advantages. The model assumes full access to the information and a person's ability to compare pros and cons of various alternatives with each other in order to make a rational and optimal decision. Utility theory is derived from axioms of preference that provide criteria for the rationality of choice. Consumers are assumed to behave as rational actors in a normative sense of having preferences that are not only ordered and known, but also invariant and consistent (Wilson and Downlatabadi, 2007).

In reality, a lot of behavior takes place under conditions of **bounded rationality**, meaning that our rationality is limited by our thinking capacity, the available information, lack of interest and laziness, risk and loss aversion, and time needed for a proper analysis. To overcome these significant barriers, people tend to use **heuristics**, which are mental shortcuts allowing people to solve problems and make judgments quickly and efficiently. People also tend to perform either a habitual behavior or choose an option which looks satisfactory for them, rather than make an optimal choice based on objective and reliable information (Pongiglione, 2011; Kowalska-Pyzalska, 2015; Lopes et al., 2012).

Therefore, as Hobman et al. (2016) pointed out, nowadays the traditional rational utility-based models of decision making have been replaced by models that take into account cognitive biases and psychological factors that cause some irrationality in humans' decision making.

These models are reviewed and described in the context of environmental or energy-related behavior in many scientific papers, such as Zhou and Yang (2016), Zhang and Nuttall (2011), Lopes et al. (2012), Ellabban and Abu-Rub (2016), Gyamfi et al. (2013), Qin et al. (2017), Stigka et al. (2014), Ek (2005), Perlaviciute and Steg (2014), Wilson and Downlatabadi (2007), and many others. Moreover, utility-based models are used in discrete or qualitative choice models, which are very common in research related to intentional and behavioral IES adoption. These models represent individuals' choices between different alternatives characterized by a number of attributes (Wilson and Downlatabadi, 2007). Choices can be made as stated preferences through survey instruments or as revealed preferences through actual purchasing behavior (see Chapter 5 for more details).

4.2.2 Theory of planned behavior

The theory of planned behavior (TPB), formerly known as the theory of reasoned action (TRA), is one of the most well-known ideas that explains the connection between people's beliefs and norms, attitudes toward activity, and behavior itself (Ajzen, 1991; Ajzen and Fishbein, 2005). According to TPB, a person's behavior is the product of their **behavioral intention**, which is created from their **individual and normative beliefs** about what their peers might think of their behavior (subjective norms) and their **perceived behavioral control** (PBC) (Ajzen and Fishbein, 2005).

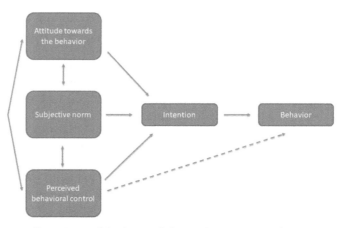

Figure 4.1. The scheme of the theory of planned behavior model (Ajzen and Fishbein, 2005).

There are three main variables included in the TPB model, as presented in Fig. 4.1: attitude, subjective norm, and perceived behavior control. An extended TPB model also often includes moral obligation.

According to TPB theory, the first significant variable that influences people's behavior intention is attitude. The more positively someone feels about an action, the more probable it is the person will engage in that behavior. Studies by Yadav and Pathak (2016), Webb et al. (2013), and Wang et al. (2016) among others have highlighted the significance of attitude in predicting people's pro-environmental behavior in a variety of contexts, such as households' energy-saving behavior, green product purchases, or green vehicle adoption behavior. An individual's attitude might be favorable or adverse depending on how they feel about engaging in a certain conduct.

Subjective norm is the second important variable to affect an individual's behavior intention. It refers to the way in which an individual perceives social pressure from one's peers regarding the performance of a given behavior. The individual tends to comply with the expectations or viewpoints of some people important to them (Gao et al., 2017). In other words, an individual's behavior intention might be based on the approval or disapproval of some people who are important to an individual (Chen et al., 2014). The higher subjective norm the individual perceives, the more likely the individual is to perform a given behavior.

Perceived behavior control is another important variable to affect an individual's behavior intention. It refers to the perceived ease or difficulty of conducting the behavior in relation to people's abilities, resources, and opportunities, which will encourage or hinder the performance (Ozaki, 2011). Some factors such as opportunity, resource, time, knowledge, and skills may not be under the control of individuals and thus influence their intention to conduct a particular behavior. If individuals have a higher degree of control over themselves, they will have a stronger intention to perform a particular behavior (Gao et al., 2017).

A good example of the controllable factors is cost: both financial and habitual. There are always consumers who are reluctant to pay extra or who are not keen to change their daily routine (Ozaki, 2011; Gadenne et al., 2011). The issue with perceived behavioral control is shown in the study of Ozaki (2011) in the case of green electricity or in the works of Gadenne et al. (2011) and Zhang and Nuttall (2011) in the case of dynamic electricity tariffs.

Other scholars, such as (Gao et al., 2017), (Abrahamse and Steg, 2009), (Yue et al., 2013), (Yadav and Pathak, 2016), (Sopha et al., 2017), and (Sopha and Kloeckner, 2016), have used TPB theory to explore individuals' pro-environmental behavior, such as green purchasing behavior, households' energy saving behavior, energy efficiency investments, and other sustainable consumption behavior in an individual setting.

Table 4.1 presents some chosen examples of research making usage of TPB to explain the incentives of people decisions to adopt certain innovative energy services or behaviors.

4.2.3 Stage-change models

Schweiger et al. (2020) pointed out that especially behavior change models, describing the process and circumstances under which the habitual behavior alter in the long term, provide a useful theoretical base for designing products and services within a smart energy system involving active consumer participation and relying on establishing new behavior or changing old behavior. In psychology, there are a few behavior change models, such as the transtheoretical model (TTM) (Ai He et al., 2010; Prochaska and Diclemente, 1982), the Fogg behavior model (FBM) (Fogg, 2009), the behavior change wheel (BCW) (Michie et al., 2014), or the self-regulated behavior change model (SSCB) (Bamberg, 2013a).

FBM includes three equally important factors of behavioral change: motivation and ability, paired with a trigger or a prompt. To induce a certain activity, the interplay of motivation and ability to do a behavior must be greater than an action threshold, so that a prompt can trigger the desired behavior (Schweiger et al., 2020; Ellabban and Abu-Rub, 2016). The target behavior cannot be encouraged in a highly motivated person who lacks ability. Similarly, a person who is perfectly capable of doing the goal activity but has no desire to do so cannot be urged to do so. When someone's

Table 4.1 The overview of the chosen studies analyzing consumer adoption and acceptance of particular IES by means of TPB model.

Object of the analysis	Sample	Main findings	References
To gain a better understanding of people's intentions to invest in wind energy	Germany, N=592, Y=2014	Investment intentions in wind energy are significantly influenced by subjective norms, perceived behavioral control, consumer profile, and investor experience, however sentiments about wind energy investments have not been found to be a significant predictor of investment intentions.	(Gamel et al., 2021)
To investigate the primary motivators for using renewable energy	Lithuania, N=1005, Y=2015	The intention to use renewable energy has been positively influenced by financial abilities, subjective norms, interaction between environmental concern and attitude toward RES, whereas attitudes to renewable energy had no effect on intention to RES.	(Liobikienė et al., 2021)
To investigate the impact of the Big Five personality traits on household energy-saving behavior	China, N=1119, Y=2021	Impact of TPB attributes depends on the residents' characteristics, e.g., PBC shows more influence on the intentions of the conservatives and the introverts.	(Liu et al., 2021)
To explain why individuals want to save energy and reduce their carbon footprint	Taiwan, N=728, Y=2012	Apart from attitudes and subjective norm, one's moral obligation plays a fundamental role in predicting one's intentions to engage in energy savings and carbon reduction behaviors. One's moral obligation may weaken or eliminate the impact of one's perceived behavioral control.	(Chen, 2016)

continued on next page

Table 4.1 continued

Object of the analysis	Sample	Main findings	References
To investigate consumers' opinions regarding solar PV and purchasing intentions using personal characteristics	Pakistan, N=311, Y=2022	Customer views toward solar photovoltaic products are positively and significantly influenced by their attitudes, product knowledge, ecological lifestyle, perceived benefits, innovativeness, and optimism.	(Hasheem et al., 2022)

motivation and ability to do the intended behavior are sufficiently high, a prompt in the environment is sufficient to elicit performance (Schweiger et al., 2020).

The behavior change wheel (BCW) is to some extent very similar to FBM and pays attention to three sources for behavior: capability, opportunity, and motivation. In contrast to the FBM, it focuses on a source of behavior that needs to alter and recommends relevant functions to handle this source (e.g., coercion, modeling). It also includes policy categories (for example, legislation and service provision) that describe how the intervention, product, or service should be implemented (Schweiger et al., 2020; Michie et al., 2014).

Next, Ai He et al. (2010) proposed a motivational framework including five stages to initiate sustainable energy consumption via feedback. These five stages correspond to the stages of change in the **transtheoretical model of (health) behavior change** (Prochaska and Diclemente, 1982), which divides motivation based on preparation, willingness, and ability to change. The model provides an outline of the phases that consumers traverse in order to live a more sustainable lifestyle. In TTM, the process of behavioral change includes progression through the following stages:

- precontemplation: lack of awareness of the problem, no need to seek or implement a solution;
- contemplation: an individual starts to be aware of the problem and decides whether to attempt to behave in a different way;
- preparation: an individual decides to alter the behavior and prepares for it;

- action: an individual perform the target action; and
- maintenance: an individual performs a new behavior and it starts to be a new routine.

Progression through these stages requires communication, support, and guidance (Ellabban and Abu-Rub, 2016). Similarly to the Diffusion of Innovation (DoI) model, in the last stage the rejection of the new behavior may appear. Falling back into old habits is called a relapse and may happen during any of the stages. When a relapse occurs, the reason should be evaluated, and the individual must be encouraged to continue with the changed behavior.

The last model that we will describe from the category of stage-change models is the model of self-regulated behavioral change, or SSCB, proposed by Bamberg (2013a). This model particularly serves to explore and analyze the adoption of a new—mainly pro-environmental—behavior. The main feature of this model is its division into four qualitatively different but interdependent stages of diffusion. The implementation of stages refers directly to the diffusion of innovation model by Rogers (2003) and a classic action phases model proposed by Heckhausen and Gollwitzer (1987); Gollwitzer et al. (1990). As a result, behavioral change, such as adoption of novel solutions, is a goal-directed and deliberate process in which individuals take little steps toward the goal. Simultaneously, the SSCB model places a greater emphasis on individual characteristics such as social norms, attitudes, and perceived behavioral control as predictors of people's engagement in the subsequent stages. Fig. 4.2 shows the phase transitions between the stages, which include:

- predecisional stage: an individual has to choose a given behavior from competing options;
- preactional stage: The individual formulates an intention to engage in a conduct. He or she analyzes the benefits and drawbacks of engaging in a particular activity and describes how the conduct will be carried out;
- actional stage: the individual implements an intention; and
- postactional stage: the individual focuses on the evaluation of an action.

Because distinct stages of behavior change involve different psychological processes, previous research has shown that consumers at different stages of the process require different methods—interventions to urge them to move on to the next phase (Bamberg, 2013a,b). Extended analysis of the interventions adjusted to specific behavioral stages is presented in the work of Ohnmacht et al. (2017). The individual tailored interventions in different areas of household energy use show that it is crucial

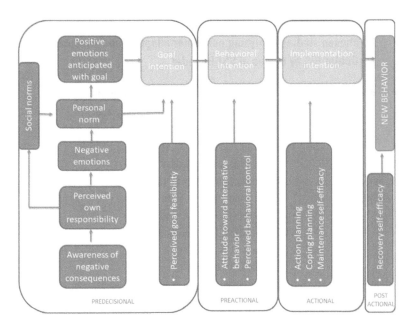

Figure 4.2. The SSCB model (Bamberg, 2013a).

to include characteristics of the targeted subgroup into the intervention design to support its success (Nachreiner et al., 2015; Ohnmacht et al., 2017; Weron et al., 2018).

The SSCB model has already been implemented to explore consumers' behavior in transportation (Bamberg, 2013b) or healthy consumption behavior (see the review by Keller et al., 2019), but recently it has also been used to analyze innovative energy services or behaviors. For example, the study of Nachreiner et al. (2015) has applied the SSCB model and analyzed whether German smart metering platforms (SMPs) are properly designed so that, through their use, energy consumers can move from one decision-making phase to another (Nachreiner et al., 2015). Similarly, the studies of Kowalska-Pyzalska and Byrka (2019), Kowalska-Pyzalska et al. (2020b) and Weron et al. (2018) made use of the SSCB model to investigate the adoption process toward SMPs.

The decision-making process would include the following stages to illustrate four phases of behavior change in the context of employing SMPs: (1) predecisional phase—when consumers decide to use SMP or engage in an energy monitoring behavior; (2) preactional phase—when consumers specify their intention to use SMP or engage in an energy monitoring behavior; (3) actional phase—when consumers use SMP or monitor energy con-

Table 4.2 The overview of the chosen studies analyzing consumer adoption and acceptance of particular IES by means of SSCB model.

Object of the analysis	Sample	Main findings	References
To investigate how people's behavior and attitudes toward energy influence how they make use of electricity, and how they might be steered through behavior change	Germany, N=592, Y=2014	This research adds to the debate on individual energy savings by establishing a hypothetical taxonomy of treatments and tying them to socio-psychological factors influencing the transition points of four phases of behavior modification.	(Ohnmacht et al., 2017)
To determine if communications congruent with the stages in which participants declared to be at a particular time are more effective than a general message or a passive control condition in pushing participants to proceed to the next stage. We also looked at how attitude and knowledge about energy monitoring affected phase shifts	Poland, N=289, Y=2018 & 2019	The intention to monitor energy is influenced by participation in the study. The longer the individuals used SMP, the more likely they were to monitor their energy consumption in the future.	(Kowalska-Pyzalska et al., 2020b)

continued on next page

sumption on a regular basis; and (4) postactional phase—when consumers assess their satisfaction with using SMP or monitoring energy consumption (Kowalska-Pyzalska and Byrka, 2019).

Other examples of implementation of the SSCB model for the analysis of IES are collected in Table 4.2.

4.2.4 Technology acceptance model

The technology acceptance model (TAM) was first proposed in 1989 by Davis (1989) and Davis et al. (1989) as an instrument

Table 4.2 continued

Object of the analysis	Sample	Main findings	References
To test the effect of environmental attitudes, knowledge, and perceived possibilities on consumers' stages of readiness to adopt SMP	Poland, N=500, Y=2018	The perceived ability to monitor energy use on a regular basis was found to be a predictor of adoption at every stage of preparedness studied. Consumers reported willingness to gain SMP know-how, indicating that general knowledge predicted development to the point of preparedness.	(Kowalska-Pyzalska and Byrka, 2019)
To explain the information design of an SM web portal built in the context of environmental psychology intervention study into the effectiveness of consumption feedback, as well as in connection to an SSCB model	German web-page	A smart meter web portal was designed supporting electricity saving in households. It guides the user in his or her migration through the action stage by combining feedback with goal setting, social norms, saving tips, and commitment.	(Mack and Tampe-Mai, 2016)

to predict the likelihood of adopting a new technology within a group or an organization. Originating in the psychological theory of reasoned action and theory of planned behavior (TPB), TAM has evolved to become one of the key models used in understanding predictors of human behavior toward potential acceptance or rejection of the innovative technology (Turner et al., 2010).

TAM is based on the concept that technology adoption and use may be explained by an individual's own beliefs, attitudes, and intentions (similar to the previously stated TPB and SSCB models). As a result, by applying the TAM when an innovative technology is launched, it should be feasible to estimate future technology utilization. The original TAM assessed the impact of four internal

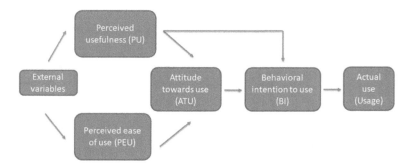

Figure 4.3. The original technology acceptance model (TAM) (Davis et al., 1989).

variables on actual technology usage (Turner et al., 2010; Davis, 1989):

- perceived ease of use (PEU);
- perceived usefulness (PU);
- attitude toward use (ATU); and
- behavioral intention to use (BI).

Apart from internal variables, the model includes a set of external ones, such as attributes of the technology, having an impact on perceived ease of use of the innovative technology, and its perceived usefulness. A graphical presentation of the TAM is shown in Fig. 4.3.

Since its origin, TAM has been modified several times, adding some new features; however, the basic concept remained unchanged. The review of Billanes and Enevoldsen (2021) provides an overview of the development of TAM and an overview of the likelihood of acceptance for the individual technologies. The Billanes and Enevoldsen (2021) review of TAM usage for the analysis of technology acceptance has shown some most influential factors associated with users' acceptance and adoption to technology, including:

- policy—with a significant effect on behavioral intention;
- self-efficacy and social influence—having impact on perceived usefulness and ease of use, attitudes, behavioral intention and actual usage;
- compatibility—with an impact on perceived usefulness, ease of use, attitude and behavioral intention to use;
- enjoyment—with an influence on perceived usefulness, ease of use, attitude and behavioral intention to use;
- trust—having influence on perceived usefulness, attitude, behavioral intentional and actual use;
- perceived risk—with an impact on perceived usefulness, ease of use, and attitude;

- demographics—having influence on perceived usefulness, ease of use, attitude and actual use;
- awareness—with an influence on attitude and behavioral intention to use; and
- knowledge—with an impact on perceived usefulness, ease of use and behavioral intention to use.

Apart from the original technology acceptance model, the literature mentions some of its extension such as, among others, unified theory of acceptance and use of technology (UTAUT) (Venkatesh et al., 2012). A literature review by Billanes and Enevoldsen (2021) revealed that most of the studies making use of TAM referred to smart energy technologies (including smart meters, small-scale renewable energy generators, and home energy management systems). Table 4.3 indicates that TAM and its extensions has been one of the most frequently applied models for explaining influential factors to users' acceptance and adoption of technology in the energy field.

4.2.5 Normative models of pro-environmental behavior

The additional set of normative models for pro-environmental behavior is based on how values and behavior interact (Stern, 2000; Dunlap et al., 2000). According to Schwartz, values are overarching psychological principles that influence a wide range of particular attitudes, beliefs, preferences, and behaviors (Stern, 2000). They might be viewed as a person's life's guiding principles (Ek, 2005; Kowalska-Pyzalska, 2015). There are plenty of models explaining the incentives of individual and collective pro-environmental behavior. The most popular ones include Schwartz's theory of basic values, the new ecological paradigm scale, value-belief-norm theory, and recently also the value-identity-personal norms model.

According to **Schwartz's theory of basic values**, values are arranged along two bipolar axes that exhibit conflicting values (tradition vs openness to change and self-transcendence versus self-enhancement) (Schwartz, 2012). According to research by Ek (2005); Perlaviciute and Steg (2014), altruistic or self-transcendence value orientations are positively correlated with pro-environmental attitudes and behaviors, but the opposite, egoistic or self-enhancement value orientations (centered on one's own riches and position) are adversely correlated. It was discovered that those with positive opinions about green energy are more worried with the negative effects of environmental issues on humans and the natural environment, presumably giving collective

Table 4.3 The overview of the chosen studies analyzing consumer adoption of IES with usage of technology acceptance model (TAM) and its extensions.

Object of the analysis	Sample	Main findings	References
To study the propensity of consumers to adopt smart meters in residential buildings, including critical factors that influence adoption and policy recommendations	Indonesia, N=400, Y=2014	Developed an index to assess customer willingness to install smart meters in residential buildings; The findings confirm that consumer views of the utility, simplicity of use, and hazards associated with SM influence customer acceptability.	(Chou and Yutami, 2014)
To improve the understanding of the socio-psychological and technological aspects that influence the use of SM	Spain, N=515, Y=2015	Subjective norms, perceived usefulness, health-related risk perception, procedural justice, time of usage, perceived distributive injustice, loss of control, and privacy-related risk perception all influence SM use.	(Guerreiro et al., 2015)
To explore the evaluation paradigm of shared benefits versus the forfeiture of personal information in case of use of smart metering technology	USA, N=300, Y=2017	Although the shared benefit of avoiding disruptions in electricity supply (brownouts) is a significant factor in electricity consumers' decisions to adopt SM, concerns about control and information privacy still matters.	(Warkentin et al., 2017)

continued on next page

or altruistic values a higher priority (Ek, 2005; Kowalska-Pyzalska, 2015). People who have a self-transcendence value orientation and who are concerned about the negative effects of environmental issues on humans and the biosphere typically believe that

Table 4.3 continued

Object of the analysis	Sample	Main findings	References
To explore the factors influencing residential customers' adoption of SM by combining electricity-saving expertise and environmental awareness with the second generation of the unified theory of technology acceptance and use	Malaysia, N=318, Y=2020	Electricity-saving knowledge and environmental awareness have influenced consumers adoption of SM	(Alkawsi et al., 2020)
To investigate the elements that influence household purchasing intentions for solar PV technology	Pakistan	Perceived usefulness and ease of use positively shape the consumer attitude toward solar PV adoption, whereas attitude influences the intention to purchase this technology. The importance of government policy and propaganda in regulating consumer attitudes and actual purchasing intention was proven.	(Ali et al., 2020)
To investigate the factors that influence renewable energy technology acceptance and to show the impact of cost and knowledge on the perceived ease of use and usefulness of renewable energy technology	Malaysia, N=784, Y=2016	The survey confirmed that perceived ease of use and perceived usefulness affect intention to use renewables	(Kardooni et al., 2016)

renewable energy has a positive impact on the environment (by, for example, reducing fossil-fuel emissions).

Because of this, these customers will favorably rate green electricity. People with a self-enhancement value orientation, on the other hand, who have worries about the negative consequences of necessary sacrifices (such as paying more), will view green energy negatively (Ek, 2005; Perlaviciute and Steg, 2014; Kowalska-Pyzalska, 2015). In the analysis by Perlaviciute and Steg (2014), the values defined which costs and benefits of energy alternatives were most vital to people and guided their acceptability ratings.

Another popular model for evaluation of pro-environmental behavior is called the **new ecological paradigm Sscale** (NEP scale); this is the successor of the new environmental paradigm (NEP) from 1978 (Dunlap et al., 2000). This paradigm is characterized by a set of guiding principles that place a focus on respecting boundaries imposed by nature and the significance of maintaining the natural world's delicate balance. The original model has undergone several revisions in order to incorporate issues relating to the likelihood of eco-crises, as well as the subscales that frame the psychological tendency to evaluate the favoring or disfavoring of the natural environment, in line with the growing awareness of global ecological problems (Ntanos et al., 2019; Dunlap, 2008). The original unidimensionality of NEP scaling toward environmental attitudes that has reflected an ecologically oriented point of view (a high NEP score reflected positiveness for the preservation of natural sources) or an anthropogenic approach (a low NEP score reflects positiveness for the exploitation of natural sources) has been modified by adding a revised NEP scaling (Ntanos et al., 2019). The revised NEP scale fulfills the psychometrically robust and contemporarily structured terminology (Dunlap, 2008).

The next model we want to mention is a model of pro-environmental consumer behavior by Stern (Stern, 2000) called the **value-belief-norm model** (VBN model). This model is based on the concept of the NEP, but it suggests that traditional, biospheric, altruistic, and egoistic values affect a person's acceptance of the NEP values, and lead to a person's ecological worldview. Values are a prominent way to strengthen intrinsic motivation to act pro-environmentally (Perlaviciute and Steg, 2014; van der Werff and Steg, 2016). As a result, according to VBN theory, personal values determine what consumers believe about the environment and the consequence of individual activities, which in turn shapes personal norms, or what the person believes is the correct thing to do. Personal norms are supposed to lead to pro-environmental behavior at home or at work (Stern, 2014).

Environmental behavior is frequently only possible by sacrificing significant quantities of resources—in terms of time, money, and brainpower. Consequently, the layout of a product or service

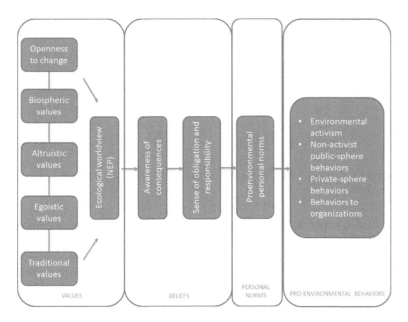

Figure 4.4. The value-belief-norm model (VBN) (Stern, 2000).

must not only address people's ideas, values, and norms in order to improve motivation, but also provide a setting in which the desired action consumes fewer resources (Steg et al., 2018). Normative beliefs have a beneficial effect on the intention to engage in environmental behavior; for example, the idea that climate change must be addressed and that everyone must do something about it, is important in the desire to engage in environmental activity (Ozaki, 2011; Stern, 2000; Kowalska-Pyzalska, 2015). Consumers feel responsibility when they comprehend what is going on and the implications of their actions. Such moral obligations improve the likelihood of adopting energy-saving habits (Ozaki, 2011; Stern, 2000; Kowalska-Pyzalska, 2015; Claudy et al., 2010).

The VBN model has also been extended into the **value-identity-personal norms model** (VIP model) (van der Werff and Steg, 2016). The VIP model, like the VBN model, believes that sentiments of moral obligation to participate in sustainable practices (personal norms) impact environmental behavior. According to the VIP model, personal norms are influenced by one's environmental self-identity, which indicates the degree to which one regards oneself as a pro-environmental person (van der Werff and Steg, 2016). Then, biospheric values influence environmental self-identity, with higher biospheric values resulting in a higher environmental self-identity (van der Werff and Steg, 2016).

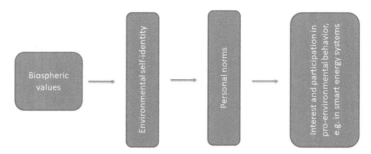

Figure 4.5. The value-identity-personal norms model (VIP) (van der Werff and Steg, 2016).

In two aspects, the VIP model differs from the VBN theory. First of all, the VIP model is more frugal than the VBN theory. Second, the VIP model addresses generic predictors of environmental activities, specifically values and environmental self-identity, with personal norms serving as a behavior-specific variable (van der Werff and Steg, 2016). A comparison of both models is presented in Figs . 4.4 and 4.5.

Finally, Table 4.4 collects some empirical surveys exploring acceptance and preferences toward IES by means of one of the abovementioned normative models of pro-environmental behavior.

4.3 Summary: what does social science tell us about diffusion of IES?

The general concepts of social science, including models and theories explaining consumers' decision making mechanism, and the transition from opinions into decisions, shed some light on the adoption process, and in the case of innovative energy services.

Each of the models pays attention to different aspects of the decision-making process, but all together they emphasize that:

- the decision process consists of a few stages, each of which involves different emotions, attitudes, and needs of the individuals;
- bounded rationality of people makes them use various heuristics and mental shortcuts influencing the final decision;
- communication channels through people's social networks play a fundamental role in the process of sharing opinions about the innovation, which influence the final intention and behavior adoption;
- motivation plays a great role in adoption process leading to a purchase of an innovation or taking a new behavior; and

Table 4.4 The overview of the chosen studies analyzing consumer adoption of IES with usage of value-believes theories and models.

Object of the analysis	Sample	Main findings	References
To deliver fresh understanding into the primary aspects that influence people's desire for solar energy	France, Germany, the UK, data from European Social Survey round 8, Y=2016	It has been demonstrated that self-transcendent ideals play a critical role in motivating desire for solar energy. The influence of efficacy beliefs and concern on such preference varies by country (beliefs are important in France and Germany, while concern serves greater guidance for French and British citizens).	(Pagliuca et al., 2022)
To assess the intention of households to use renewable energy sources	Sardinia, N=432, Y=2016	The most powerful predictors of the intention to utilize renewable energy devices were moral norms and informational influence (i.e., trust in friends/relatives and neighbors). The effects of injunctive and descriptive social norms on intention to use were largely indirect.	(Fornara et al., 2016)
To measure and analyze citizens' NEP score in a Greek area with reference to the further development of RES	Greece, N=366, Y=2017	NEP score has occurred to be correlated with respondents' willingness to pay for renewable energy expansion	(Ntanos et al., 2019)

continued on next page

- heterogeneous consumers are motivated by different factors (both financial and nonfinancial).

In practice, the factors that influence the rate and direction of an innovation's adoptions are determined by the interaction

Table 4.4 continued

Object of the analysis	Sample	Main findings	References
To investigate the elements that influence the acceptability of energy policies aimed at reducing CO_2 emissions by households and to assess the extent to which VBN theory predicts acceptability judgments	Denmark, N=112, Y=2005	The findings validated the causal order of the variables in VBN theory, progressing from relative stable general values to views about human-environment relations, which affect behavior specific beliefs and norms, as well as acceptability judgments.	(Steg et al., 2005)
To investigate the links between household energy usage and householders' aim to reduce consumption of energy on the one hand, and psychological and socio-demographic characteristics on the other	Denmark, N=7,000, Y=2001	Household consumption of energy proved to be most closely connected to socio-demographic variables (income, household size, and age), with attitudinal variables and self-transcendence values (tradition/security and power/achievement) also playing a role.	(Abrahamse and Steg, 2011)

continued on next page

of several factors that may be classified as (Karakaya et al., 2014; Kowalska-Pyzalska, 2018b):

- demand-side factors (customer perceptions and preferences, and willingness to pay, social network and influence);
- cross-country factors (culture, religion, opinion leaders); and
- supply-side factors (access to the information, relative advantage of the innovation, barriers to adoption, feedback and trust between providers and customers).

All of the aforementioned factors may have a substantial impact on the success rate of the innovation.

Table 4.4 continued

Object of the analysis	Sample	Main findings	References
To prove that Schwartz's individually measured motivational types of values predict people's proenvironmental behavior	15 European countries, N=9,710, y=2010	Individual-level values are better predictors of environmental attitudes. Consumers who have strong altruistic beliefs are more likely to act in an environmentally beneficial manner. Egoistic values, such as the desire for personal success and dominance over others (power and achievement), are less likely to be related with proenvironmental behavior. Consumers with higher degrees of environmental concern, which indicates their understanding and contemplation of environmental issues, are more likely to take specific ecologically favorable actions.	(Primc et al., 2021)

4.4 References and proposed additional reading

Theory of planned behavior model:

- Ajzen (1985) From intentions to actions: a theory of planned behavior. In: Kuhl, J. and Beckmann, J. (eds) Action Control. SSSP Springer Series in Social Psychology. Springer, Berlin, Heidelberg. (Ajzen, 1985)
- Ajzen (1991) The theory of planned behavior. Organ. Behav. Hum. Decis. Process. 50, 2, 179–211 (Ajzen, 1991)
- Chen (2016) Extending the theory of planned behavior model to explain people's energy savings and carbon reduction behavioral intentions to mitigate climate change in Taiwan—moral obligation matters. Journal of Cleaner Production 112, 2, 1746–1753 (Chen, 2016)

- Chen et al. (2014) How does individual low-carbon consumption behavior occur? An analysis based on attitude process. Applied Energy 116, 376–86 (Chen et al., 2014)
- Gamel et al. (2021) Financing wind energy projects: an extended theory of planned behavior approach to explain private households' wind energy investment intentions in Germany. Renewable Energy 182, 592–601 (Gamel et al., 2021)
- Gao et al. (2017) Application of the extended theory of planned behavior to understand individuals' energy saving behavior in workplaces. Resources, Conservation and Recycling 127, 107–113 (Liao et al., 2017)
- Hasheem et al. (2022) Factors influencing purchase intention of solar photovoltaic technology: an extended perspective of technology readiness index and theory of planned behavior. Cleaner and Responsible Consumption 7, 100079 (Hasheem et al., 2022)
- Liobikienė et al. (2021) The determinants of renewable energy usage intentions using theory of planned behaviour approach. Renewable Energy 170, 587–594 (Liobikienė et al., 2021)
- Liu et al. (2021) Are you an energy saver at home? The personality insights of household energy conservation behaviors based on theory of planned behavior. Resources, Conservation and Recycling 174, 105823 (Liu et al., 2013)
- Mack and Tampe-Mai (2016) An action theory-based electricity saving web portal for households with an interface to smart meters. Utilities Policy 51–63 (Mack and Tampe-Mai, 2016)
- Sopha and Kloeckner (2011) Psychological factors in the diffusion of sustainable technology: a study of Norwegian households' adoption of wood pellet heating. Renewable and Sustainable Energy Review 15, 2756–2765 (Sopha and Kloeckner, 2016)
- Wang et al. (2016) Predicting consumers' intention to adopt hybrid electric vehicles: using an extended version of the theory of planned behavior model. Transportation 43, 1, 123–143 (Wang et al., 2016)
- Webb et al. (2013) Self-determination theory and consumer behavioral change: evidence from a household energy-saving behavior study. J. Environ. Psychol. 35, 59–66 (Webb et al., 2013)
- Yadav and Pathak (2016) Young consumers' intention towards buying green products in a developing nation: extending the theory of planned behavior. J. Clean. Prod. 135, 732–739 (Yadav and Pathak, 2016)
- Yue et al. (2013) Factors influencing energy-saving behavior of urban households in Jiangsu Province. Energy Policy 62, 665–675 (Yue et al., 2013)

Technology acceptance models:

- Ali et al. (2020) Determining the influencing factors in the adoption of solar photovoltaic technology in Pakistan: a decomposed technology acceptance model approach. Economies 8, 108 (Ali et al., 2020)
- Alkawsi et al. (2020) Empirical study of the acceptance of IoT-based smart meter in Malaysia: the effect of electricity-saving knowledge and environmental awareness. IEEE Access 8, 42794–42804 (Alkawsi et al., 2020)
- Billanes and Enevoldsen (2021) A critical analysis of ten influential factors to energy technology acceptance and adoption. Energy Reports 7, 6899–6907 (Billanes and Enevoldsen, 2021)
- Chou and Yutami (2014) Smart meter adoption and deployment strategy for residential buildings in Indonesia. Applied Energy 128, 336–349 (Chou and Yutami, 2014)
- Davis (1989) Perceived usefulness, perceived ease of use, and user acceptance of information technology. MIS Quarterly 13(3), 319–340 (Davis, 1989)
- Davis et al. (1989) User acceptance of computer technology: a comparison of two theoretical models. Management Science 35(8), 982–1003 (Davis et al., 1989)
- Guerreiro et al. (2015) Making energy visible: sociopsychological aspects associated with the use of smart meters. Energy Efficiency 8, 1149–1167 (Guerreiro et al., 2015)
- Kardooni et al. (2016) Renewable energy technology acceptance in Peninsular Malaysia. Energy Policy 88, 1–10 (Kardooni et al., 2016)
- Keller et al. (2019) Lessons learned from applications of the stage model of self-regulated behavioral change: a review. Frontiers in Psychology 10, 1091 (Keller et al., 2019)
- Turner et al. (2010) Does the technology acceptance model predict actual use? A systematic literature review. Information and Software Technology 52(5), 463–479 (Turner et al., 2010)
- Venkatesh et al. (2012) Consumer acceptance and use of information technology: extending the unified theory of acceptance and use of technology. MIS Quarterly 36(1), 157–178 (Venkatesh et al., 2012)
- Warkentin et al. (2017) Shared benefits and information privacy: what determines smart meter technology adoption? Journal of the Association for Information Systems 18(11) (Warkentin et al., 2017)

Stage-change models:

- Bamberg (2013) Applying the stage model of self-regulated behavioral change in a car use reduction. Journal of Environmental Psychology 33, 68–75 (Bamberg, 2013a)

- Bamberg (2013) Changing environmentally harmful behaviors: a stage model of self-regulated behavioral change. Journal of Environmental Psychology 34, 151–159 (Bamberg, 2013b)
- Fogg (2009) A behavior model for persuasive design. In: Proceedings of the 4th International Conference on Persuasive Technology—Persuasive '09, ACM Press, New York, USA (Fogg, 2009)
- Gollwitzer et al. (1990) From weighing to willing: approaching a change decision through pre- or postdecisional mentation. Organizational Behaviour and Human Decision Processes 45, 41–65 (Gollwitzer et al., 1990)
- He et al. (2010) One size does not fit all: applying the transtheoretical model to energy feedback technology design. In: Proc. 28th International Conf. Hum. factors Comput. Syst.—CHI'10, 927–936 (Ai He et al., 2010)
- Heckhausen and Gollwitzer (1987) Thought contents and cognitive functioning in motivational versus volitional states of mind. Motivation and Emotion 11, 101–120 (Heckhausen and Gollwitzer, 1987)
- Keller et al. (2019) Lessons learned from applications of the stage model of self-regulated behavioral change: a review. Frontiers in Psychology 10, 1091 (Keller et al., 2019)
- Kowalska-Pyzalska and Byrka (2019) Determinants of the willingness to energy monitoring by residential consumers: a case study in the city of Wroclaw in Poland. Energies 12, 907 (Kowalska-Pyzalska and Byrka, 2019)
- Kowalska-Pyzalska et al. (2020) How to foster the adoption of electricity smart meters? A longitudinal field study of residential consumers. Energies 13, 4737 (Kowalska-Pyzalska et al., 2020a)
- Mack et al. (2019) Bridging the electricity saving intention-behavior gap: a German field experiment with a smart meter website. Energy Res. Soc. Sci. 3, 34–46 (Mack et al., 2019)
- Michie et al. (2014) The Behaviour Change Wheel. A Guide to Designing Interventions, Silverback Publishing (Michie et al., 2014)
- Nachreiner et al. (2015) An analysis of smart metering information systems: a psychological model of self-regulated behavioral change. Research & Social Science 9, 85–97 (Nachreiner et al., 2015)
- Ohnmacht et al. (2017) Rethinking social psychology and intervention design: a model of energy savings and human behavior. Energy Research & Social Science 26, 40–53 (Ohnmacht et al., 2017)

- Prochaska and Diclemente (1982) Transtheoretical therapy: toward a more integrative model of change. Psychother.: Theory Res. Practice 19, 3, 276–288 (Prochaska and Diclemente, 1982)
- Weron et al. (2018) The role of educational trainings in the diffusion of smart metering platforms: an agent-based modeling approach. Physica A, Statistical Mechanics and its Applications 505, 591–600 (Weron et al., 2018)

Normative models of pro-environmental behavior:
- Abrahamse and Steg (2011) Factors related to household energy use and intention to reduce it: the role of psychological and socio-demographic variables. Research in Human Ecology 18, 1, 30–40 (Abrahamse and Steg, 2011)
- Claudy et al. (2010) Consumer awareness in the adoption of microgeneration technologies. An empirical investigation in the Republic of Ireland. Renewable and Sustainable Energy Reviews 14, 154–2160 (Claudy et al., 2010)
- Dunlap et al. (2000) New trends in measuring environmental attitudes: measuring endorsement of the new ecological paradigm: a revised NEP scale. Journal of Social Issues 56, 3, 425–442 (Dunlap et al., 2000)
- Dunlap (2008) The new environmental paradigm scale: from marginality to worldwide use. Environ. Educ. 40, 3–18 (Dunlap, 2008)
- Ek (2005) Psychological determinants of attitude towards "green" electricity: the case of Swedish wind power. Energy Policy 33, 1677–1689 (Ek, 2005)
- Fornara et al. (2016) Predicting intention to improve household energy efficiency: the role of value-belief-norm theory, normative and informational influence, and specific attitude. Journal of Environmental Psychology 45, 1–10 (Fornara et al., 2016)
- Kowalska-Pyzalska (2015) Social acceptance of green energy and dynamic electricity tariffs—a short review. In: International Conference on Modern Electronic Power Systems (MEPS) 2015, Wroclaw, Poland (Kowalska-Pyzalska, 2015)
- Ntanos et al. (2019) An application of the new environmental paradigm (NEP) scale in a Greek context. Energies 12, 339 (Ntanos et al., 2019)
- Ozaki (2011) Adopting sustainable innovation: what makes consumers sign up to green electricity? Business Strategy and the Environment 20, 1–17 (Ozaki, 2011)
- Pagliuca et al. (2022) Values, concern, beliefs, and preference for solar energy: a comparative analysis of three European countries. Environmental Impact Assessment Review 106722 (Pagliuca et al., 2022)

- Perlaviciute and Steg (2014) Climate change and individual decision making: an examination of knowledge, risk-perception, self-interest and their interplay. Renewable and Sustainable Energy Review 35, 361–181 (Perlaviciute and Steg, 2014)
- Primc et al. (2021) How does Schwartz's theory of human values affect the proenvironmental behavior model? Baltic Journal of Management 16(2) 276–297 (Primc et al., 2021)
- Steg et al. (2014) Factors influencing the acceptability of energy policies: a test of VBN theory. Journal of Environmental Psychology 25, 415–425 (Steg et al., 2018)
- Stern (2000) Towards a coherent theory of significant environmental behavior. Journal of Social Issues 56(3), 407–424 (Stern, 2000)
- Stern (2014) Individual and household interactions with energy systems: toward integrated understanding. Energy Research and Social Science 1, 41–48 (Stern, 2014)
- van der Werff and Steg (2016) The psychology of participation and interest in smart energy systems: comparing the value-belief-norm theory and the value-identity-personal norm model. Energy Research & Social Science 22, 107–114 (van der Werff and Steg, 2016)

Others:
- Arts et al. (2011) Generalizations on consumer innovation adoption: a meta-analysis on drivers of intention and behavior. Int. J. Res. Market. 28, 2, 134–144 (Arts et al., 2011)
- Ellabban and Abu-Rub (2016) Smart grid customers' acceptance and engagement: an overview. Renewable and Sustainable Energy Reviews 65, 1285–1298 (Ellabban and Abu-Rub, 2016)
- Hobman et al. (2016) Uptake and usage of cost-reflective electricity pricing: insights from psychology and behavioral economics. Sustainable Energy Reviews 57, 455–467 (Hobman et al., 2016)
- Karakaya et al. (2014) Diffusion of eco-innovations: a review. Renewable and Sustainable Energy Reviews 33, 1935–1943 (Karakaya et al., 2014)
- Kowalska-Pyzalska (2018) What makes consumers adopt to innovative energy services in the energy market? A review of incentives and barriers. Renewable and Sustainable Energy Reviews 82, 3, 3570–3581 (Kowalska-Pyzalska, 2018b)
- Krantz and Tversky (1971) Conjoint-measurement analysis of composition rules in psychology. Psychological Review 78, 2, 151–169 (Krantz and Tversky, 1971)

- Lopes et al. (2012) Energy behaviors as promoters of energy efficiency: a 21st century review. Renewable and Sustainable Energy Reviews 16, 4095–4104 (Lopes et al., 2012)
- Schweiger et al. (2020) Active consumer participation in smart energy systems. Energy and Buildings 227, 110359 (Schweiger et al., 2020)
- Qin et al. (2017) Selection of energy performance contracting business models: a behavioral decision-making approach. Renewable and Sustainable Energy Reviews 72, 422–433 (Qin et al., 2017)
- Wilson and Downlatabadi (2007) Models of decision making and residential energy use. Annu. Rev. Environ. Resour. 32, 169–203 (Wilson and Downlatabadi, 2007)
- Zhou and Yang (2016) Understanding household energy consumption behavior: the contribution of energy big data analytics. Renewable and Sustainable Energy Reviews 56, 810–819 (Zhou and Yang, 2016).

5

Consumer acceptance and engagement toward IES: practical experiences and findings

5.1 Introduction

According to the European Commission, in order to achieve climate policy objectives, consumers must be involved and approve offered solutions. To that end, empirical and simulation studies are being conducted all over the world with the goal of proposing various innovative products, services, and business models, as well as appropriate strategies for their implementation, in order to meet consumer interest and acceptance. Pilot initiatives are also often established to test the efficacy of the proposed solutions.

In this chapter, we will discuss the practical experiences and findings from the pilot programs, field experiments, modeling, and simulation studies regarding acceptance, preferences, and willingness to adopt and pay with reference to various IES among consumers. In summary, we will provide the main incentives and barriers regarding consumers' engagement with future energy systems and their developments.

5.2 Research methods and areas

5.2.1 Methods of data collection and analysis

Many scientific publications have been written about the investigation and modeling of consumers' energy behavior, including the diffusion of certain innovative energy services (IES) (e.g., RES or dynamic electricity tariffs). Together with the acceleration of the energy transition observed in a recent decade, the scientific interest toward social acceptance and consumers' willingness to adopt and pay for the IES has increased significantly. This topic

Diffusion of Innovative Energy Services. https://doi.org/10.1016/B978-0-12-822882-1.00011-1

has a multidisciplinary character, connecting social, environmental, and engineering researchers together. The scientists keep exploring the incentives and barriers of smooth energy transition from various points of view, proving that without social support and engagement, the efficiency of the transition and moving into sustainable energy system is impossible.

There are four main groups of methods used in research regarding diffusion and adoption, and acceptance of innovative energy services (Engelken et al., 2016; Kowalska-Pyzalska, 2018b). The first group of methods is based on **gathering empirical evidence** of a certain phenomenon. To collect data necessary for scientific analysis, various experimental **quantitative and qualitative methods** popular in social science are implemented. The most popular methods include:

- field experiments (for example, Ma et al., 2015; Gans et al., 2013; Allcott, 2011; Nolan et al., 2008);
- survey questionnaire, both online and by telephone (for example, Kowalska-Pyzalska, 2018a; Chawla et al., 2020b; Gerpott and Mahmudova, 2010; Zoric and Hrovatin, 2012; Fouad et al., 2022);
- semistructured or in-depth interviews (for example, Ozaki, 2011; Nygren et al., 2015; Fouad et al., 2022);
- focus groups (for example, Paetz et al., 2012; Buchanan et al., 2016; Bertoldo et al., 2015); and
- data collected directly among energy suppliers (e.g., in the study of Nachreiner et al., 2015), and others.

The second group of methods examines consumers' stated preferences—that is, overall evaluation—for a certain product or a service by means of either the **contingent valuation method** (CVM), such as in studies by Nomura and Akai (2004); Paravantis et al. (2018); Yoo and Kwak (2009); Gerpott and Mahmudova (2010); Zhang and Wu (2012); Zoric and Hrovatin (2012); Zhou et al. (2018); Lim et al. (2017); Wiser (2007); Xie and Zhao (2018), or **discrete choice experiment** (DCE), for example, in Bartczak et al. (2017); Borchers et al. (2007); Ozbafli and Jenkins (2016); Su et al. (2018); Knapp and Ladenburg (2015); Kashintseva et al. (2018); Ek and Soederholm (2008). These methods are commonly used to measure consumers' willingness to pay (WTP) (Oerlemans et al., 2016; Gerpott and Paukert, 2013; Zoric and Hrovatin, 2012; Kowalska-Pyzalska, 2019; Zhang and Wu, 2012) and willingness to accept (WTA), discussed later in this chapter. The CVM is very popular mainly due its relative simplicity and availability to develop various scenarios in which goods are presented (Oerlemans et al., 2016; Kowalska-Pyzalska, 2019). The main disadvantage of this method includes hypothetical bias, which means that what people say is different to what they actually do, which may influence the obtained results.

Respondents in the DCE approach, on the other hand, are presented with their favorite option among two or more products. Several attributes, such as price, quality, distribution, and so on, are used to define these products (Oerlemans et al., 2016). The respondent's role is to determine which product they would purchase. The fundamental distinction between the CVM and the DCE is that in the CVM, the product qualities are fixed across respondents, whereas in the DCE, the product attributes vary experimentally.

Apart from the CVM and DCE, the literature proposes also **conjoint analysis** (CA) to study consumer preferences regarding a given good. Utility theory, which is used to describe and explain consumer behavior, serves as the theoretical and methodological foundation for all variations of conjoint techniques (Krantz and Tversky, 1971). The main objective of the CA is to determine preferences for the researched variants before calculating the partial contributions of each feature. The ability to determine the relative importances for qualities and the so-called part worths for all factor levels is one of this method's key benefits (Agarwal et al., 2015; Kowalska-Pyzalska et al., 2022). Conjoint analysis was used by Poortinga et al. (2003) for the investigation of energy-savings measures, by Duetschke and Paetz (2013) to explore consumers' preferences toward dynamic electricity pricing, or by Kaufmann et al. (2013) to explore consumer value of smart metering. CA design was also used to analyze the impact of behavioral factors in the renewable energy investment decision-making process in work by Masini and Menichetti (2012).

The next collection of methods covers all types of **intellectual study, evaluating numerous theories and lines of inquiry and putting out fresh theoretical and behavioral models**. Such works often have one of two objectives: either they examine the state of the art and address novel concepts (e.g., Gadenne et al., 2011; Lopes et al., 2012) or they provide some policy recommendations (e.g., Sorrell, 2015). Below we present some examples of such papers, mentioning their aim and area of research:

- an overview of the main issues and challenges associated with energy demand reduction (Sorrell, 2015);
- an overview of demand response potentials and benefits in smart grids (Siano, 2014);
- a comprehensive "socio-techno-economic" review, classification, analysis of DR barriers and enablers in a smart grid, and a intellectual framework for further analysis (Good et al., 2017);

- an examination of cognitive biases and psychological quirks that may affect how customers react to electricity price, as well as some achievable and affordable solutions that address these factors to get the best results for both customers and the energy industry (Hobman et al., 2016);
- a presentation of the concept of the energy efficiency market, with an analysis of market barriers (Bukarica and Tomšić, 2017);
- an overview the concept of diffusion of eco-innovation (Karakaya et al., 2014);
- a review of agent-based modeling applications in comparison to other methods in the context of energy-efficient residential technologies (Moglia et al., 2017);
- a review of various social intervention literature related to energy-user behavior transition (Iweka et al., 2019);
- an overview of drivers, barriers, and opportunities of business models for renewable energy (Engelken et al., 2016);
- a synthesis of existing research findings into a simple and accessible framework of influences on household adoption and rejection of energy technology (Chadwick et al., 2022);
- a proposal of a new self-regulated behavioral change model together with its application (Bamberg, 2013a); and
- a critical review of concepts, benefits, risks, and politics of smart home technologies in Europe (Sovacool and Furszyfer Der Rio, 2020).

Finally, researchers also employ **modeling and simulation** techniques to track the manner and environment in which the goods or services disseminate in the market. **Agent-based modeling** (ABM) has undoubtedly been one of the most widely used modeling techniques recently, despite the fact that many different modeling techniques are being used. Because it starts with micro behaviors (agents, customers) and moves upward through macro behaviors (societies, populations), ABM is becoming more and more popular (Rixen and Weigand, 2014; Stummer et al., 2015). Such an approach enables the simulation of consumer behavior with regard to different products and the identification of the effects of social influence, social influence, network topologies, and external factors, such as mass media advertising or governmental policies, on the diffusion time and schedule (Rixen and Weigand, 2014; Stummer et al., 2015; Kowalska-Pyzalska et al., 2014; Ringler et al., 2016; Przybyła et al., 2014).

There is a great number of papers that examine and explain the diffusion with reference to innovative energy services, such as smart metering and smart grids (Rixen and Weigand, 2014; Ringler et al., 2016). As Ringler et al. (2016) indicate, ABM is used for modeling: (a) competitive wholesale markets, (b) electricity consumer behavior, e.g., Zhang and Nuttall (2011); Kowalska-Pyzalska et al. (2014), (c) impact of policies on market penetration (Ringler et al., 2016), and (d) diffusion of products, such as smart meters (Zhang and Nuttall, 2011; Rixen and Weigand, 2014; Chou et al., 2015; Ringler et al., 2016), SM platforms (Kowalska-Pyzalska, 2016), dynamic tariffs (Kowalska-Pyzalska et al., 2014), storage devices (Zheng et al., 2014), PV systems (Palmer et al., 2015), novel biomass fuel (Guenther et al., 2011), residential energy-efficient behaviors by means of smart technologies (Moglia et al., 2017), or general eco-innovations (Byrka et al., 2016; Karakaya et al., 2014).

The examples below present the goals of the studies that implement ABM to search for the determinants and conditions of the successful diffusion of IES:

- an evaluation of policy options for inducing innovation adoption of smart meters (Rixen and Weigand, 2014);
- a study of temporal dynamics of consumer opinions and decisions regarding switching to dynamic electricity tariffs (Kowalska-Pyzalska et al., 2014);
- an examination of the impact of educational programs and trainings on the diffusion of smart metering platforms (SMPs) (Weron et al., 2018);
- evaluating the potential of agent-based modeling to understanding energy transitions from a social-scientific perspective (Hansen et al., 2019);
- evaluating government's policies on promoting smart metering diffusion (Zhang and Nuttall, 2011);
- modeling the diffusion of residential photovoltaic systems (Palmer et al., 2015); and
- predicting the performance of different residential distributed PV solar models with respect to stakeholders' objectives (Mittal et al., 2019).

To summarize, one of the main advantages of the ABM approach is its cost-effectiveness. Computer modeling and simulation does not involve expensive and time-consuming field experiments. It allows one to investigate various scenarios and to perform a complex sensitivity analysis. Hence, the ABM framework can be a great test-bed for analyzing innovative concepts and paradigms in the field of smart grids and markets (e.g., demand response) (Ringler et al., 2016). On the one hand, ABM can be used as a substitute for costly social experiments.

It can occasionally be impossible to plan and carry out a worthwhile social experiment using a sizable, representative sample of customers. This is especially true in the energy market, where customers' behavior can be studied either by assessing their preferences (see, for example, Gerpott and Paukert, 2013; Duetschke and Paetz, 2013; Buryk et al., 2015) or by determining how responsively they are to different pricing incentives or social norms. However, in the latter scenario, collaboration with the energy supplier or power system operator is a requirement (see, for example, Star et al., 2010; Allcott, 2011; Nolan et al., 2008).

On the other hand, a social experiment can be used to calibrate and validate a model, as was the case, for instance, in reference (Sopha et al., 2017). It's also feasible to construct and test an ABM before planning a legitimate social experiment. In such a situation, the variables can be altered using ABM, and some methods (such as customized marketing interventions) can be evaluated prior to being applied to responders.

5.2.2 Pilot programs

Last but not least, the practical solutions are tested in the real world by means of **pilot programs**. As mentioned earlier, the presence of IES in energy systems does not meet with consumers' interest, engagement, and acceptance. In contrast, in most cases consumers remain uninterested, indifferent, and not willing to involve much. At the same time, the suppliers of IES are often obliged to increase the presence of a given food in the power grid due to the legislative regulations and energy policy. To overcome social resistance, suppliers and regulators often decide on so-called pilot programs, in which they provide a given good in a limited area. The examples of such pilot projects include:

- Home Energy Report letters sent in 2009 to the households by the company OPOWER in order to compare a household's energy use to that of similar neighbors and provide energy conservation tips;
- EcoGrid-EU project run among 800 households in 2016–2019 in the Bornholm Island; flexible power consumption in private households, controlled by aggregators, was tested (Neska and Kowalska-Pyzalska, 2022);
- LINEAR pilot, a large-scale research and demonstration project focused on the introduction of demand response at residential premises in the Flanders region in Belgium (D'hulst et al., 2015);
- GridFlex Heeten project run among 47 households in 2017–2020 in the Netherlands; local storage, using sea salt batteries and flexible pricing strategies, such as variable network tariffs and collective and individual pricing mechanisms, were tested (Neska and Kowalska-Pyzalska, 2022);

- Hoog Dalem 2.0 project run among 16 households between 2019 and 2020 in the Netherlands; energy was traded locally by households via blockchain in which all transactions were recorded (Neska and Kowalska-Pyzalska, 2022); and
- a review of current DR pilot projects in China, identifying the main barriers in implementing these projects and proposing recommendations to make it successful across the country (Tahir et al., 2020; Chen et al., 2021).

Pilot programs, also known as feasibility studies or experimental trials, are short-term tests that can help a company learn how a larger-scale project might work in practice. They provide a platform for a firm to test logistics and spot any potential deficiencies before the further development of the project. In other words, a pilot program allows companies and providers to test the effectiveness of a planned solution on a smaller scale. Pilot programs are widely used also in cases of launching new services or business models in the energy markets. Within the pilot program, the participating households can get experience of a given good and experiment with it, without bearing the financial cost of investment. The organizers of these programs also learn which set of parameters of a given good is mostly beneficial for them from technical, organizational, and economic points of view. After the pilot program finishes, the participants may opt for an innovation and decide to continue using it, or they may resign from it.

5.2.3 Analytical tools used in data analysis

Apart from a variety of tools used to collect the data, scientists use many analytical methods to explore the obtained data sets. Dependent on the aim of the research, the data are usually analyzed by the means of statistical and econometric tools, such as:

- regression models, such as probit models (Nakamura, 2016; Cantono and Silverberg, 2009), logit models (Diaz-Rainey and Tzavara, 2015; Kowalska-Pyzalska and Byrka, 2019; Krishnamutri et al., 2012; Chawla et al., 2020a; Weiss et al., 2016; Buryk et al., 2015; Henn et al., 2019; Ntanos et al., 2018), or tobit models (Chawla and Kowalska-Pyzalska, 2019);
- analysis of variance ANOVA or multivariate analysis of variance MANOVA (Gölz and Hahnel, 2016; Sohn and Kwon, 2020); or
- principle component analysis (Ma et al., 2015; Ozaki, 2011; Gadenne et al., 2011; Chawla and Kowalska-Pyzalska, 2019), and others.

The choice of the regression model depends on the type of a data set. For example, Mengaki (2012), Ma et al. (2015), and Zoric and Hrovatin (2012) include variants of models of discrete choice that can be used to estimate consumers' WTPs. They mention, among other models, multinominal or nested logit models, fixed effect logit models, conditional logit models, tobit or censored regression models, ordered probit models, and mixed models.

Recently, tools of big data analysis, such as machine learning, have also been used, such as in the work of Zhou and Yang (2016), where the usefulness of energy big data analysis for understating household energy consumption behavior was presented.

5.2.4 Overview of research areas regarding IES and consumer behavior

Diffusion of IES and their perception and acceptance among electricity consumers have been studied for years from various points of view. Researchers have focused their efforts on explaining the incentives and barriers of IES adoption, investigating social awareness, acceptance, opinion formation, and decision making toward innovative goods in the future energy systems. Special attention has been paid to investigation of consumers' willingness to accept/adopt and the analysis of consumers' preferences that may allow the IES to be designed in a suitable way. Secondly, willingness to pay for access to the innovative energy service has been broadly studied.

Most of these studies refer to some extent to the aspects of social acceptance of the future energy systems. This is because, as mentioned in previous chapters, smooth diffusion of any innovation in the market requires some level of social acceptance (Gouws and Van Rheede van Oudtshoorn, 2011). **Social acceptance** is a very broad concept and can be categorized on various levels, each with its own perspective. Wuestenhagen et al. (2007) have given a categorization of social acceptance, which distinguishes three, occasionally symbiotic, categories: **socio-political acceptance**—this, most general and the broadest level is concerned with the acceptance of technologies and policies by the people, key stakeholders, and policy makers; **community/public acceptance**: this concerns the acceptance of procedures by law and trust building; and **customer/consumer/ market acceptance**—this concerns the acceptance of innovation by the individual consumers, investors, and intra-firms (Wuestenhagen et al., 2007; Wolsink, 2014; Chawla and Kowalska-Pyzalska, 2019; Kowalska-Pyzalska, 2015; Claudy et al., 2010; Perlaviciute and Steg, 2014).

Dependent on the investigated type of the acceptance, the attention moves from the macroscopic analysis of acceptance among public and key stakeholders, together with the policy makers in the socio-political acceptance, to microscopic analysis of acceptance among individual consumers and investors in customer/ market acceptance. In community acceptance, the point of view of local stakeholders, such as residents and local authorities understood as a community or a group of people with a common interest, is investigated. From the point of view of this book, the author's attention is focused on market/customer acceptance, known also as **consumer acceptance**.

To clarify the differences between three types of acceptance, in Table 5.1 the areas of research with some findings for each type of acceptance have been summarized on the examples of renewable energy (Kowalska-Pyzalska, 2015; Wolsink, 2014; Wuestenhagen et al., 2007).

There are many examples from the literature explaining the relationship between the successful diffusion of IES and social acceptance consisting of three areas: socio-political, public, and consumer/market. There are many studies examining social acceptance of small-scale renewable energy sources or green electricity tariffs and programs. We can mention, for example, Hansla et al. (2008); Hobman and Frederiks (2014); Kowalska-Pyzalska (2018a); Ozaki (2011) and Stigka et al. (2014), who investigated the relation between the consumer acceptance and adoption rates and diffusion. This point of view is very important, because acceptance on the private and public level is a precondition of the smooth diffusion of these energy sources in the market.

Apart from the investigation of consumer acceptance of RES and green electricity tariff, recently, a lot of studies have been carried out to explore the social acceptance and awareness of smart grids and smart metering (Chawla and Kowalska-Pyzalska, 2019; Chawla et al., 2020c). From the point of view of consumers, awareness about the opportunities they get and knowledge on how to use SMP are fundamental. Without any awareness, knowledge, and acceptance of smart metering together with SMP, this novelty will never spread successfully in the market (Wolsink, 2014; Claudy et al., 2010; Krishnamutri et al., 2012; Kowalska-Pyzalska and Byrka, 2019), leading to an insufficient increase of energy efficiency.

The analysis of social acceptance is a starting point of many different analyses. For example, while examining consumer acceptance of SM, various aspects can be explored, including:

- an overview of consumers' acceptance and engagement toward smart grid solutions (Ellabban and Abu-Rub, 2016);
- consumers' expectations and perceptions about SM (Krishnamutri et al., 2012);

Table 5.1 Three dimensions of social acceptance on the three examples with reference to RES.

Ex.	Social-political acceptance	Community/public acceptance	Customer/Consumer/Market acceptance
(1)	The accurate spatial planning system to stimulate collaborative decision making	Sitting decisions regarding location of RES project may raise NIMBY (Not In My Backyard) problems leading to social resistance to RES investments if they are too close to residential buildings	Investigation of the individual preferences and opinions toward location of RES projects
(2)	The effective public financial support for renewable technologies to create incentives for investment	The division between collective and individual costs and benefits from RES requires focus on fairness-related characteristics of the RES projects, such as fair procedure (procedural and distributional justice), trust building, information sharing, and compensation strategies	Psychological factors like values, norms and personal identity with the location of the RES project influence acceptance
(3)	The role of policies and social and educational campaigns on awareness, knowledge, and acceptance	Community-based approach toward RES project	Market segmentation allows to identify different needs and expectations of various consumer groups and adjust the RES projects or offers to their needs
Ref.	(Wolsink, 2020; Leonhardt et al., 2022; Robert, 2019; Wuestenhagen et al., 2007)	(Radl et al., 2020; Koirala et al., 2016; Lennon et al., 2019; Coy et al., 2021; Perlaviciute and Steg, 2014)	(Koirala et al., 2018; Kowalska-Pyzalska, 2018a; Ntanos et al., 2018; Claudy et al., 2010)

- effectiveness of feedback provided by SM together with some enabling technologies (such as in-home displays or smart metering platforms) (Kowalska-Pyzalska and Byrka, 2019); (Nachreiner et al., 2015; Gans et al., 2013; Burchell et al., 2016; Ma et al., 2018; Podgornik et al., 2016; Schleich et al., 2017; Foulds et al., 2017);
- effectiveness of education and training in SM and SMP context (Weron et al., 2018); and
- incentives or barriers to SM adoption (Good et al., 2017; Kahma and Matschoss, 2017; Kowalska-Pyzalska, 2018b).

Finally, Table 5.2 summarizes and gives an overview of the broadness of the research areas and goals regarding IES based on the recent literature. We can see the combination of various kind of studies, ranging from the in-depth literature reviews and meta-analysis, research surveys, and field experiments to mathematical models.

The review of the research agenda's diversity reveals the issues that interest and matter to scholars. It also makes it possible to identify current trends in this field of study. It is obvious that researchers concentrate on the factors that influence successful spread. The fact that the investigations are multidisciplinary attracts attention. The authors mix approaches, models, and variables from environmental and electrical engineering as well as social science (economic, sociology, psychology, and environmental psychology). Multidisciplinarity brings many positive effects, leading to a broader perspective of the investigation and to a synergy effect.

5.3 Practical experience and research findings

In this chapter, we will discuss the research findings with regard to the:
- determinants of consumer acceptance and willingness to accept/adopt IES;
- willingness to pay for IES;
- determinants of energy-efficient behaviors in the context of IES; and
- determinants of IES market diffusion.

At the end of this chapter, we will summarize the incentives and barriers regarding IES adoption.

Table 5.2 Research areas and goals of the chosen studies related to IES.

Research question	Reference
Technologies based on renewable energy	
Define a set of individual values linked with biofuel support	(Khachatryan et al., 2013)
Cover the gap in literature regarding consumers' awareness	(Claudy et al., 2010)
Fill the knowledge gap in the literature about consumer awareness	(Perlaviciute and Steg, 2014)
Describe the motivators and constraints affecting business models for renewable energy sources, as well as the exciting opportunities available in various parts of the world	(Engelken et al., 2016)
Gain understanding of various multiple criteria decision-making techniques with regard to applications for renewable energy	(Kumar et al., 2017)
Examine the literature to discover the patterns in the evaluation of RES investments	(Strantzali and Aravossis, 2015)
Simulate the spread of small home PV systems in the future under various circumstances	(Palmer et al., 2015)
Create an agent-based simulation approach to examine how different marketing strategies and policies affect consumer uptake	(Guenther et al., 2011)
Green electricity tariffs	
Examine the contingent validation method and its potential sources of errors with regard to WTP for green electricity	(Oerlemans et al., 2016)
Determine the interests of consumers and their willingness to participate in green electricity initiatives	(Borchers et al., 2007)
Identify the kind of factors that are more or less likely to prevent people from enrolling in green power programs or tariffs	(Hobman and Frederiks, 2014)
Describe the factors that influence customer adoption of green power prices	(Ozaki, 2011)
Investigate empirically the variables that affect people's desire to switch to green power pricing	(Gerpott and Mahmudova, 2010)
Create a model that explains the noticeable discrepancies between the actual adoption of green power pricing and the declared intention to do so	(Diaz-Rainey and Tzavara, 2012)

continued on next page

Table 5.2 continued

Research question	Reference
Demand response and demand management systems	
Determine the best methods for delivering dynamic pricing to maximize customer uptake and usage over a wider demographic range	(Hobman et al., 2016)
Analyze and research consumer preferences for dynamic pricing strategies	(Buryk et al., 2015; Duetschke and Paetz, 2013)
Examine obstacles to effective voluntary demand reduction	(Gyamfi et al., 2013)
Review, classify and analyze demand response barriers and enablers	(Good et al., 2017)
Apply an agent-based model to commercially available storage technologies and tariffs to conduct DR optimization and economic viability evaluations	(Zheng et al., 2014)
Smart metering, smart metering information platforms	
Evaluate policy options, including regulatory interventions for inducing innovation adoption of SM by simulation analysis	(Rixen and Weigand, 2014)
Define how reduction of electricity consumption may be encouraged by smart meter information systems and the informational concepts associated with them	(Nachreiner et al., 2015)
Examine the effect of usage feedback on residential consumption	(Gans et al., 2013)
Examine the efficacy of regulations encouraging the use of smart meters	(Zhang and Nuttall, 2011)
Determine the extent to which consumer views of specific SM feature facets and general environmental consciousness can account for disparities in WTP for smart meters (SM)	(Gerpott and Paukert, 2013)
Compare and contrast the consumer uptake of smart meters in the four Asian countries	(Chou et al., 2015)
Review, quantify, and explain empirically the determinants of consumer behavior in relation to electricity consumption	(Batalla-Bejerano et al., 2020)
To test the effect of environmental attitudes, knowledge, and perceived possibilities on consumers' stages of readiness to adopt SMP	(Kowalska-Pyzalska and Byrka, 2019)

continued on next page

Table 5.2 continued

Research question	Reference
Examine how houesholds that are equipped with SM use these devices on a regular basis	(Bertoldo et al., 2015)
Assess the present outlook for SM roll-out in India based on consumer interest and willingness to install it	(Chawla et al., 2020c)
Energy-efficient behaviors	
Explore the effect of customized consumption feedback and tailored information on energy-efficient behavior patterns and energy saving	(Podgornik et al., 2016)
Analyze how and why feedback mitigates inefficient energy consumption caused by habits	(Lee et al., 2020)
Study the effectiveness of feedback and examine the goals which motivate households to use web-based feedback about their electricity consumption	(Gölz and Hahnel, 2016)
Explore a proper design of feedback software that leads to a behavioral change and consumer satisfaction	(Wood et al., 2019)
Examine affective and behavioral responses to energy-sharing situations incorporating different types of energy displays	(Leygue et al., 2014)
Investigate the impact of a bonus system to reward responsible consumption of energy	(Flambard et al., 2021)
Review, explain and predict household energy use by means of psychological and behavioral economics	(Frederiks et al., 2014)
Identify the main issues and challenges associated with energy demand reduction	(Sorrell, 2015)
Establish a framework of behavior-oriented energy consumption behavior	(Zhou and Yang, 2016)
Analyze the influence of consumers' environmental beliefs and attitudes on energy-saving behavior	(Gadenne et al., 2011)

5.3.1 Determinants of consumer acceptance and willingness to accept

There is a wide list of factors that may determine consumer acceptance for IES. The literature review indicates that these factors can be divided into several categories, such as: (1) demographics,

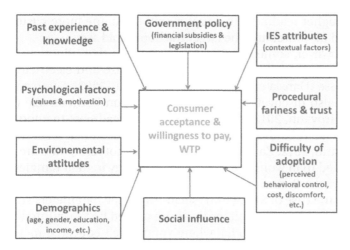

Figure 5.1. Set of determinants for consumers' acceptance and willingness to pay.

(2) environmental attitudes and behaviors, (3) values and norms, (4) social influence, (5) past experiences and knowledge in the energy market, (6) procedural fairness and trust, (7) perceived difficulty of adoption, and (8) financial support and legislation. In addition, there are contextual factors, meaning the attributes of a given innovation that impact the consumer's acceptance and willingness to adopt.

A graphical representation of the complexity of factors influencing both consumers' acceptance and willingness to accept, adopt, and pay is shown in Fig. 5.1. These factors influence also intention and behavior adoption of IES, leading first to formation of an opinion regarding IES and then to a decision to adopt or reject.

Below, we briefly explain the impact of each group of factors on consumer acceptance.

Demographics

Numerous surveys have looked into how customers' willingness and choice to install small-scale green energy sources are influenced by their income, expenditure on electricity bills, and household size. While the majority of the data show that a consumer's willingness rises with money (see Ropuszyńska-Surma and Weglarz, 2016; Zarnikau, 2003), the impact of other variables is less certain. According to Ropuszyńska-Surma and Weglarz (2016), the readiness to switch to green energy is favorably connected with both the electricity cost and the size of the household.

The higher readiness to adopt is said to be, the more customers spend for power and the larger the household size.

However, some empirical data suggests that adoption readiness may actually decline as household size and electricity bills increase (Hansla et al., 2008; Borchers et al., 2007). Some authors have also discovered a negative association between age (Zoric and Hrovatin, 2012; Zarnikau, 2003) and readiness to adopt/pay, as well as a positive correlation between education level (Zoric and Hrovatin, 2012; Zarnikau, 2003). Last but not least, men are more inclined than women to install green energy in their families (Ropuszyńska-Surma and Weglarz, 2016).

In the case of SM or SMP, socio-economic parameters seem to play a role too. Sometimes these are caused by the cultural background, such as in India, where young, well-educated men, in a good financial situation, living in a city rather than in a village, have been found to be mostly interested in SM and conscious usage (Chawla et al., 2020c). Generally, the studies have shown that knowledge and experience with energy markets in general, and SM and conscious energy consumption in particular, rise with the level of education.

Environmental attitudes and psychological factors

Environmental attitudes are beliefs a person has about the effects of engaging in a particular conduct based on how they value such effects in terms of protecting the environment. Therefore, behavioral beliefs generate attitudes, whether positive or negative. There is ample proof that adopting green energy is supported by pro-environmental attitudes and ideas (Ozaki, 2011; Stern, 2014). According to Ozaki (2011), a belief that green energy is a clean energy source may convince consumers to pay more. Gerpott and Mahmudova (2010) indicate that individuals' readiness to switch to green electricity is most strongly influenced by their opinions regarding environmental protection problems. In addition to attitudes, other psychological factors, e.g., individual or collective values, influence evaluation and adoption of green energy (Ajzen and Fishbein, 2005; Perlaviciute and Steg, 2014). Finally, normative beliefs have a positive impact on the intention to adopt a certain environmental behavior; see, e.g., Stern (2014); Ozaki (2011). It has also been proved that green activities, such as recycling, conserving energy, and utilizing electro-rubbish, are positively correlated with willingness to adopt green energy (such as becoming a prosumer; see, e.g., Ropuszyńska-Surma and Weglarz, 2016).

The impact of environmental believes and concerns on SM acceptance is ambiguous. Generally, people who are aware of climate change are more willing to accept SM as a useful and energy-efficient technology (Bugden and Stedman, 2019).

Values and norms

There is also a wide range of psychological factors, including both individual and collective values that may influence the evaluation of decision's alternatives regarding, e.g., green energy technologies (Sopha and Kloeckner, 2016; Perlaviciute and Steg, 2014). Hansla et al. (2008), Sopha and Kloeckner (2016), and Stern (2014) indicate that self-transcendence values (i.e., interest in the welfare of others rather than one's own well-being) increase willingness to accept and adopt green energy solutions. The same studies show that self-enhancement values correlate negatively with acceptance (Kowalska-Pyzalska, 2018a). Thus, a consumer's decision-making process and assessment of the IES are influenced by whether they place a higher priority on the welfare of society as a whole (collective, self-transcendence values) or their own financial security (individual, self-enhancement values). Most of the time, consumers regard energy services more favorably from a group perspective than from an individual one. Individual values are significant early adoption drivers, according to Frank et al. (2015), because they provide as driving forces for pursuing objectives and intentions that are pertinent to the early adoption process.

When deciding whether to accept an innovation, people take into account the innovation's meaning to them and how it represents their identity, image, values, and social norms in addition to its functionality, usability, costs, and desired outcomes (Ozaki, 2011). The value-belief-norm theory emphasizes the impact of norms on attitudes and behavior (Stern, 2000). This theory claims that the intention to adopt environmental behavior is positively influenced by normative beliefs. Recycling, according to Ozaki, is a good illustration of how a concern for the environment may become a standard practice (Ozaki, 2011). The likelihood that a particular activity will develop into a habit is higher the more consumers who are persuaded that waste segregation is good for the environment start doing it.

Social and community influence

Many researchers have shown that strong social norms are needed to encourage adoption (Ozaki, 2011; Gadenne et al., 2011; Allcott, 2011; Nolan et al., 2008; Nyczka and Sznajd-Weron, 2013; Przybyła et al., 2014). Most people want to adjust to their peers because they need social approval. Without social norms, people cannot judge whether adopting a new energy service is accepted or not. The role of social influence is important: people show their sense of membership by taking up activities that are regarded as norms within the group they belong to Ozaki (2011).

The work of Nolan et al. (2008) highlighted the influence of the social norm. The authors argued that a social norm has more of an impact than other nonnormative incentives, such as saving money, protecting the environment, or even helping society (Nolan et al., 2008). Additionally, they showed a mismatch between reported motivation and actual conduct. According to the study, the least significant motivator in the self-reported motivation stage was "because others are doing it." On the other hand, it was confirmed that there was a strong association between people's present conservation behavior and their perception of whether or not their neighbors practiced it (Kowalska-Pyzalska, 2018b).

Furthermore, a high number of research studies suggests that consumers are cordially motivated by the opinions and behaviors of their family, friends, and associates as well as by cultural values (Bollinger and Gillingham, 2012; Jager, 2006; Gangale et al., 2013; Ajzen and Fishbein, 2005; McMichael and Shipworth, 2013; Schultz et al., 2007; Sidiras and Koukios, 2004). Many studies have shown that normative social influence has a positive effect on the intention to engage in environmental behaviors, like the acceptance of green energy or energy conservation behavior (Ozaki, 2011; Allcott, 2011; Nolan et al., 2008; Kowalska-Pyzalska et al., 2014). In the work of Bollinger and Gillingham (2012), the authors perceived social interaction through peer effects as a potentially crucial factor in the diffusion of new services in the energy market. The peer impacts on household decisions regarding the installation of solar photovoltaic (PV) panels in the energy market were examined in this particular case. It was discovered that the likelihood of adoption and new PV installation increased dramatically with a rise in the average number of PV installed in a given area (Bollinger and Gillingham, 2012). The investigations by Ayers et al. (2013) and Allcott (2011) also looked into and examined the strength of social influence. The authors analyzed the results of the large-scale program sponsored by the company OPOWER, in which "Home Energy Report" letters were given to residential utility customers, comparing their electricity use to that of their neighbors (Kowalska-Pyzalska, 2015).

This marketing intervention allowed energy consumption to be reduced by 2%. Both studies showed that combining the descriptive and injunctive messages (in this case, emoticons: happy or sad faces) reduced energy consumption and lessened the undesirable boomerang effect, which is the phenomenon in which people who unintentionally use less energy than their neighbors start to use more. Ayres et al. (2013) came to the conclusion that, on the one hand, knowing that our neighbors conserve more (less) energy could increase (decrease) guilt emotions about contributing to society problems, which would affect individual preferences and motivations to conserve energy (Gerpott and Paukert, 2013). Learning from neighbors' behavior, on the other hand, may provide consumers with information about viable alternative consumption options and the relative benefits of those choices (Kowalska-Pyzalska, 2015).

Past experiences and knowledge in the energy market

Environmental drivers include procedural knowledge and understanding which are necessary to turn attitudes and beliefs into concrete actions, consumer feelings of guilt or moral obligation, sense of social responsibility, ease of adoption, and personal relevance (Pongiglione, 2011). Consumers are now aware of the potential contribution that RES could make to environmental protection, but they are also unaware of the best ways to encourage the growth of RES. This is especially true in the cases of green electricity programs and tariffs. In many countries where the majority of electricity is produced from fossil fuels, we still observe the generally low level of knowledge of consumers about the energy market, and a lack of interest and engagement. Additionally, it might be argued that these customers view green electricity as a public good, leading them to believe that the federal government and local governments should be in charge of continuing to develop RES without charging end users any additional fees (Ropuszyńska-Surma and Weglarz, 2016; Kowalska-Pyzalska, 2019).

In the cases of SM and SMP, familiarity of this technology is also low. Consumers mistake SM with other smart home devices. Knowledge of and exposure to SM may, in part, be linked to an increase in worries about the drawbacks of these technologies. However, they may also increase interest in and readiness for monitoring energy consumption (Krishnamutri et al., 2012; Kahma and Matschoss, 2017; Raimi and Carrico, 2016; Foulds et al., 2017). A positive relation between the increase of consumers' knowledge about the energy market and general smart grid solutions (including SM, SMP, and DSM/DR) and smart meters and SMP acceptance has been found in the work of Chawla et al. (2020c).

This study has shown that consumers experienced with SM had the highest level of knowledge about SM and smart grids, which is quite natural. Moreover, this consumer segment cared about the experiences and opinions about SM of their friends and acquaintances. In addition, information about the lack of negative effects on health caused by SM had an impact on the SM owner. Consumers who were in the process of SM installation were mainly those who lived in a city center or urban areas, rather than in villages.

According to findings in Chawla et al. (2020a), understanding of SM has increased as the ages of individuals have risen, suggesting that young people know less about SM. Those who were active on social media sites like Facebook and LinkedIn had a higher likelihood of knowing about SM than those who were not. Consumers who own basic items like Wifi or home internet access, laptops or cell phones, and home appliances were also more probable to accept SM. In Indonesia, consumers do not have to pay to upgrade to SM, according to the current policy, and an emphasis on factors such as energy saving, resulting in savings in the cost of electricity and how consumers could achieve these savings, would push consumers toward accepting SM (Chawla et al., 2019).

Procedural fairness and trust

Access to and influence over the decision-making process are two aspects of procedural fairness. It shows if someone has control over a particular action or process, in this case, SM data usage and transmission (Bugden and Stedman, 2019; Good et al., 2017). As Immonen et al. (2020) emphasize, the empowerment of the consumers will never succeed without giving consumers more control over their electricity and transmission fees. This control can be achieved thanks to the high penetration of IoT devices and artificial intelligence (AI) technologies, and distributed ledger technology (DLT) (Dogaru, 2020; Petri et al., 2020; Summeren et al., 2021), which enables near real-time and remote control of consumer electricity consumption. At the same time, the security of consumers' private data is a vital condition of success.

Privacy concerns come from their perception that utilizing SM, which discloses extensive information about household activities, may result in a loss of privacy. The actions of people inside their homes (habits, usage, the kind of home appliances they own, etc.) may be revealed by data gathered through SM. SM data may be utilized improperly by both authorized and unauthorized individuals in the event of poor cyber security (Bugden and Stedman, 2019; Razavi and Gharipour, 2018; Hmielowski et al., 2019; Chen et al., 2017). Addressing data privacy concern through advances in technology, installations of proper security systems, and visits from a company representative to deal with any doubts of consumers may become vital determinants of SM acceptance (Chawla et al., 2020a).

Privacy concern and procedural fairness connect with trust in energy suppliers (whether they will secure the personal information and will not share it with third parties) (Bugden and Stedman, 2019; Chen et al., 2017). A reluctance to adopt may be caused by a lack of **trust** in energy suppliers, doubts whether green energy is really a clean source, and worries that the energy provided to the household was not generated using green energy sources (Hobman and Frederiks, 2014; Kowalska-Pyzalska, 2018b). Switching experiences, particularly the perception of switching difficulty, may have an impact on the willingness to adopt green electricity among consumers with low electricity consumption levels(Gerpott and Mahmudova, 2010). This segment of consumers can be encouraged to change to a green electricity tariff if they believe that an energy supplier is acting in a socially responsible manner (Gerpott and Mahmudova, 2010).

Difficulty of adoption

The following behavioral barriers to SM acceptance have been most frequently mentioned in the literature: Bounded consumer rationality, difficulty making decisions due to a lack of expert advice, negative perceptions primarily due to ignorance and underestimation, negative word-of-mouth (spreading unfavorable information on social networks), denial of climate change, discomfort with use, and privacy and security concerns (Good et al., 2017; Kowalska-Pyzalska, 2018b; Kahma and Matschoss, 2017; Ellabban and Abu-Rub, 2016).

Next, especially in the case of adoption of RES, the strongest barriers include large initial investment costs and expected long pay-back times Hobman and Frederiks (2014); Negro et al. (2012). People also suffer from insufficient information, lack of professional help and advice, and lack of time (Gadenne et al., 2011; Kowalska-Pyzalska et al., 2014; Sidiras and Koukios, 2004; Perlaviciute and Steg, 2014; Stern, 2014). People make more or less consciously a cost-benefit analysis of the alternatives, and weigh pros and cons, both financial and nonfinancial, to maximize their benefits (Lopes et al., 2016). If the perceived costs exceed the benefits, people usually refuse to adopt the innovation.

The tendency to delegate environmental preservation duties to other organizations, such as local governments, the government, or even neighbors, reduces the desire to adopt (Hobman and Frederiks, 2014; Kowalska-Pyzalska, 2018b). Adoption can occasionally be hampered by supply-side barriers (such as the technical difficulties of installing a green small-scale generator at the household or the lack of green power rates in the supplier's offer) Hobman and Frederiks (2014); Kowalska-Pyzalska (2018b).

In the case of SM, acceptance rises with the belief in a positive result of cost-benefit analysis of consumer engagement in the energy market (taking into account financial and nonfinancial aspects, e.g., discomfort of usage). At the same time, data security and privacy, ignorance of the nature of control, and low benefits versus high initial cost are the main barriers to acceptance (Fouad et al., 2022).

Finally, Siano (2014) gave a review of the possibilities and advantages of demand response in smart grids, along with a discussion of enabling technology and systems. The domestication of a technology is thought to be more crucial than the actual acquisition of that technology. Consumers must incorporate new options and technologies into their daily routines (Verbong et al., 2013). As Vázquez-Canteli and Nagy (Vázquez-Canteli and Nagy, 2019) pointed out, demand response's future is strongly dependent on incorporating human feedback into the control loop.

Financial subsidy and legislation

Finally, grants, subsidies, discounts, rewards, and educational programs may increase the willingness to adopt by decreasing the financial and nonfinancial difficulty of adoption Masini and Menichetti (2012); Negro et al. (2012). Environmental opinions are not always influenced by government regulations, subsidies, and index subsidies, according to studies of Masini and Menichetti (2012). This might be a sign that green customers don't have faith in their governments to follow through on their promises of stronger regulations and cost-covering subsidies. It has also been discovered that convincing consumers to invest in particular renewable energy technology depends heavily on their confidence in policies and their justice and righteousness. Because of this, effective government programs must reassure citizens that, in the long term, taking action to protect the environment will be more beneficial than costly.

A number of customers are concerned that the installation of SM may result in higher energy costs (more accurate readings). However, some of them might expect SM to start saving money right once, which is a bit unreasonable (Bugden and Stedman, 2019; Krishnamutri et al., 2012; Lineweber, 2011; Mack et al., 2019).

The combination of perceived personal benefits from adopting the innovative energy service, compatibility with a consumer's values, identity, and social references, strong social influence and normative beliefs, a sense of control over costs and associated inconveniences associated with switching over, no perceived risk or uncertainty, and finally good information is what drives people from the intention to adopt to actual adoption (Kowalska-Pyzalska, 2018b).

The modern energy policy consists of four dimensions: security of supply, economics, and environment, together with social acceptance (Schweiger et al., 2020). Hargreaves pointed out that the impact of new technologies such as smart meters on energy demand and demand flexibility depends heavily on social variables such as individual preferences, social relations, or daily routines in a household (Hargreaves et al., 2010).

5.3.2 Willingness to pay (WTP)

The true adoption of such products will only be possible if the social acceptance is accompanied by the consumers' engagement and willingness to pay (WTP), understood as a willingness to contribute (by paying more for green energy, by becoming a prosumer, by switching to the dynamic tariffs program) (Kowalska-Pyzalska, 2015). Due to this, we will explore several WTP-related challenges in this subsection using IES as our chosen examples.

Definition of the WTP concept

As mentioned in Chapter 3, after becoming aware of an innovative good and forming an opinion about it, consumers may express their willingness or readiness to adopt it. The literature of innovation diffusion as well as of the nonmarket goods' evaluation distinguishes various methods of determining consumers' willingness to adopt (Diaz-Rainey and Tzavara, 2012; Zoric and Hrovatin, 2012; Stigka et al., 2014). In most cases, **stated willingness to adopt** (SWA) is measured in monetary terms as so-called **willingness to pay** (WTP) (Stigka et al., 2014; Oerlemans et al., 2016; Zarnikau, 2003). WTP expresses the additional premium that a consumer is ready to pay in order to obtain a given good, and what makes it a popular concept in goods appraisal and in consumer choice (Oerlemans et al., 2016). In that sense, WTP can measure individual as well as public preferences (Kowalska-Pyzalska, 2019). Apart from SWA and WTP, the literature also mentions **willingness to accept** (WTA) (Sundt et al., 2020; Nicolson et al., 2017), discussed in the previous chapter. In the case of early adopters, i.e., consumers who are the first to become interested in a new innovative good, the literature considers also the **innate willingness to pay** (IWTP) for innovations; see, for example, the work by Karakaya et al. (2014).

The literature also differentiates between **feasible adoption** (usually lower than SWA) and actual adoption, mainly because of some supply-side problems and regulatory failures (Diaz-Rainey and Tzavara, 2012) or rejection of innovation after some trials. In other words, obtaining positive (above zero) WTP, does not mean that consumers will actually decide for a given good. WTP informs only about consumers' declarations, which can be but do not have to be the same as the real consumers' decisions and actions. However, WTP is still one of the most popular means of identifying the level of appraisal of a product among consumers. Below, we will discuss the results of studies that explored all kinds of willingness, concentrating mainly on either WTP or WTA. The main difference between these approaches is that in WTP, the results are presented in monetary terms, whereas WTA provides a statistical analysis of factors that positively/negatively influence the probability of high/low WTA.

How to evaluate WTP

Consumers' WTP can be calculated either as a percentage of the current electricity bill (see, e.g., Liu et al., 2013; Kowalska-Pyzalska, 2017) or as an absolute value (e.g., an increase in the cost of an electricity bill (Zhang and Wu, 2012; Zoric and Hrovatin, 2012) or an increase in the price per kWh of electricity supplied (Borchers et al., 2007; Hansla et al., 2008). While the CVM generates values for the products as a whole, the CE elicits values for the goods' individual features (Ma et al., 2015). The manner in which the respondents are presented with the WTP question is a crucial component of any CVM design (Kowalska-Pyzalska, 2019).

In the literature, typically four WTP elicitation formats are popular (Oerlemans et al., 2016; Kowalska-Pyzalska, 2019):

- bidding or bargaining format (a respondent is asked to accept or reject a proposed WTP value and, based on their decision, higher or lower bids are offered);
- payment scale format (all respondents choose different values from a predefined and ordered list, as in e.g., Ntanos et al., 2018; Zhang and Wu, 2012; Liu et al., 2013);
- open-ended format (a respondent is asked to choose their own WTP valuation, unbounded and unprompted, as in, e.g., Zoric and Hrovatin, 2012);
- dichotomous choice format (a respondent receives a randomly assigned bid (or bids) and is invited to accept or reject it, as in Yoo and Kwak (2009).

The format of the question may have an influence on the results obtained (Oerlemans et al., 2016). In the case of green electricity, WTP is usually expressed in relative or absolute terms, as either an increase in the amount of an electricity bill or an increase in the price per kWh of electricity supplied (Kowalska-Pyzalska and Byrka, 2019).

The objects for WTP evaluation

Most of the research regarding WTP focuses on green electricity understood as a willingness to contribute (by paying more for green electricity, by becoming a prosumer, by switching to green electricity tariffs or programs), and has been performed for consumers from a given country. See, for example, the following studies investigated WTP among consumers in a particular country:

- Germany by Gerpott and Mahmudova (2010); Wuestenhagen and Bilharz (2006); Tabi et al. (2014);
- Poland by Kowalska-Pyzalska (2019); Ropuszyńska-Surma and Weglarz (2016); Bartczak et al. (2017);
- Lithuania by Su et al. (2018);
- Sweden by Hansla et al. (2008);
- Slovenia by Zoric and Hrovatin (2012);
- Greece by Ntanos et al. (2018);
- China by Zhang and Wu (2012); Zhou et al. (2018); Xie and Zhao (2018);
- Japan by Murakami et al. (2015); Nomura and Akai (2004);
- South Korea by Yoo and Kwak (2009);
- The U.S. by Zarnikau (2003); Wiser (2007); and
- Australia by Hobman and Frederiks (2014).

Apart from the specific studies for a given country, including country-specific conditions, e.g., legislation, purchasing power of the citizens, and their preferences regarding RES, many studies have reviewed and compared findings from different parts of the world (Frank et al., 2015; Ma et al., 2015; Oerlemans et al., 2016; Sundt and Rehdanz, 2015; MacDonald and Eyre, 2018; Krishnamurthy and Kriström, 2014).

Among various studies, the authors often do not specify renewable energy source for the generation of green electricity; see, e.g., the study by Borchers et al. (2007). In such a case, respondents are asked to value generic green electricity. In other cases, electricity from wind or solar is explicitly mentioned (Oerlemans et al., 2016), mostly because consumers are familiar with these sources.

In the case of other IES, such as smart meters or dynamic electricity tariffs, most studies focus on willingness to accept (WTA) rather than classical WTP. For example, WTA was a focus of research by Chawla et al. (2019) in the case of smart metering rollout in Indonesia. Gosnell and McCoy (2021) measured households' willingness to accept compensation for smart meter installation in the UK following exposure to various treatments aimed at overcoming two relevant market failures: imperfect information and learning by using. They investigated whether the household adopts the smart meter without compensation, or with the subsidy (Gosnell and McCoy, 2021). WTA for time-of-use tariffs was investigated by Sundt et al. (2020). Classical WTP for smart meters was measured by Gerpott and Paukert (2013).

General findings of the WTP studies

Although these studies differ in terms of survey periods, countries, institutional contexts, survey typology, methods of elicitation, and the methodology and econometric techniques applied, they give some common results (Oerlemans et al., 2016; Sundt and Rehdanz, 2015; Stigka et al., 2014; Ma et al., 2015). Mainly, two sorts of variables are included in the WTP analysis, no matter which IES is taken into account. The large group of attributes represents demographics (i.e., income, financial expectations, savings orientation, or education). The second large group consists of attitudinal and psychological variables (e.g., environmental awareness, knowledge to capture the differences in perception of RES or social norms, uncertainty avoidance, importance of status symbols) (Su et al., 2018; Ozaki, 2011; Perlaviciute and Steg, 2014; Paravantis et al., 2018; Ek, 2005; Xie and Zhao, 2018).

Karakaya et al. (2014) emphasized that WTP, especially among early adopters, can also be affected by country and cultural context (population size, macroeconomic parameters, cultural values, e.g., individual vs. collective decision making). As a consequence, a consumer's final decision regarding an innovative product or service depends on his or her satisfaction, which is based on perceived quality, competitive advantages, values, initial quality expectations, public brand image, and social recognition (Karakaya et al., 2014; Kowalska-Pyzalska, 2018b). In many cases, the prices for new products and services are higher than for established ones, which is why high willingness to pay is a precondition for early adoption of innovations (Karakaya et al., 2014; Kowalska-Pyzalska, 2018b). Frank et al. (2015) additionally states that WTP around early adopters tends to be positively influenced by income (satisfaction), financial expectations, and importance of status symbols, and negatively influenced by female gender, savings orientation, and stress avoidance. Below we present the specific results of WTP for (1) green electricity tariffs and programs, and (2) smart meters and dynamic electricity tariffs.

Determinants for WTP for green electricity tariffs/programs

As Zoric and Hrovatin (2012) indicate, there are three main types of studies of WTP with reference to green electricity. The first group estimated percentage premiums or absolute amounts that households are willing to contribute for "generic" green electricity Zarnikau (2003); Kowalska-Pyzalska (2018b). The second utilized choice experiments to investigate the willingness to support different types of renewables (Buryk et al., 2015; Borchers et al., 2007). The third used a contingent valuation method in combination with choice experiments to evaluate the WTP (Roe et al., 2001). Some research looked into economic factors such as price premium, or the proportion and types of households ready to pay different premiums, as well as the nonlinear relationship between the amount of energy generated from renewable sources and the premium amount (Zarnikau, 2003; Roe et al., 2001; Hobman and Frederiks, 2014). Other studies examined psychological predictors of willingness and intention to purchase green electricity (Clark et al., 2003; Hansla et al., 2008).

Table 5.3 presents the antecedents of WTP for green electricity divided into those with effects that are positive, negative, or ambiguous.

In general, consumers' level of WTP is influenced by their familiarity and experience with RES (Borchers et al., 2007). Solar energy, for example, is chosen over general green and wind energy, although biomass and hydro power are the least preferred options (Borchers et al., 2007; Ma et al., 2015; Zoric and Hrovatin, 2012). It was established that WTP is increasing in the share of fossil fuels that is replaced by renewables, indexrenewable, where a 1 kWh increase in the use of renewables increases the WTP by 2 Euro cents on average (Zoric and Hrovatin, 2012). Finally, while researching the distinctions between mandatory and voluntary programs, it was discovered that the latter has a greater WTP (Borchers et al., 2007).

WTP estimates for green electricity

The WTP estimates range significantly between countries due to major variances in economic growth, environmental awareness, social norms, and cultural origins. The results also differ due to changes in sample sizes, time periods, techniques, and questionnaires utilized, see Oerlemans et al. (2016), Zoric and Hrovatin (2012), and Mengaki (2012)). The actual value of the WTP is frequently higher when customers are questioned about specific energy sources (e.g., wind generators or solar panels) or specific demand response tools or technologies (e.g., smart meters) rather than generic RES or generic DR instruments (Gerpott and Paukert, 2013; Borchers et al., 2007; Zoric and Hrovatin, 2012).

Finally, Sundt and Rehdanz (2015) reported that the mean WTP, found in various studies, was around USD 13.3 per household per month, and the median WTP was USD 11.67. In another meta-analysis, a summary WTP estimate on the level of USD 7.16 per month was obtained (Soon and Ahmad, 2015). The minimum and

Table 5.3 The comparison of antecedents of WTP for green electricity (Kowalska-Pyzalska, 2018b).

Effect on WTP	Antecedents	References
Positive	attitudes toward the environment and RES, social norms, higher household income, being a home owner, being risk seeking, higher level of education, knowledge of technical aspects of energy systems and knowledge about RES	Bartczak et al. (2017); Borchers et al. (2007); Claudy et al. (2010); Gerpott and Mahmudova (2010); Hansla et al. (2008); Mengaki (2012); Paravantis et al. (2018); Yoo and Kwak (2009); Zarnikau (2003); Zoric and Hrovatin (2012); Ek and Soederholm (2008); Clark et al. (2003); Xie and Zhao (2018); MacPherson and Lange (2013)
Negative	age (older people seem to have a lower WTP), values focused on one's own happiness and comfort, a perceived difficulty of switching an energy supplier, risk and loss aversion	Bartczak et al. (2017); Perlaviciute and Steg (2014); Zarnikau (2003); Zhang and Wu (2012); Zoric and Hrovatin (2012)
Ambiguous	prior experience with RES, household size (WTP tends to decrease with household size, but there are exceptions), gender (some studies report that WTP is lower for males than females), electricity prices and bills (sometimes, the higher the price, the lower the WTP), share or source of green electricity	Sundt and Rehdanz (2015); Yoo and Kwak (2009); Borchers et al. (2007)

the maximum WTP were equal to USD 1 and USD 43.01, respectively (see Sundt and Rehdanz, 2015). If WTP is expressed in kWh, then the mean WTP was 3.18 US-cents per kWh and the median WTP was 1.95 per kWh. The review by MacDonald and Eyre (2018) pointed out that some WTP results are specific for a given country. For example, it was found that in China, some consumers may be attracted to the idea of "premium" electricity and be willing to pay more (Ek, 2005; Krishnamurthy and Kriström, 2014). On the other hand, there is some evidence that consumers in some countries are skeptical of particular types of renewables and consequently express a lower willingness to pay (Zhang and Wu, 2012; Ma et al., 2015). This may be particularly true for countries with large amounts of hydroelectric power, where studies have found consumers to be less receptive to green electricity that is generated from hydro due to ecological concerns such as the impact on waterways (Larsen, 2013).

Kowalska-Pyzalska (2018a) and Kowalska-Pyzalska (2019) are examples of studies presenting an empirical survey designed and conducted on a representative sample of N=502 adult Poles. In Kowalska-Pyzalska (2018a), first the factors influencing the acceptance and adoption of innovative products related to RES among households were investigated. In Kowalska-Pyzalska (2019), attention was paid to the factors that affect willingness to pay for green electricity. This study also focused on answers to two additional questions: do Polish consumers want to support the development of renewable energy by accepting higher electricity bills (assuming that electricity is generated in RES) and what socio-economic and psychological factors affect consumers' willingness to pay?

While examining the acceptance of green electricity by consumers, it was assumed that consumers can contribute to the development of renewable energy sources in the following way: (a) deciding to pay more for electricity if its part or the whole comes from RES; (b) be ready to become a prosumer, i.e., to invest in a small installation based on RES, for example, photovoltaic panels or for switching energy suppliers, if it offers so-called green electric tariffs (this is the so-called willingness to accept); and (c) already being a prosumer—that is, generating electricity for one's own needs.

Based on the literature, it was proposed to verify four research hypotheses stating that consumers are willing to support the development of renewable energy (activities (a)–(c)) when: their income is high; they are well-educated and young; they are characterized by pro-ecological attitudes and behaviors; their friends and acquaintances support their decision to install renewable energy or to switch to green electricity tariffs; and they have knowledge of the energy market. Detailed results were presented by Kowalska-Pyzalska (2018a); however, it should be mentioned here that statistical analysis allowed all hypotheses to be confirmed, except for the positive impact of pro-ecological behavior on the willingness to support renewable energy.

The research also showed that for 56% of respondents, financial support (e.g., subsidies) and a quick return on investment (30%) are the most important stimuli that may lead individuals to invest in a home installation for the production of electricity. As many as 53% of respondents claimed that the lack of sufficient knowledge about the possibilities of supporting renewable energy was the biggest barrier to supporting RES.

In turn, in research by Kowalska-Pyzalska (2019), the focus was on an in-depth study of factors affecting willingness to pay (WTP) for green electricity. To investigate WTP, the study used the contingent valuation method (CVM), which consisted of two questions: (1) If part or all of the electricity supplied would come from RES, would you be willing to change the energy supplier? (possible answers: yes, no, I do not know); and (2) How much would you be willing to pay extra for electricity, knowing that part or all of it is generated in RES?

The analysis of the answers obtained allowed the authors to estimate the average consumer's willingness to pay for green electricity (about PLN 13 per month that is c.a. 3 euro) and to indicate the basic economic and social factors responsible for both the acceptance of RES and the willingness to pay for it. Using the tools of statistical analysis, including regression models (logit, ordered logit, and tobit), it was shown that consumers' interest in supporting green energy is affected by: their level of income, knowledge and information about green electricity tariffs, peer support, pro-ecological attitudes, and age (support decreases with age) (see Kowalska-Pyzalska, 2019).

In turn, the level of willingness to pay increases along with pro-ecological attitudes and income level, but also along with knowledge of the energy market and green tariffs, social support, level of education, and type of place of residence (those who live in houses support more renewable energy), and decreases with age (Kowalska-Pyzalska, 2019).

From the point of view of enterprises, the results obtained clearly indicate which segments of consumers may be primarily interested in RES (for both the installation of small household energy sources and green electric tariffs). These are young, pro-ecological consumers, who perceive their current financial situation well, have an orientation on the energy market, are generally well-educated, and for whom peer support for their activities on the RES market is important. These observations can be particularly helpful for companies supplying electricity and for RES-based technology providers, for example, when constructing green electricity tariffs or other product and marketing innovations based on green energy.

In order to overcome the barriers to innovation acceptance and diffusion, educational and social campaigns should certainly be developed, aimed at increasing levels of awareness and knowledge, the lack of which is currently an acute problem. Suppliers and sellers of electricity could offer trial contracts and participation in pilot programs, which in other countries have effectively raised the level of knowledge and reduced concerns related to unknown products and services. Subsequently, as the social impact has been shown to be an important factor in the implementation of RES-related innovations, companies may consider introducing elements of competition between consumers in the same segment (as has already been successfully implemented for actions to increase energy efficiency) or in a given tariff group.

Willingness to pay for SM and dynamic electricity tariffs

In the case of SM and DSM/DR tools, especially dynamic electricity tariffs, the majority of studies focus on evaluation of willingness to accept (WTA) (see, for example, Chawla et al., 2019, Gosnell and McCoy, 2021, or Sundt et al., 2020) rather than measuring explicitly consumers' willingness to pay, such as in the work by Gerpott and Paukert (2013). This is caused by the fact that in most countries, consumers do not have to permit or pay for the installation of the smart meter. The roll-out of smart meters is being regulated by national law and international directives. This is why researchers focus instead on evaluation of consumers' willingness to accept SM, meaning a decision to use it for controlling and monitoring of energy consumption.

In the study by Chawla et al. (2019), the authors showed that financial savings can be achieved due to the exchange of the meter from the analog to the smart one, addressing data privacy concerns, and positive social influence enhances the acceptance level of SM. Moreover, attitudes of consumers toward energy-efficient purchases or willingness to pay more for energy-saving appliances had a major direct effect on a consumer's acceptance of SM. In the work of Sundt et al. (2020), the authors additionally showed that WTA of private consumers toward time-of-use tariffs varied dependent on the time of peak tariff. A high level of heterogeneity of preferences toward the time of the peak tariff was stated (i.e., a significant share of respondents always neglected inconveniences of peak time pricing; a smaller share reacted only to discounts). In particular, the authors confirmed that consumers with low energy literacy acted with bounded rationality when making decisions about SM acceptance (Sundt et al., 2020). Gosnell and McCoy (2021) developed an incentive-compatible online experiment to elicit a large and representative panel of UK households' willingness to accept compensation for SM installation following exposure to various treatments such as: (a) whether the household is willing to adopt SM without compensation; and (b) if and what subsidy level is necessary for nonadopting households to become willing to adopt. The results suggested that £10, £50, and £75 subsidies would induce additional adoption of 4, 24, and 34 percentage points, respectively, from a baseline of 22% adoption without a subsidy. Pairing these subsidies with a social benefits information campaign enhances these effects by 4.2, 4.9, and 6.6 percentage points, respectively, effectively doubling the impact of the £10 incentive and contributing an additional 20% of the impact of the £50 and £75 incentives. Our evidence suggests that neither a private benefits campaign (mirroring the policy approach to date) nor a campaign focused on societal learning and resultant technological improvements influences adoption rates.

A more accurate study of WTP for SM was conducted by Gerpott and Paukert (2013). The authors measured WTP by asking participants to indicate their WTP in euro interval for: (1) a one-time SM provision fee; (2) a monthly recurring SM use charge; and (3) the purchase of a software, which makes it possible to analyze personal Sm data on a computer. The received results confirmed relatively low WTP toward SM. An additional empirical survey measured the impact of five determinants on consumers' appraisal of SM including: (1) expecting savings; (2) a personal intention to change usage behavior; (3) usefulness of consumption feedback; (4) trust in data protection; and (5) environmental awareness. The authors identified that financial savings were not the strongest determinant of WTP for SM. Consumers do not perceive SM as a potential investment leading to some direct cost reductions. At the same time, consumers believe that an SM allows energy utilities to better control the effectiveness of energy supply and consumption by keeping the privacy of the data safe. Finally, the study showed that personal value perception of an SM and hence consumer's WTP for such a device is affected by the extent to which an electricity consumer perceives the opportunity obtained through SM installation for a mechanism for self-controlled actions to reduce electricity consumption and costs in one's household. In that sense, SM can be shown to the public as an instrument allowing better control over one's costs and a guide for a behavioral change, for example, using more energy-efficient appliances (Gerpott and Paukert, 2013).

A recent study in Finland has shown that although about half of the respondents were willing to allow third-party device control, several fears and obstacles were identified in the survey that have a negative impact on the respondents' willingness to enable third-party control or to invest in energy-saving, and potentially also energy-producing, units (Immonen et al., 2020). The results of this research show that Finnish consumers are currently not familiar with the concept of "demand flexibility" or do not understand why or how they could become active market players themselves. On the other hand, consumers seemed to be very interested in developments in the energy market and were aware of how their own behavior can affect their energy consumption. Studies indicate that there is limited awareness, knowledge, and interest regarding SM among consumers, and customers have shown concerns regarding the acceptance of the same (Buchanan et al., 2016; Kahma and Matschoss, 2017; Krishnamutri et al., 2012). Customer concerns regarding SM include privacy and security of data, network connections in remote areas with lower or no mobile coverage, installation visits and doorstep selling, effects on health, disconnection of meters on a prepayment basis, and the option to switch between suppliers and keep "smart functionality" (Good et al., 2017; Hinson et al., 2019; Nachreiner et al., 2015).

Even though SM could be seen as a step toward consumers gaining more access and control over their energy consumption (Kowalska-Pyzalska and Byrka, 2019; Weron et al., 2018), many studies indicate a low level of knowledge, awareness, and engagement toward new solutions available in the energy markets (Ellabban and Abu-Rub, 2016; Claudy et al., 2010; Verbong et al., 2013; van der Werff and Steg, 2016). In particular, many studies have shown a relatively low level of consumers' knowledge and interest about smart metering (Buchanan et al., 2016). Most consumers are not even familiar with the terms "smart grid" and "smart metering." However, at the same time, they declare a willingness to save energy while being informed about electricity prices and ways of consumption reduction (Ellabban and Abu-Rub, 2016; Paetz et al., 2012). It was also found that only those consumers who were already interested or involved in energy savings were willing to use SM combined with some feedback devices, such as SMP, and learn from them (Wallenborn et al., 2011). Even if consumers have an initial interest in SMP, it is uncertain whether such engagement will persist over a longer period of time (Kowalska-Pyzalska and Byrka, 2019; Ma et al., 2018; Hargreeaves et al., 2013).

Currently, one of the main reasons for the slow SM diffusion is consumers' reluctance and lack of engagement, but another is the lack of legal regulations and arrangements provided by the national authorities Chawla et al. (2020b). Hence, to enhance the SM deployment, some regulatory support is needed. However, this is not enough. Society will benefit from this enrollment only if consumers learn how to use the information provided by SM—in particular, how to monitor energy consumption based on the information provided by the enabling technology, such as smart metering information systems (platforms) or in-home displays

(Kowalska-Pyzalska and Byrka, 2019; Foulds et al., 2017; Ma et al., 2018; Schleich et al., 2017). The first step in this process is connected with the increase of consumers' awareness and engagement regarding energy-efficiency issues (Verbong et al., 2013; Ellabban and Abu-Rub, 2016; Burchell et al., 2016; Gans et al., 2013).

5.3.3 Energy efficiency among residential consumers

Some studies have investigated the determinants of acceptance and adopting energy-efficient behavior such as energy saving, or monitoring of energy consumption. Usually this type of research focuses on one type of IES, such as smart meters or DSM/DR tools. For example, it has been shown that rising knowledge about the benefits and options given by SM and SMP may lead to positive behavioral changes (i.e., lower energy consumption or shifting the consumption from peak to off-peak hours). The potential of SM is especially emphasized if energy companies provide additional DSM/DR tools such as dynamic electricity tariffs. In that case, feedback received by means of SM and SMP, regarding one's electricity consumption and the current electricity prices, may have a significant impact on the increase of energy efficiency (Foulds et al., 2017; Schleich et al., 2017). On the other hand, it is not certain whether consumers' engagement will persist over a longer period of time or not (Chawla and Kowalska-Pyzalska, 2019; Ma et al., 2018; Kowalska-Pyzalska and Byrka, 2019).

The main conclusion from the literature is that consumers' environmental behavior is influenced by motivational, contextual, and habitual factors. Environmental behavior is strongly connected not only with consumers' general environmental beliefs and attitudes, but also with environmental norms, drivers, and barriers, perceived financial and nonfinancial costs and benefits, individual and collective values, social and community influence (moral and normative concerns), government policy, and affection (Lopes et al., 2012; Gangale et al., 2013; Kowalska-Pyzalska, 2015; Masini and Menichetti, 2012; Pongiglione, 2011; Gadenne et al., 2011; Frederiks et al., 2014; Chen et al., 2014; Rodriques-Barreiro et al., 2013). The authors indicate that these different perspectives are not mutually exclusive and all of them should be taken into account when predicting environmental behaviors.

The literature provides a number of findings from the recent studies in which either:

- willingness to monitor energy and responsiveness to the energy feedback is investigated (Kowalska-Pyzalska and Byrka, 2019; Buchanan et al., 2014; Foulds et al., 2017; Hargreaves et al., 2010; Gangale et al., 2013; Ma et al., 2018; Bertoldo et al., 2015; Gölz and Hahnel, 2016; Lee et al., 2020); or
- willingness to reduce energy consumption with help of some enabling technologies is studied (Chen, 2016; Gao et al., 2017; Gadenne et al., 2011; Ohnmacht et al., 2017; Liu et al., 2021; Bator et al., 2019; Sheau-Ting et al., 2013; Allcott, 2011; Tiefenbeck et al., 2013; Batalla-Bejerano et al., 2020).

Energy monitoring as one of the energy-efficient behaviors involving usage of a smart metering platform (SMP) has been investigated in the work by Kowalska-Pyzalska and Byrka (2019). The survey was conducted using the computer-assisted telephonic interview (CATI) method on a sample of N=500 adult residents of one of Poland's biggest cities. In recent years, the DSO company operating in this region of the country has carried out a comprehensive exchange of energy meters among households, from analog to smart ones, thus allowing them access to data on energy consumption through a free web-page and mobile phone application, called e-licznik.

In order to examine the level of knowledge and interest of consumers toward this application, hereinafter referred to as SMP, the authors analyzed: demographic data, pro-ecological commitment, knowledge of the energy market, previous experience and behaviors aimed at monitoring energy consumption, stages of readiness for SMP use (according to the SSCB model), and attitudes and behavior toward monitoring energy consumption. The following four behavioral stages based on the stage model of behavioral change (SSCB) were identified: predecisional or F1 ("I am not interested whether I have a smart meter installed and I never use a SMP. I do not intend to change my behavior"); preactional or F2 ("I would like to monitor energy consumption more often, but I am not sure how to achieve this goal"); actional or F3 ("My goal is to organize my time to monitor energy consumption, e.g., through SMP. I am going to check if I have a smart meter installed and access to SMP"); and postactional or F4 ("I often monitor the energy consumption in my household through SMP. I intend to continue this action in the coming months and even intensify it"). A five-point Likert scale was used for each phase to determine the extent to which the respondent agreed with the statement (Kowalska-Pyzalska and Byrka, 2019).

It was found that as many as 25% of respondents do not monitor energy consumption at all, and more than 40% use traditional methods based on tracking electricity bills. Only 4% of respondents use innovative solutions. The initial correlation analysis as well as the estimation of factors affecting the individual four stages of readiness for accepting SMP using the logit model showed that the predecisional F1 stage is negatively related to pro-ecological attitudes and perceived ease of monitoring implementation (perceived behavioral control). This means that the more pro-ecological a person is, the less they see any difficulty in implementing regular energy consumption monitoring, and the less it will be positively related to the F1 stage. A positive relation between a respondent's perceived ability to monitor energy consumption with stages F2–F4 was revealed. Knowledge of the energy market has proved to be important only in the case of stage F3, in which the consumer expresses the will to obtain additional information allowing him or her to improve the process of monitoring energy consumption.

In all phases, it was shown that the perceived possibility of monitoring energy consumption (both in the traditional way and with the help of SMP) is crucial when consumers engage in this type of behavior. This means that for the suppliers of SMP and other intelligent solutions on the energy market (e.g., smart plugs), it is necessary to show consumers the simplicity and advantages of those products when monitoring energy consumption.

The results obtained show that in order to introduce SMP to the market successfully, companies should first of all ensure the level of consumer awareness about the product itself and the benefits of its use (marketing innovation). The willingness to monitor energy consumption is also correlated with pro-ecological attitudes, knowledge of the energy market, and a sense of control, which should be used by enterprises in the design of the innovations themselves as well as marketing strategies accompanying their implementation (Kowalska-Pyzalska and Byrka, 2019).

Additionally, in the case of energy monitoring, Buchanan et al. (2014) revealed that the effect of feedback differs dependent on the segment of consumers. Those with an increased sense of personal control were less empowered, as were those confronted with an environmental problem. Those who had already encountered various problems (e.g., "horrendous bills") were more empowered, along with those who had already activated certain motives such as a desire to save money (Buchanan et al., 2014). Consumers must put some time and effort into familiarizing themselves with the energy consumption pattern and notice that this is an area for improvement.

Achieving energy efficiency goals at the energy consumption level requires the behavioral response of consumers to the feedback they receive. Providing information on people's consumption, smart meters can change deep-seated habits and implicit consumption beliefs (Bertoldo et al., 2015). Kowalska-Pyzalska and Byrka (2019) pointed out that perceived possibilities to monitor energy consumption on a regular basis was found to be the predictor of adoption of SMP. Many of the empirical studies have shown how personalized nudges increase the effectiveness of feedback from the energy monitors that consumers receive (Leygue et al., 2014; Flambard et al., 2021; Wood et al., 2019; Herrmann et al., 2021).

Finally, the literature shows that consumers' ecological and/or energy-efficient behavior is strongly associated not only with professed values and opinions, but also with objective and subjective barriers and difficulties with accepting new behaviors, and legal regulations and support systems (Allcott, 2011; Byrka et al., 2016; Gadenne et al., 2011; Nolan et al., 2008; Avancini et al., 2019). Moreover, consumer engagement in energy conservation is influenced by social and personal norms (Allcott, 2011; Ayers et al., 2013; Schultz et al., 2007; Byrka et al., 2016). To achieve the best results in behavioral change in terms of energy monitoring and conservation, both normative and descriptive norms should be combined (Allcott, 2011; Ayers et al., 2013; Nolan et al., 2008). That is why the social pressure cannot be neglected in diffusion of green energy and dynamic tariffs. Seeking information from personal contacts, referred to as the mobilization of social capital, could potentially promote the diffusion of energy-reducing innovations.

5.4 Diffusion of IES in simulating and modeling

5.4.1 Consumers' adoption rates

Actual adoption rates that describe what part of the population has actually adopted a specific innovation differ dependent on the given IES. The highest adoption rates are observed in cases of small-scale renewable energy sources, such as solar PV. More and more people, especially in Europe, are deciding to install solar PV on their roofs and hence not only decrease their electricity bills but also become more independent from the power system (Wicki et al., 2022). Annual increases in installed photovoltaic capacity are impressive. For example, worldwide, in 2020, around 139 GW of solar PV capacity was added, constituting as much as 58% of new RES power capacity. At the begining of 2023, the total capacity of PV installations has already reached 1,185 GW (Wicki et al., 2022; REN21, 2021). For example, in Germany, by the end of

2022, the total installed solar PV capacity was equal to 66.5 GW, distributed over 2.65 million individual installations, including households, industrial sites, and commercial installations.[1]

Next, according to market data, the actual take-up of green electricity tariffs is quite low, even in countries where consumers claim to be pro-environmental and eager to support the development of RES. For example, in Australia in 2014, only 7% of the population had signed up to a green electricity program, although people claimed to be in favor of RES. Among the reasons mentioned by nonparticipants were financial cost, negative perceptions, limited knowledge and awareness, limited accessibility or other external constraints, indifference and resistance to change, disbelief in climate change, no perceived personal responsibility, etc. (Hobman and Frederiks, 2014). The data from Europe and the US are even worse. In the US, average rates are estimated to be at or below 2%, though some of the best-performing regional programs have achieved penetration rates between 5% and 17% (Diaz-Rainey and Tzavara, 2015). In Europe, only modest levels of green electricity tariff adoption by consumers have been observed, with the Netherlands providing a notable exception.

Adoption rates for dynamic electricity tariffs are even worse. Pilot programs indicate that dynamic pricing may succeed in reducing peak demand (even to 44%, if enabling technologies are installed (Kowalska-Pyzalska, 2018b)), but only if a certain percentage of the population get engaged. Currently the adoption rates are rather low, which makes demand response among consumers insignificant in terms of power system operation (Siano, 2014; Hobman and Frederiks, 2014; Faruqui and Sergici, 2010; O'Connell et al., 2014). An example for Illinois, in the US, in the AIU Power Smart Pricing Program shows the significance of the enrollment problem. Namely, only 18% of customers, where the pilot program was run, were aware of it. Then, only 10% of them understood the program and only 5% were interested in it. In the end, less than 1% of customers decided to enroll in the program (Star et al., 2010). Similar results were obtained in other pilot programs in the US or in Western Europe, in countries where people are relatively aware of and sensitive to environmental issues (Gerpott and Paukert, 2013). Pongiglione (2011) mentioned the results of a survey in Italy where 70% of respondents declared a willingness to increase energy saving, but only 2% were currently reducing their use (Pongiglione, 2011). In Central Europe, as the report of ATKearney revealed (ATKearney, 2012), 60–75% of consumers

[1]https://metsolar.eu/blog/renewable-energy-trends-prosumers-expansion-europe-scenario/ (accessed December 7, 2022) (REN21, 2021).

were not aware of the existence of smart grids and were not willing to shift their consumption to off-peak hours.

On the other hand, the official data regarding smart metering roll-out, at least in some European countries, look optimistic, as some EU countries have either completed or achieved at least 80% of SM deployment (Mengolini et al., 2017; Vitiello et al., 2022). Regulatory decisions regarding SM implementation are made on a national level based on the assessment of long-term costs and benefits. If the assessment is positive, then at least 80% of households should be equipped with smart metering systems by 2020 (Crispim et al., 2014). Although an SM roll-out has indisputable advantages, its implementation is in different stages, depending on the location (Zhou and Brown, 2017; Avancini et al., 2019). Whereas in many European countries, such as Denmark, Sweden, Finland, France, Italy, and Estonia, the SM roll-out is already finalized, and in countries such as Norway, Italy, Slovenia, and France, it is at an advanced stage (Sovacool et al., 2017; Zhou and Brown, 2017; Vitiello et al., 2022), other countries, such as Germany, the Czech Republic, Greece, and Ireland, show a lower commitment level toward SM deployment (European Commission, 2018). In those countries, the governments have usually not formally decided to have a national SM roll-out, mainly because of negative or inconclusive results of cost-benefit analysis (CBA) (Chawla et al., 2020b; Vitiello et al., 2022). According to the Agency for the Co-operation of Energy Regulators (ACER), in late 2018, only 37% of EU consumers were equipped with SM, but in 2020, this number reached around 50%, and at the end of 2022 56%; this is however still not enough, according to a benchmark of at least 80% in 2020.[2]

5.4.2 Intention-behavior gap

One of the reasons for relatively low engagement of consumers is the phenomenon of the **intention-behavior gap** (IBG), also known as the **value-action gap**, which shows the discrepancy between people's attitudes or beliefs and consumers' willingness to pay for certain products and their actual behaviors. The basic observation of psychology is that people's attitudes toward some ideas or products do not have to be confirmed by actual decisions and behaviors. This creates a discrepancy between intention adoption and actual behavior adoption.

This social phenomenon has been empirically documented also in cases of smart energy systems and services (Star et al.,

[2]https://ses.jrc.ec.europa.eu/smart-metering-deployment-european-union (accessed December 7, 2022).

2010; Gadenne et al., 2011; Pongiglione, 2011; Zhang and Nuttall, 2011; Kowalska-Pyzalska et al., 2014; MacPherson and Lange, 2013; Diaz-Rainey and Tzavara, 2012). For example, there is a gap between stated willingness to accept (SWA) and actual adoption. Generally, high WTP between 40–60% and SWA between 30–60% for green energy in Europe and in the US does not transform into high numbers of consumers switching to green tariffs (the average adoption rate in US is below 2% and in Europe this figure is even lower). For example, a survey carried out in Italy showed that while 70% of respondents were willing to increase energy savings, only 2% were currently reducing their use (Pongiglione, 2011). In the US, 78% of Americans opposed gasoline tax and 60% opposed business energy taxes. At the same time, 52% of Americans claimed to support the Kyoto Protocol, which was an international agreement that aimed to lower greenhouse gas (GHG) and carbon dioxide (CO_2) emissions from human activity. However, if they had to pay an extra 50 dollars per month, then they would oppose it (Pongiglione, 2011). Thus, people are in favor of an idea as long as it has no consequences for themselves. In another study, 74% of American respondents expressed WTP at least 1.63–1.72 dollar per month, whereas only 9,5% of them made such a payment. In Switzerland, as many as 73% of respondents claimed to have positive attitudes toward green energy, while only 10% had actually switched to green electricity. In Finland, 30% of households claimed to be interested in green energy, while only 0.2% demonstrated purchasing behaviors relating to this (Zhang and Wu, 2012). Finally, in Australia, 80% of respondents claimed to support RES, but only 7% subscribed to green electricity (Hobman and Frederiks, 2014).

The same problem has been noticed in the case of dynamic tariffs; for example, in the UK, only about 5% of consumers opt for a simple dynamic time-of-use (TOU) tariff with peak and off-peak prices (Buryk et al., 2015). In the US, higher recruitment rates were for default offer (78–87%) in contrast to opt-in offers (5–28%). Consumers, generally, do not want to shift consumption (Ofgem, 2011).

Koirala et al. (2018) investigated the role of citizens in community energy systems. The authors found that 80% of participants were aware of local energy projects and 53% were willing to participate, but only 8% were willing to steer different activities within the community. It may be concluded from this that only every second consumer was actually willing to get actively involved.

There are several reasons for the presence of IBG. As Diaz-Rainey and Tzavara (2012) and Ozaki (2011) have argued, among factors that may cause stated preferences to diverge from the actual behavior, the following can be mentioned:

- unstable consumers' opinions;
- lack of knowledge of the green power availability;
- confusion generated by the complexity of tariffs;
- lack of guidelines and advice;
- lack of sufficient supply;
- a hesitancy to switch from one electricity supplier to another;
- distrust of energy product suppliers and cost concerns;
- search cost involved in switching; and
- a free rider problem, meaning a kind of a market failure that ccurs when those who benefit from common or public resources, do not pay for them or under-pay.

The problem of IBG has been illustrated in work by Kowalska-Pyzalska et al. (2014), which aimed to show how consumers' personal characteristics (especially the level of their conformism or indifference to social impact), as well as the level of advertising and financial incentives, encourage consumers to form positive opinions about dynamic electricity tariffs (innovative products and an important element of innovative energy management systems), and finally also to make decisions about switching to these tariffs (from, e.g., traditional tariffs characterized by a fixed amount of electricity fee). In the developed simulation model, two blocks were distinguished: a block of opinions and a block of decisions. It was assumed that the condition for making a decision is to have a stable opinion on a given product (in this case, a dynamic electricity tariff) for a certain period of time.

Similarly to the work of Przybyła et al. (2014), based on the decision rules regulating agents' (i.e., households or firms) behavior in the system introduced in the model, by averaging the Monte Carlo simulation (MCS) results, the following outcomes were obtained. Firstly, it was shown that with the currently high level of consumer indifference regarding dynamic electric tariffs (parameter p in the agent-based model), it is very difficult to achieve a satisfactory level of innovation diffusion.

As Fig. 5.2 (bottom panel) shows, the level of advertising (parameter h in the model) has a slight influence on the degree of product spread on the market. The top panel in Fig. 5.2 shows the difference between the level of opinions and decisions depending on the level of consumer indifference. It is easy to see that at $p > 0.4$, positive opinions outweigh positive decisions. In other words, there is a gap between opinions and decisions (known as the intention-behavior gap), when positive opinions do not translate into decisions about undertaking a given action. With a high level of indifference, it is difficult to maintain the stability of a pos-

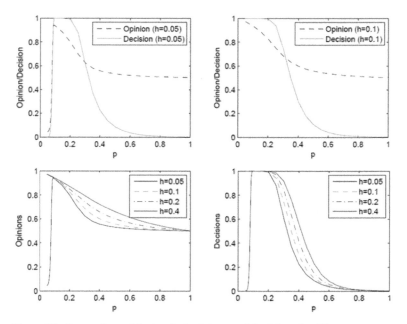

Figure 5.2. Comparison of the level of opinions and decisions for different parameters' sizes: p and h, where p is the probability of the agent's indifference, and h is the probability of the impact of advertising (Kowalska-Pyzalska et al., 2014).

itive opinion on innovation, which in the model is a condition for making the decision to switch to dynamic electricity tariffs. In turn, in the case of a low level of indifference in society, opinions and decisions are convergent (the gap disappears).

On the basis of the conducted analysis, it is recommended for companies implementing dynamic electricity tariffs to undertake activities aimed at reducing the gap between opinions and decisions regarding innovative products and services on the energy market. It should be emphasized that currently the level of indifference among consumers is high. Therefore, to increase the level of engagement and interest of consumers one should: (a) provide consumers with clear and complete information on the products offered, their advantages and possible barriers to use (e.g., the need to adapt activity to the changing price of electricity in order to reduce electricity bills), what should reduce uncertainty and lack of consumer confidence, and what should increase public awareness about the existence of a given innovation; and (b) reduce the time needed to make a decision (e.g., by facilitating the change of energy supplier or offering trial contracts for a specified period of time) (Kowalska-Pyzalska et al., 2014).

Kowalska-Pyzalska et al. (2014) studied the IBG between consumers attitudes and behaviors toward dynamic electricity tariffs using an agent-based model (ABM) of opinion and decision formation. It has been noted that three main parameters—agent's conformity or indifference (lack of interest and engagement), social influence, and product's features—impact the opinion dynamics of consumers. The main conclusion is that the gap is generally caused by the instability of consumers' opinions (one day a consumer may be in favor of the dynamic pricing and a few days later he or she may be against it). Secondly, the higher the level of consumers' indifference and disengagement toward IES is, the larger the gap is: even positive opinions about the tariffs do not make consumers switch from a traditional flat tariff to the dynamic one (Kowalska-Pyzalska et al., 2014).

5.4.3 Impact of social influence

Recent studies have shown that **normative social influence** is one of the most significant types of influence, having a positive effect on the intention to engage in environmental behaviors and purchasing decisions (Ozaki, 2011; Nolan et al., 2008; Allcott, 2011; Ayers et al., 2013; McMichael and Shipworth, 2013; Moglia et al., 2017). It has been found that strong social norms encourage the adoption of various pro-environmental behaviors and goods, e.g., acceptance of green energy or energy conservation behavior; see Ozaki (2011). The literature suggests that consumers are favorably influenced by the opinions and actions of their peers (Kowalska-Pyzalska et al., 2014; Jager, 2006; Sidiras and Koukios, 2004; Gangale et al., 2013; Ayers et al., 2013; Przybyła et al., 2014; Sznajd-Weron et al., 2014a). Therefore, the social dimension of consumer behavior and engagement needs to be taken into account carefully in the context of innovation diffusion (Allcott, 2011).

Secondly, as Ozaki (2011) noted, **social and personal identity and values** can be represented by a person's level of consumption or adoption of green electricity. In the work of Bollinger and Gillingham (2012), social interaction through so-called peer effects was recognized as a potentially important factor in the diffusion of new products. In that study, the impact of peer effects on household decisions about the installation of solar photovoltaic (PV) panels has been shown. The more PV were installed on average in a certain area, the higher the probability was of the adoption and further increase of new installations (Bollinger and Gillingham, 2012).

Thirdly, Nolan et al. (2008) have argued that a **social norm has a greater impact that other nonnormative motivations** such as protection of the environment, benefiting society, or even saving money. Moreover, in that study, the inconsistency between stated motivation and actual behavior was revealed. Because "others are doing it" was judged to be the least important reason at the self-reported motivation stage. The highest correlation with actual conservation behavior was a person's belief about whether or not their neighbors were doing it.

The impact of neighbors' behavior has also been revealed in the studies of Allcott (2011) and Ayers et al. (2013). Both studies reported on a large-scale program, run by the company OPOWER, which sent Home Energy Report letters to residential utility customers comparing their electricity use to that of their neighbors. By the means of this action, energy consumption has been reduced by 2%. It was shown that combining the descriptive and injunctive messages (in this case, emoticons: happy or sad faces) lowered energy consumption and reduced the undesirable boomerang effect (that those who happened to use less energy in comparison with the neighbors started to increase their consumption); see Allcott (2011). According to Ayers et al. (2013), learning that neighbors consume less (or more) energy could increase (or decrease) feelings of guilt about contributing to social problems and thereby impact private preferences and motivations to conserve. Alternatively, learning the behavior of neighbors might provide information about the possibility of alternative consumption choices and the relative benefits of those choices.

The impact of social influence has also been shown in the work by Kowalska-Pyzalska (2016) in the context of smart metering platforms. The results from an agent-based model showed that social influence can either increase or decrease adoption and the market share of SMP, dependent on the market price of the good (in relation to other substitutes available in the energy market). If the market prices are high, people are more likely to share negative information about the SM platform, so word of mouth (WOM) will strengthen the negative impact of the perceived difficulty of adoption and weaken the positive effect of the advertisement. If the market prices are low, WOM strengthens the positive effect of advertisement and reduces the negative impact of difficulty of adoption. This knowledge could be used by energy suppliers when designing IES. Conditional on a targeted market penetration level and a market price of the good, they should aim at strengthening or weakening the WOM effect, in particular by encouraging the individualistic (to minimize the impact of WOM) or collective (to maximize the social influence) decision-making and market behavior of consumers (Kowalska-Pyzalska, 2016; Kowalska-Pyzalska et al., 2016; Kowalska-Pyzalska, 2018b).

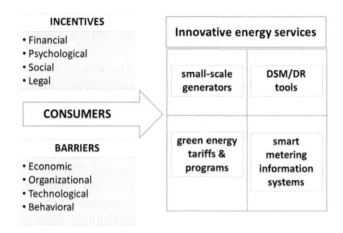

Figure 5.3. Incentives and barriers to IES adoption (Kowalska-Pyzalska, 2018b).

5.5 Summary: incentives and barriers of consumers' engagement, acceptance, and willingness to adopt in the energy market

Incentives and barriers to IES adoption can be divided into various categories, as shown in Fig. 5.3. The final decision of the consumer about whether to adopt or not depends on the consumer's preferences and perception regarding the set of IES attributes (contextual factors) and the interactions between social, economic, technological, and psychological parameters.

5.5.1 Incentives for IES acceptance and adoption

The challenge to increase adoption rates of IES is high, because most consumers are not motivated enough to get interested in these products. People do not talk about them, and do not exchange experiences. These goods are also not commonly advertised in the mass media. However there are some incentives that may motivate consumers to use energy services. As research surveys have shown, consumers increase their engagement firstly because of economic reasons (they find a certain investment in renewables, energy-efficient technologies to be costly effective, promising savings on electricity bills, high return on investment, or extra incomes from selling domestically produced energy to the energy retailer), and secondly because of social pressure from their peers and neighbors who have already adopted a certain product, service, or behavior (Stern, 2014; Kowalska-Pyzalska et al., 2014; Zheng et al., 2014; Palmer et al., 2015; Guenther et al., 2011).

Environmental motivations are found to be helpful in convincing people to adopt, but they do not seem to play a major role in diffusion of IES (Ajzen and Fishbein, 2005; Palmer et al., 2015). Finally, many authors mention that psychological factors, to which individual and collective values belong, affect evaluations of the IES alternatives, e.g., among renewable technologies (Nachreiner et al., 2015; Pongiglione, 2011; Duetschke and Paetz, 2013; Frederiks et al., 2014). As Kowalska-Pyzalska (2018b) emphasized, the strength of the effects of values and the processes through which they influence evaluations and acceptability might differ depending on the unique characteristics of each IES (which in turn is likely to depend on the contextual factors, e.g., price, availability, service).

To encourage consumers to adopt, governmental support (e.g., legislation, subsidies, educational programs) may be needed. As Negro et al. (2012) reported, differences in policy needs are determined by the phase in which the innovation service is. Dependent on the type and maturity of the IES, there are other specific problems related to the technology, such as acquisition of financial resources, distance to market, and strength of the networks or international playing field (Negro et al., 2012). Even though IES differ from one to another, we argue that when designing strategies and legislation, policy makers should keep in mind the whole portfolio of IES and try to propose such solutions that may bring a synergy effect by implementing a package of these services. Financial incentives, grants, discounts, subsidies, and other intrinsic and extrinsic rewards can be helpful in changing consumer behavior, but as the literature suggests, they are not enough (Masini and Menichetti, 2012; Gadenne et al., 2011; Diaz-Rainey and Tzavara, 2015; Frederiks et al., 2014). They should be combined with some of the other factors, such as pro-environmental attitudes, social influence, and lack of environmental barriers (Stern, 2000).

The main incentives of adoption toward IES include:

- financial savings, e.g., lower electricity bills (Gerpott and Paukert, 2013);
- "being like others", adopting social norms and peers' behavior (Khachatryan et al., 2013; Perlaviciute and Steg, 2014; Ayers et al., 2013);
- satisfaction from being pro-environmental (Gangale et al., 2013; Ozaki, 2011; Hansla et al., 2008);

- personal values, beliefs, and attitudes toward environmental protection issues (Gangale et al., 2013; Ozaki, 2011; Gadenne et al., 2011; Perlaviciute and Steg, 2014); and
- government subsidies and other financial support (Ozaki, 2011; Gadenne et al., 2011; Negro et al., 2012).

In addition to the issues mentioned above, adoption is highly influenced by factors on the demand side, such as consumer attitudes toward environmental protection issues, perceived difficulty of switching one's electricity supplier, customers' expectations that their behaviors are ethically proper, perceived differences between offerings, and access to reliable data about substitutes (e.g., comparison of pros and cons of various tariffs); see Hu et al. (2015), Nolan et al. (2008), Ellabban and Abu-Rub (2016), and Nachreiner et al. (2015). On the supply side, among factors influencing diffusion, typical aspects of marketing mix can be defined, such as price level, distribution channels, service, and promotion of new offers (Jager, 2006).

5.5.2 Barriers to IES acceptance and adoption

Even if future energy systems, from the perspective of the deployment of IES, look promising, the questions are whether consumers are aware of all these new opportunities and whether they are ready and willing to contribute to the efficiency and sustainability of the energy system. Moreover, it is not clear **how to convince consumers to change their energy behaviors and adopt IES in their daily routines.** Finally, how can consumers be persuaded to pay more for green electricity or to sign to the dynamic pricing programs, which are a crucial type of DSM/DR tool? How can they be convinced to adopt products that often generate either higher bills for electricity (i.e., green electricity programs or tariffs) or discomfort of usage in daily routine (i.e. adjustment of electricity demand to the current electricity prices by means of demand response tools)? Further, what influences the social acceptance of these products?

All these and other similar questions have been asked for years by scientists from various disciplines: electricians, psychologists, economists, environmentalists, and others, who have discussed and explored the motivations of consumers' energy behaviors (Chou et al., 2015; Krishnamutri et al., 2012; Geelen et al., 2013; Moreno-Munoz et al., 2016). However, no clear solution has yet been identified. Consumers are heterogeneous, having various needs and motivations. Hence, it is extremely challenging to convince them to adopt certain products, services, or ideas when economic incentives do not play a fundamental role, and other signals than price must be used to make people accept and adopt IES.

For example, recently some surveys have shown that consumers have become more environmentally conscious and in many cases they declare their willingness to contribute to environment protection in their daily routine (Peters et al., 2018; Ozaki, 2011). At the same time, however, many investigators argue whether and how these environmental beliefs and attitudes result in more environmental behavior, such as energy conservation by choosing dynamic electricity tariffs or paying more for electricity, for example, just because it is green, i.e., it comes from RES (Pongiglione, 2011). Some empirical results have even shown that strong environmental beliefs and pro-environmental attitudes do not always lead to environmental behavior. This is known as the intention-behavior gap (Stigka et al., 2014; Pongiglione, 2011; Ozaki, 2011), which causes additional challenges for policy makers and energy utilities.

Immonen et al. (2020) indicated that although the energy market has changed substantially, many consumers are still passive users of electricity in the power grid. This stage is caused by various factors, such as:

- lack of knowledge and awareness of the opportunities that consumers have;
- lack of interest and engagement;
- lack of technical feasibility (e.g., to install small-scale generator); and
- a negative results of cost-benefit analysis, meaning that the perceived financial and behavioral costs of adoption outweigh the potential benefits.

Consumers' engagement may involve not only decisions to invest in a given product or a service (e.g., a small-scale generator or in-home display), but also decisions to switch to another energy supplier offering another type of green or dynamic electricity tariff, or decisions to change a given behavior (e.g., decision to regularly monitor electricity consumption, a decision for participation in demand response services).

Despite the obstacles to consumers' engagement in the energy market, future power systems will involve the active participation of consumers. Nowadays, as Schweiger et al. (2020), Shaukat et al. (2018), Coy et al. (2021), and Immonen et al. (2020) have emphasized, the revolution in thinking about the power system has created an advantageous environment for active consumer involvement in the energy market as never before. Future energy systems will make use of flexible management that includes extraordinary role of individual consumers, microgrids, and virtual power plants as important market players. However, first the current incentives and barriers to adoption and active involvement of consumers in the energy market must be realized, understood, and improved or removed, respectively.

Finally, barriers to acceptance and adoption responsible for slow diffusion of IES can be divided into four categories: economic, organizational, technological, and behavioral:

- **Economic barriers:** (1) The market fails to operate properly due to imperfect information, including lack of knowledge and awareness; (2) imperfect competition and uncertainty (Karakaya et al., 2014); (3) limited access to capital and hidden transaction costs, including the cost of negotiating and enforcing contracts, and lack of appropriate long-lasting financial and legal support (Good et al., 2017; Negro et al., 2012; Bukarica and Tomšić, 2017); (4) lack of appropriate market structure, meaning property rights are not comprehensively assigned (Negro et al., 2012; Good et al., 2017; Tabi et al., 2014); (5) difficulty in proper pricing of services; and (6) financial costs of investment, service, and maintenance (Hobman and Frederiks, 2014; Tabi et al., 2014).
- **Organizational barriers:** (1) Lack of agreement about how demand response should be measured and remunerated (Nygren et al., 2015; Hu et al., 2015); (2) political and regulatory barriers (Karakaya et al., 2014); (3) limited availability, including program unavailability and inaccessibility (Frederiks et al., 2014); (4) misconceptions between consumers and energy service designers or suppliers (Hu et al., 2015); (5) lack of supporting social structures (Gadenne et al., 2011; Nygren et al., 2015); and (6) lack of supply chains, services, and conventions (Gerpott and Paukert, 2013; Negro et al., 2012).
- **Technological barriers:** (1) Limited supply of energy (Sorrell, 2015); (2) technological "lock-in" (Good et al., 2017); (3) integration of IES with the power grid (Zhou and Yang, 2016); (4) need for standardization, in terms of metering, computing the large quantity of data (Good et al., 2017; Gerpott and Paukert, 2013; Frederiks et al., 2014; Nygren et al., 2015); (5) lack of procedural fairness and clear procedures (Hess, 2014; Chen et al., 2017; Bugden and Stedman, 2019); and (6) communication and private data security (Good et al., 2017; Gans et al., 2013; Sopha and Kloeckner, 2016; Tabi et al., 2014; Hess, 2014).
- **Behavioral and cognitive barriers:** (1) Cognitive-biases and heuristics in the decision-making process due to bounded rationality and limited processing capacity (Hobman and Frederiks, 2014; Frederiks et al., 2014; Stenner et al., 2017); (2) risk aversion and resistance to change (Duetschke and Paetz, 2013;

Perlaviciute and Steg, 2014); (3) confusion of choice (lack of professional advice) (Nolan et al., 2008; Frederiks et al., 2014); (4) negative perceptions and word of mouth (i.e., negative information shared within a social network about the innovation) (Khachatryan et al., 2013; Hobman and Frederiks, 2014; Allcott, 2011; Byrka et al., 2016); (5) credibility and trust (e.g., disbelief in climate change) (Frederiks et al., 2014; Good et al., 2017; Hobman and Frederiks, 2014); (6) no perceived responsibility (no moral obligation to subscribe or to participate in energy efficiency behavior) (Perlaviciute and Steg, 2014; Good et al., 2017); and (7) discomfort of usage (Star et al., 2010).

5.5.3 Possible areas for improvement

In particular, the conducted studies, making use of various behavioral models and theories, have shown the following:

- Pro-environmental attitudes and beliefs do not always translate into environmental behavior (intention-behavior gap). This is due to a lack of strong social norms and personal relevance, inconvenience of switching, uncertainty about the quality of green electricity or confusion about choosing between various dynamic electricity tariffs, and lack of accurate information and advice.
- To increase the chance of effective adoption by consumers, it is necessary to overcome obstacles of behavioral change, such as perception, self-interest, and limited knowledge (including awareness, understanding, and procedural knowledge of the innovation) (see, e.g., Pongiglione, 2011).
- To fill the gap between intentions and actual behavior, the benefits from adoption need to have personal relevance to encourage potential adopters to take action.
- From various promoting strategies of more efficient energy behaviors, those based on feedback mechanisms seem to bring the best results (Lopes et al., 2012; Nolan et al., 2008; Allcott, 2011). This is the case because people compare themselves to their neighbors and the motivation "because others are doing it" seems to be crucial.
- Social norms and innovations influence each other: when more people adopt an innovation, the innovation itself becomes a norm, which encourages even more people to adopt it (see, e.g., Ozaki, 2011).
- Strategies promoting DSM or green energy policy and programs must be designed according to the consumer profile to make them more effective. Market segmentation and market analysis are needed (see, e.g. Claudy et al., 2010; Lopes et

al., 2012). The level of consumers' awareness of the innovation should be investigated and the marketing strategy and promotion should be designed according to this.

- Green electricity is not generated generically, but often it is promoted generically. Research has shown that consumers do not perceive green energy sources as equivalent, and that it is important to specify the source of green power when estimating preferences and utility (Borchers et al., 2007).
- Finally, to make the adoption of innovative green energy and dynamic tariffs effective, consumers must perceive more benefits and positive consequences from adopting than costs. They must think that adopted products are in agreement with their values, beliefs, and current practices. They should have a feeling of control and accept paying more money for the adopted products or suffering from discomfort (of rescheduling their daily routine). Last but not least, they have the support of other members of the community who are also becoming adopters (social influence and norms) (Kowalska-Pyzalska, 2015).

5.6 References and proposed additional readings

Willingness to pay:
- Borchers et al. (2007) Does willingness to pay for green energy differ by source? Energy Policy 5, 3327–3334 (Borchers et al., 2007)
- Gerpott and Paukert (2013) Determinants of willingness to pay for smart meters: an empirical analysis of household customers in Germany. Energy Policy 61, 483-495 (Gerpott and Paukert, 2013)
- Kowalska-Pyzalska (2019) Do consumers want to pay for green electricity? A case study from Poland. Sustainability 11, 5, 1310 (Kowalska-Pyzalska, 2019)
- Ma Ch., et al. (2015) Consumers' willingness to pay for renewable energy: a meta-regression analysis. Resour. Energy Econ. 42, 93–109 (Ma et al., 2015)
- Oerlemans L.A.G., et al. (2016) Willingness to pay for green electricity: a review of the contingent valuation literature and its source of error. Renewable and Sustainable Energy Reviews 66, 875–885 (Oerlemans et al., 2016)
- Ozbafli and Jenkins (2016) Estimating the willingness to pay for reliable electricity supply: a choice experiment study. Energy Economics 56, 443–452 (Ozbafli and Jenkins, 2016)

- Su et al. (2018) Valuating renewable microgeneration technologies in Lithuanian households: a study on willingness to pay. Journal of Cleaner Production 191, 318–329 (Su et al., 2018)
- Xie and Zhao (2018) Willingness to pay for green electricity in Tianjin, China: based on the contingent valuation method. Energy Policy 114, 98-107 (Xie and Zhao, 2018)
- Yoo and Kwak (2009) Willingness to pay for green electricity in Korea: a contingent valuation study. Energy Policy 37, 5408–5416 (Yoo and Kwak, 2009)
- Zhang and Wu (2012) Market segmentation and willingness to pay for green electricity among urban residents in China: the case of Jiangsu Province. Energy Policy 51, 514–523 (Zhang and Wu, 2012)
- Zhou and Brown (2017) Smart meter deployment in Europe: a comparative case study on the impacts of national policy schemes. Journal of Cleaner Production 144, 22–32 (Zhou and Brown, 2017)
- Zoric and Hrovatin (2012) Household willingness to pay for green electricity in Slovenia. Energy Policy 47, 180–187 (Zoric and Hrovatin, 2012)

Reviews:
- Aghaei and Alizadeh (2013) Demand response in smart electricity grids equipped with renewable energy sources: a review. Renewable and Sustainable Energy Reviews 18, 64–72 (Aghaei and Alizadeh, 2013)
- Avancini et al. (2019) Energy meters evolution in smart grids: a review. Journal of Cleaner Production 217, 702–715 (Avancini et al., 2019)
- Chadwick et al. (2022) The role of human influences on adoption and rejection of energy technology: a systematised critical review of the literature on household energy transitions. Energy Research & Social Science 89, 102528 (Chadwick et al., 2022)
- Ellaban O. and H. Abu-Rub. 2016. Smart grid customers' acceptance and engagement: an overview. Renewable and Sustainable Energy Reviews 65, 1285–1298 (Ellabban and Abu-Rub, 2016)
- Engelken et al. (2016) Comparing drivers, barriers and opportunities of business models for renewable energy: a review. Renewable and Sustainable Energy Reviews 60, 795–809 (Engelken et al., 2016)
- Good, N., K. Ellis, and P. Mancarella (2017) Review and classification of barriers and enablers of demand response in the smart grid. Renew. Sust. Energy Rev. 16, 57–72 (Good et al., 2017)

- Hobman et al. (2016) Uptake and usage of cost-reflective electricity pricing: insights from psychology and behavioral economics. Renewable and Sustainable Energy Reviews 57, 455–467 (Hobman et al., 2016)
- Hua et al. (2022) Applications of blockchain and artificial intelligence technologies for enabling prosumers in smart grids: a review. Renewable and Sustainable Energy Reviews 161, 112308 (Hua et al., 2022)
- Iweka et al. (2019) Energy and behaviour at home: a review of intervention methods and practices. Energy Research and Social Science 57, 101238 (Iweka et al., 2019)
- Karakaya et al. (2014) Diffusion of eco-innovations: a review. Renewable and Sustainable Energy Reviews 33, 1935–1943 (Karakaya et al., 2014)
- Kowalska-Pyzalska (2018) What makes consumers adopt to innovative energy services in the energy market? A review of incentives and barriers. Renewable and Sustainable Energy Reviews 82, 3, 3570–3581 (Kowalska-Pyzalska, 2018b)
- Siano (2014) Demand response and smart grids—a survey. Renewable and Sustainable Energy Reviews 30, 461–478 (Siano, 2014)
- Sorrell (2015) Reducing energy demand: a review of issues, challenges and approaches. Renewable and Sustainable Energy Reviews 47, 74–82 (Sorrell, 2015)
- Stigka et al. (2014) Social acceptance of renewable energy sources: a review of contingent valuation applications. Renewable and Sustainable Energy Reviews 32, 100–006 (Stigka et al., 2014)
- Strantzali and Aravossis (2015) Decision making in renewable energy investments: a review. Renewable and Sustainable Energy Reviews 55, 885–898 (Strantzali and Aravossis, 2015)
- Sovacool and Furszyfer Der Rio (2020) Smart home technologies in Europe: a critical review of concepts, benefits, risks and policies. Renewable and Sustainable Energy Reviews 120, 10966 (Sovacool and Furszyfer Der Rio, 2020)

Agent-based modeling:
- Guenther et al. (2011) An agent-based simulation approach for the new product diffusion of a novel biomass fuel. J. Oper. Res. Soc. 62, 12–20 (Guenther et al., 2011)
- Kiesling et al. (2012) Agent-based simulation of innovation diffusion: a review. Central European Journal of Operations Research 20(2), 183–230 (Kiesling et al., 2012)
- Kowalska-Pyzalska et al. (2014) Turning green: agent-based modeling of the adoption of dynamic electricity tariffs. Energy Policy 71, 164–174 (Kowalska-Pyzalska et al., 2014)

- Mittal et al. (2019) An agent-based approach to designing residential renewable energy systems. Renewable and Sustainable Energy Reviews 112, 1008–1020 (Mittal et al., 2019)
- Moglia et al. (2017) A review of agent-based modelling of technology diffusion with special reference to residential energy efficiency. Sustainable Cities and Society 31, 173–182 (Moglia et al., 2017)
- Palmer et al. (2015) Modeling the diffusion of residential photovoltaic systems in Italy: an agent-based simulations. Technological Forecasting & Social Change 99, 106–131 (Palmer et al., 2015)
- Przybyła et al. (2014) Diffusion of innovation within an agent-based model: Spinsons, independence and advertising. Advances in Complex Systems 17(1), 1450004 (Przybyła et al., 2014)
- Ringler et al. (2016) Agent-based modelling and simulation of smart electricity grids and markets—a literature review. Renewable and Sustainable Energy Reviews 57, 205–215 (Ringler et al., 2016)
- Rixen and Weigand (2014) Agent-based simulation of policy induced diffusion of smart meters. Technological Forecasting and Social Change 85, 153–167 (Rixen and Weigand, 2014)
- Weron et al. (2018) The role of educational trainings in the diffusion of smart metering platforms: an agent-based modeling approach. Physica A, Statistical Mechanics and its Applications 505, 591–600 (Weron et al., 2018)
- Zhang and Nuttall (2011) Evaluating government's policies on promoting smart metering diffusion in retail electricity markets via agent-based simulation. Journal of Product Innovation Management 28, 169–186 (Zhang and Nuttall, 2011)

Conjoint analysis and discrete choice experiment:
- Agarwal et al. (2015) An interdisciplinary review of research in conjoint analysis: recent developments and directions for future research. Customer Needs and Solutions 2(1) 19–40 (Agarwal et al., 2015)
- Danne et al. (2021) Analyzing German consumers' willingness to pay for green electricity tariff attributes: a discrete choice experiment. Energ. Sustain. Soc. 11, 15 (Danne et al., 2021)
- Duetschke and Paetz (2013) Dynamic electricity pricing—which programs do consumers prefer? Energy Policy 59, 226-234 (Duetschke and Paetz, 2013)
- Kaufmann et al. (2013) Customer value of smart metering: explorative evidence from a choice-based conjoint study in Switzerland. Energy Policy 53, 229–239 (Kaufmann et al., 2013)

- Masini and Menichetti (2012) The impact of behavioral factors in the renewable energy investment decision making process: conceptual framework and empirical findings. Energy Policy 40, 23–38 (Masini and Menichetti, 2012)
- Tabi et al. (2014) What makes people seal the green power deal? Customer segmentation based on choice experiment in Germany. Ecological Economics 107, 206–215 (Tabi et al., 2014)

Social acceptance:
- Chawla and Kowalska-Pyzalska (2019) Public awareness and consumer acceptance of smart meters among Polish social media users. Energies 12, 2759 (Chawla and Kowalska-Pyzalska, 2019)
- Paravantis et al. (2018) Social acceptance of renewable energy projects: a contingent valuation investigation in Western Greece. Renewable Energy 123, 639–651 (Paravantis et al., 2018)
- Wolsink (2014) Distributed generation of sustainable energy as a common pool resource: social acceptance in rural setting of smart (micro-) grid configurations. In: New Rural Spaces: Towards Renewable Energies, Multifunctional Farming, and Sustainable Tourism; editors: B. Frantál and S. Martinát, University of Amsterdam: Amsterdam, the Netherlands, 36–47 Wolsink (2014)
- Wolsink (2020) Distributed energy systems as common goods: socio-political acceptance of renewables in intelligent microgrids. Renew. Sustainable Energy Rev. 127, 109841 (Wolsink, 2020)
- Wuestenhagen et al. (2007) Social acceptance of renewable energy innovation: an introduction to the concept. Energy Policy 35, 2683–2691 (Wuestenhagen et al., 2007)

Energy-efficient behavior:
- Anda, M. and J. Temmen (2014) Smart metering for residential energy efficiency: the use of community based social marketing for behavioural change and smart grid introduction. Renew. Energ. 67, 119–127 (Anda and Temmen, 2014)
- Batalla-Bejerano, J., E. Trujillo-Baute, and M. Villa-Arrieta (2020) Smart meters and consumer behaviour: insights from the empirical literature. Energ. Policy 144, 111610 (Batalla-Bejerano et al., 2020)
- Bertoldo, R., M. Poumadère, and L.C. Rodrigues Jr. (2015) When meters start to talk: the public's encounter with smart meters in France. Energy Res. Soc. Sci. 9, 146–156 (Bertoldo et al., 2015)
- Buchanan, K., R. Russo, and B. Anderson (2014) Feeding back about eco-feedback: how do consumers use and respond to energy monitors? Energ. Policy 73, 138–146 (Buchanan et al., 2014)

- Buchanan K., R. Russo, and B. Anderson (2015) The question of energy reduction: the problem (s) with feedback. Energ. Policy 77, 89–96 (Buchanan et al., 2016)
- Gaspari, J., E. Antonini, L. Marchi, and V. Vodola (2021) Energy transition at home: a survey on the data and practices that lead to a change in household energy behavior. Sustainability-Basel 13(9), 5268 (Gaspari et al., 2021)
- Gölz, S. and U.J.J. Hahnel (2016) What motivates people to use energy feedback systems? A multiple goal approach to predict long-term usage behaviour in daily life. Energy Res. Soc. Sci. 21, 155–166 (Gölz and Hahnel, 2016)
- Kowalska-Pyzalska, A. and K. Byrka (2019) Determinants of the willingness to energy monitoring by residential consumers: a case study in the city of Wroclaw in Poland. Energies 12(5), 907 (Kowalska-Pyzalska and Byrka, 2019)
- Lee, E., M. Kang, J. Song and M. Kang (2020) From intention to action: habits, feedback and optimizing energy consumption in South Korea. Energy Res. Soc. Sci. 64, 101430 (Lee et al., 2020)
- Leygue, C., E. Ferguson, A. Skatova, and A. Spence (2014) Energy sharing and energy feedback: affective and behavioral reactions to communal energy displays. Front Energy Res. 2(29), 1–12 (Leygue et al., 2014)
- Zeng et al. (2014) China's promoting energy-efficient products for the benefit of the people program in 2012: results and analysis of the consumer impact study. Appl. Energy 133, 22–32 (Zeng et al., 2014)

Social influence:
- Abrahamse and Steg (2013) Social influence approaches to encourage resource conservation: a meta-analysis. Global Environ. Change 23, 1773–1785 (Abrahamse and Steg, 2013)
- Allcott (2011) Social norms and energy conservation. Journal of Public Economics 95, 9–10, 1082–1095 (Allcott, 2011)
- Ayers et al. (2013) Evidence from two large field experiments that peer comparison feedback can reduce residential energy usage. The Journal of Law, Economics and Organization 29(5), 992–1022 (Ayers et al., 2013)
- Ek and Soederholm (2008) Norms and economic motivation in the Swedish green electricity market. Ecological Economics 68, 169–182 (Ek and Soederholm, 2008)
- Gumz et al. (2022) Social influence as a major factor in smart meters' acceptance: findings from Brazil. Results in Engineering 15, 100510 (Gumz et al., 2022)
- Nolan et al. (2008) Normative social influence is underdetected. Personality and Social Psychology Bulletin 34, 913–923 (Nolan et al., 2008)

- Schultz et al. (2007) The constructive, destructive and reconstructive power of social norms. Psychological Science 18, 429–434 (Schultz et al., 2007)
- Spandagos et al. (2021) Social influence and economic intervention policies to save energy at home: critical questions for the new decade and evidence from air-condition use. Renew. Sustain. Energy Rev. 143, 110915 (Spandagos et al., 2021)

Pilot programs:
- D'hulst et al. (2015) Demand response flexibility and flexibility potential of residential smart appliances: experiences from large pilot test in Belgium. Applied Energy 155, 79–90 (D'hulst et al., 2015)
- Neska and Kowalska-Pyzalska (2022) Conceptual design of energy market topologies for communities and their practical applications in EU: a comparison of three case studies. Renewable and Sustainable Energy Reviews 169, 112921 (Neska and Kowalska-Pyzalska, 2022)
- Star et al. (2010) The dynamic pricing mousetrap: why isn't the world beating down our door? ACEEE Summer Study on Energy Efficiency in Buildings 2010, Proceedings 2, 257–268 (Star et al., 2010)
- Tahir et al. (2020) Significance of demand response in light of current pilot projects in China and devising a problem solution for future advancements. Technology in Society 63, 101374 (Tahir et al., 2020).

6

Behavioral strategies and marketing interventions: policy recommendations and practical advice

6.1 Introduction

As Saviotti and Pyka (2017) emphasize, the essence of innovation effectiveness is its market verification, i.e., acceptance from the demand side. The lack of demand for new products not only is a barrier related to the implementation of innovations, but it can also discourage a company from seeking new solutions and improvements.

The many research areas of contemporary market consumer behavior in the context of introducing innovations to the market include:

- diffusion of innovation (the impact of network topologies, social influence, knowledge, and advertisement on the spread of innovation);
- the impact of socio-economic factors, as well as norms and values on adopting innovations (willingness to accept, buy, and pay for a new good, consumer preferences and expectations); and
- models of consumer acceptance of innovations (external and internal factors favoring the acquisition of innovation or causing resistance and opposition to them).

It should be emphasized that such an analysis can be extremely useful for enterprises whose foundation of success is the effective introduction of innovations to the market. Knowing the needs of consumers, characterizing their socio-economic factors and their willingness to pay for a given good, can help to target innovation properly in order to increase market attractiveness and thus positively influence the purchasing behavior of consumers.

Fig. 6.1 presents the background of the analysis of consumers' acceptance and willingness to pay and its impact on IES diffusion

Diffusion of Innovative Energy Services. https://doi.org/10.1016/B978-0-12-822882-1.00012-3

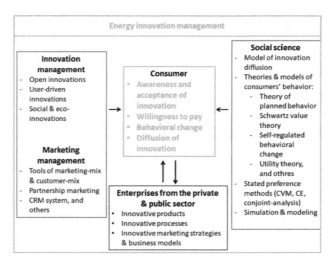

Figure 6.1. The framework of the energy innovation management including the bilateral impact of consumers and enterprises.

as a part of energy innovation management (EIM). EIM takes insights from the social sciences in order to learn about consumers' attributes, motivations, and preferences. Moreover, it makes use of a variety of tools provided by innovation and marketing management. As a result, energy companies as well as all other enterprises who are or want to become active in future energy systems are given hints about how to design an innovative energy service (IES) in order to achieve a successful level of diffusion. High adoption rates, which correlate with successful diffusion, bring advantages to suppliers (in terms of high revenues and profits, better social visibility, etc.) and for whole societies and communities by providing social and ecological benefits (lower air pollution, reduced electricity bills, etc.).

Information on consumer behavior is important for companies for two reasons. First of all, it is an excellent source of information on the effectiveness of transforming potential demand into an effective one, which translates into sales results and revenues of the company as well as its position in the market. Second, based on consumer preferences, enterprise can create innovations and the structure of its components.

There is no doubt that thanks to the implementation of innovations (e.g., product or marketing), a company can increase its competitive advantage in the market. The energy market is a very complex one in technical, economic, and legal terms. Consumers are the final recipients of it, who only recently have been able to play on it not only a passive, but also an active role. Socio-economic changes, increased awareness of the need to protect the environment and climate, and very restrictive requirements set for this industry in terms of increasing efficiency and energy efficiency force enterprises to implement many changes. Among these changes are innovative products and services that are the subject of interest here.

In this chapter, we will provide a description and comparison of behavioral strategies and marketing interventions that may enhance consumers' interest, engagement, and willingness to adopt various IES, and hence participate actively in energy transition. We will also discuss the proposal of marketing tools that can be used to encourage consumers' participation in the energy market. Finally, we will provide some policy recommendations and future agenda for research.

6.2 The overview of the interventions

From the discussion provided in the previous chapters (see Chapters 2–5), it is clear that what consumers need to get engaged in the energy market are: (1) information, (2) motivation, and (3) strategy and tools. Thus, consumers must first get informed to become aware of the opportunities they have. Based on this information, they should be able to form an opinion toward an offered product or a service. In the second step, consumers must find intrinsic or extrinsic motivation to engage in a given behavior or to make a certain decision (e.g., to invest in solar PV or to decide on the participation in green electricity program or to shift the tariffs from flat to dynamic ones). Finally, theories and models of consumers' decision making, discussed in Chapter 4, clearly show that without proper behavioral or marketing strategies, the broader social adoption of IES will not be feasible (Lopes et al., 2012; Jager, 2006; Gyamfi et al., 2013; Kowalska-Pyzalska, 2018b). Hence, the product or service offered to consumers must be designed in such a way that consumers will be given tools and directions/advice on how to proceed with a given innovation. At this time, proper marketing strategies are especially necessary to help consumers decide on a given behavior and to maintain this decision in the long term.

The successful diffusion of IES require multilevel incentives consisting of institutional changes, networks of communication, proper maintenance and other services by retailers, unbiased information provision, education, encouraging policies, legislation and administration, and a positive atmosphere (Nygren et al., 2015; Nachreiner et al., 2015; Darby and McKenna, 2012; Connor et al., 2014; McKenna et al., 2012). As Rixen and Weigand (2014) point out, designing effective and efficient incentives is challenging. Ineffective or inefficient policies may cause nonadoption and/or uncontrollable costs. That is why **behavioral strategies (interventions)** require considerable deliberation before implementation. The most common objective of these interventions is to promote energy conservation through either providing rewards that make pro-environmental decisions more attractive or targeting individuals' perceptions, preferences, and abilities in order to induce certain behavior (Zhou and Yang, 2016).

Generally, intervention strategies aiming at improving energy efficiency and stimulating energy savings can be categorized into three major types:

- **Structural interventions** aim to influence contextual variables and behavior (e.g., by altering the advantages and disadvantages of potential solutions or legal tools) (Lopes et al., 2012). They may include price policies (e.g., energy or product tax), subsidies (e.g., cost-cutting funds), loans (e.g., green loans), and legislation (i.e., building regulation, procedures), as well as a variety of program structures (e.g., fixed monthly premiums, leasing or ownership of photovoltaic energy) (Zhou and Yang, 2016; Lopes et al., 2012; Kowalska-Pyzalska, 2018b).
- **Antecedent interventions** are designed to change factors that precede behavior. They usually cover information-intensive strategies aiming to increase consumer knowledge and awareness. Such interventions include tailored marketing, promotional materials, and education efforts, as well as interpersonal word of mouth, demonstration (by celebrities, by energy suppliers familiar with a specific customer sector), giving away free products (trails), and lastly goal-setting. These motivational-based informational strategies aim to alter perceptions, motivations, knowledge, and social norms without really altering the external context in which the choices are made (Hobman and Frederiks, 2014; Zhou and Yang, 2016; Lopes et al., 2012; Iweka et al., 2019; Słupik et al., 2021; Kowalska-Pyzalska, 2018b).
- **Consequence interventions** include mainly feedback (from energy use appliances or from energy supplier) and rewards (i.e., monetary) (Foulds et al., 2017; Buchanan et al., 2014; Lopes et al., 2012; Kowalska-Pyzalska, 2018b). These interventions focus on modifying the consequences of behaviors, with the notion that when favorable outcomes (i.e., rewards) are attached with them, more efficient energy activities will become more appealing (Lopes et al., 2012).

A variety of interventions have already been tested in various empirical studies. The findings show that economic incentives belonging to structural interventions have an ambiguous impact on the behavioral change. Spandagos et al. (2021) mention that whereas several studies demonstrate their effectiveness in encouraging savings (Abrahamse et al., 2005), others associate them with negative effects, such as increased consumption (Delmas et al., 2013), free-riding (Houde and Aldy, 2017), and the rebound effect (Alberini et al., 2016).

The general observation is that interventions that include a social influence element are likely to succeed most (Abrahamse and Steg, 2013; Spandagos et al., 2021). Social influence is usually included in either antecedent or consequence interventions, such as informative strategies, gamification, or feedback. This is why in this chapter we will focus on the analysis and discussion of these types of marketing and behavioral strategies.

6.3 Rising awareness of information-intensive strategies

The general problem with broader diffusion of IES concerns the lack of consumers' knowledge and hence interest and acceptance. As Trotta (2020) emphasize, consumer inattention and lack of information are ubiquitous, especially in household energy-related settings. With the currently observer envisioned growth in the residential electricity demand and increased share of intermittent renewables in the supply mix, **consumers will need to be better informed** about their electricity consumption. Only the provision of general and tailored information may allow consumers to play an active role in managing their electricity use (Trotta, 2020).

The provision of information to householders can make consumers more aware about helpful tips, guides, and newly introduced technologies, mechanisms, and approaches (Iweka et al., 2019). Information can be provided in many different ways, such as through:

- brochures (Gangale et al., 2013);
- energy consultancy services, auditing, and fairs (Taylor et al., 2014; Iwasaki, 2019; Gangale et al., 2013);
- workshops and educational programs;
- energy labels (Burgess and Nye, 2008; Girod et al., 2017b; Brucal and Roberts, 2019);
- visual prompts (Elsharkawy and Rutherford, 2015);
- benchmarking;
- Energy Performance Certificates (Backhaus et al., 2011; Adjei et al., 2011; Gonzalez-Caceres et al., 2020); and
- mass or social media campaigns (Mankoff et al., 2010).

The aforementioned and commonly used approaches can create or increase awareness about problems linked with energy or adoptable energy conservation procedures. They may be used separately or combined (Iweka et al., 2019), dependent on the target and marketing strategies. However, it is important to remember that communication channels play a vital role in the diffusion of information as well as addressing consumers' concerns (Rogers, 2003). At the same time, people have different needs and an information and communication channel does not have to be similarly efficient and convincing for everybody.

For example, in 2009, a case study for understanding the impact of social capital on information diffusion, for adoption of household energy efficiency measures, was carried out among three communities in the UK (McMichael and Shipworth, 2013). The results showed that **standard campaigns** account for approximately two-thirds of information-seeking behavior, but this may not address the rest of the community, who prefer to receive information from people they know. It was also concluded that the **likelihood of acceptance toward innovations increases up to four times in cases where the information is shared through personal contact**. This implies that it is very important to tailor the diffusion or awareness campaigns to communities' communication channel preferences, to have more efficient results (McMichael and Shipworth, 2013).

In another experiment conducted by Trotta (2020), more than two-thirds of the total number of respondents confirmed a willingness to receive additional information about energy consumption and hints how to save energy. However, the authors discovered a significant portion of "electricity unaware" respondents who were not only unwilling to receive such information, but were also unaware of their own knowledge deficits. This experiment has proved how important it is to know consumers also in terms of their knowledge deficits. This can allow decision makers to design proper strategies dedicated to this type of consumer.

Another way to make people save energy is by **informing them that "comparable others" save more** (Graffeo et al., 2015; Ayers et al., 2013; Nolan et al., 2008). In a survey conducted by Graffeo et al. (2015), the authors investigated whether one can further improve this effectiveness of this informative incentive by manipulating who the "comparable others" are. The experiment setup looked as follows:

- (1) The authors asked participants to imagine receiving feedback stating that their energy consumption exceeded that of "comparable others" by 10%.

- (2) The subject "comparable others" were in a 2 × 2 design: they were either a household that was located either in the same neighborhood as the respondents, or in a different neighborhood, and its members were either identified (by names and a photograph) or unidentified.
- (3) The experiment included two control conditions: one where no feedback was provided, and one where only statistical feedback was provided (feedback about an average household).

The results of this study revealed that it matters who the "comparable others" are. The most effective feedback was when the referent household was from the same neighborhood as the individual, and its members were not identified (Graffeo et al., 2015).

In another field experiment designed by Bator et al. (2019), the authors have promoted **summer electricity conservation** among low- to moderate-income households that do not pay for energy. Both experiments were conducted during summer months when electricity use increases, and both focused on reducing use of air-conditioning. The authors have tested two experiment interventions and measured their effectiveness in terms of energy conservation: (1) **face-to-face communications** that provided normative feedback (comparison to neighbors' energy use), an indoor ambient room thermometer, energy saving tips to reduce window air-conditioning use, free compact fluorescent lamps (CFLs), and a written commitment—results showed a reduction in average summer electricity use of 2.7% compared to a control condition; and (2) **provision of materials under residents' doors** instead of face-to-face communication. They were informed, among others, about the relation between energy use, smog, and childhood asthma (Bator et al., 2019). Such a survey setup has resulted in average short-term savings of 1.4% but there was no evidence of longer-term savings (Bator et al., 2019).

In conclusion, the authors stated that **normative interventions** can be used to promote electricity conservation, even when there is no direct financial benefit to participants. This kind of intervention can be cost-effective if metering is already set up to monitor energy use at the household level. It also amply proves that environmental behavior can be driven by factors other than financial gain (Bator et al., 2019).

6.3.1 Tailoring

The above discussion has shown that communication channels as the information itself should be adjusted to the particular needs and preferences of a given group of consumers. Energy systems and their interfaces affect consumers differently. To achieve any consumer behavior change, it is important to understand consumer needs and preferences and to deliver the service accordingly. For example, services aligning with consumer values—focusing on sustainability when people's biospheric values are high, and on personal gains when their egoistic values are high—will have a greater impact on consumer behavior than services that are misaligned to consumer values (Schweiger et al., 2020).

In addition to considering what is important to a consumer, it is also crucial to take into account what a consumer can do. Some people are skilled in utilizing complex mobile applications, while others become discouraged when required to use one. Similar to this, some people can spend more time and others less time interacting with a product or service. As suggested in cocreation approach, it is crucial to involve potential users in the design process. Such an approach guarantees that they will be pleased with the final solution (Schweiger et al., 2020).

Tailored information avoids overloading householders with too much information by giving them personal information only. Tailored information can be made available after a home audit by professionals in order to establish the needs, opportunities, and obstacles of a given household. In other words, knowing the consumer matters.

Lastly, as Schweiger et al. (2020) point out, the starting point of consumers matters. Are they already planning to change their energy consumption and simply do not quite know how to do so, or are they not even aware of any problems arising from their behavior? Answering this question, as we will show later on, has a tremendous impact on the choice of the marketing strategies and interventions.

6.3.2 Nudges

A prime example of cleverly designed context to stimulated desired behavior without demanding many resources are **nudges** (Rathi and Chunekar, 2015). Nudging is a soft push, that can make people act or react—and consume less energy—because they are told their neighbors or peers do so, for instance, by changing the default settings of energy devices. Nudges function by modifying the path of least resistance and serve as reminders to highlight opportunities. They are transparent cues that are placed in the environment to encourage desired behavior without the use of coercion or alternative behavior punishment (Rathi and Chunekar, 2015). Nudges are a type of nonfiscal, noncoercive behaviorally informed intervention that consists of changing aspects of how choices are presented to promote a specific decision (Caballero and Ploner, 2022). Nudges have also been tested to reduce peak demand consumption (Pratt and Erickson, 2020), and proposed as tools to increase uptake of solar energy by households (Colasante et al., 2021).

Recently different kind of nudges were gathered by the NUDGE project,[1] funded by the European Horizon 2020 program, aiming at investigating the potential of behavioral interventions toward achieving higher energy efficiency, paving the way to the generalized use of such interventions as a worthy addition to the policy-making toolbox.

Nudges can be divided into six categories, as follows:

- **facilitating nudges**—facilitate desirable behavior by diminishing the physical or mental effort of individuals (e.g., personalized push notifications to either switch to manual or automated management of temperature setting);
- **fear nudges**—attempt to generate fear or uncertainty (e.g. inform that free PV energy is available for two more hours and provide a discount on installing monitoring equipment to allow saving energy later);
- **confronting nudges**—seek to prevent an unwanted behavior by instilling doubt about it (e.g., implement time buffer between decision and action and remind on the consequences of the actions);
- **reinforcement nudges**—aim to reinforce behaviors by pointing out desired behaviors at a suitable time and provoking feelings of compassion to stimulate desired behavior;
- **deceive nudges**—favor desirable behavior by deceiving users' perceptions about the alternatives (e.g., visualizing the nonenergy efficient choices impact through dramatic visualizations); and
- **social influence nudges**—draw on humans' desire to comply with what they perceive as others' expectations of them (e.g., compare behavior with other peers).

The findings from five pilot trials within the NUDGE project have shown that to deliver long-term energy efficiency behavior changes and impact, the following conditions should be fulfilled: (1) the engagement of users achieved thanks to remarkable efficiency improvements (i.e., users motivation and engagement have increased after they have seen that their behavioral change leads to positive outcomes); (2) combination of collective and social factors for local energy community members; (3) employment of energy monitoring tools to evaluate energy consumption and/or production; and (4) employment of digital user interfaces

[1] https://www.nudgeproject.eu/the-project/ (accessed data January 5, 2023).

to enable interaction with end consumers but also the operationalization of behavioral interventions.

6.3.3 Feedback

Feedback is one of the most spectacular and effective interventions. In simple words, feedback is a kind of information about the amount of energy a household consumes in a given period of time (Buchanan et al., 2014). The aim of energy feedback is to raise awareness and to provoke reflection about consumer energy usage by means of specific home appliances, and its relevance to one's own behavior. Apart from real-time data, proper energy feedback should also include access to and comparison of the historical data of electricity consumption to encourage self-reflection and improvement (Voelker et al., 2021; Gaspari et al., 2021).

Nowadays, feedback for electricity end-users is provided mainly by means of smart meters and energy displays (Leygue et al., 2014; Gölz and Hahnel, 2016; Weiss et al., 2016). According to Martin (2020), "energy feedback is positioned as a catalyst capable of transforming an ostensibly passive and unaware public into energy-conscious microresource managers," mainly because of the delivery of real-time information about household energy consumption and generation and the ability to combine it with DSM/DR tools, such as dynamic electricity tariffs.

Feedback is often subdivided into direct, indirect, and inadvertent, depending on how the information is disseminated, on the type, quality, and quantity of data presentation, and on interaction and control by the energy user (Lopes et al., 2012; Gans et al., 2013). Successful feedback has to capture consumers' attention, draw a close link between specific actions and their effects, and activate various motives that may appeal to different consumer groups (Lopes et al., 2012). As Nachreiner et al. (2015) emphasize, consumer behavior doesn't have to be changed by feedback alone. The most successful designs integrate a variety of feedback and analysis choices, including historical comparisons, motivating strategies, and information about, for instance, energy conservation. In particular, feedback regarding the customers' results, e.g., in redaction of electricity consumption in comparison to the results achieved by, e.g., neighbors or similar customers' segment have been found to be effective in changing behavior (Allcott, 2011; Nolan et al., 2008; Hargreaves et al., 2010).

Although energy feedback seems to be a very effective intervention, the literature shows that there are some determinants responsible for its effectiveness. First of all, empirical research reveals that the proper design of energy feedback is essential. As

Gölz and Hahnel (2016) point out, the heterogeneity of consumers in terms of their needs, preferences, and fears means that energy monitors cannot be based only on financial goals, neglecting other nonmonetary motivation that people may have. The literature clearly shows that among goals with reference to energy feedback, learning how to save electricity, control and reduction of costs, or avoiding inconvenience due to perceived negative impacts of feedback usage also matter (Gölz and Hahnel, 2016). A variety of needs and preferences leads to the necessity of adjusting feedback to the consumer profiles, not simply providing one type of uniform energy feedback (Lee et al., 2020; Chawla and Kowalska-Pyzalska, 2019; Olmos et al., 2011; Ozawa et al., 2017). Other findings from the literature indicate that the effectiveness of energy feedback correlates with the prior environmental motivation (Wallenborn et al., 2011; Henn et al., 2019) or prior knowledge of energy in general, and energy monitoring and conservation in particular (Kowalska-Pyzalska and Byrka, 2019).

Finally, the literature pays attention to the role of social influence and interactions in terms of popularity of energy monitoring by means of SM or SMP, and changing behaviors in order to save energy in particular (Chadwick et al., 2022; Gumz et al., 2022; Chawla and Kowalska-Pyzalska, 2019; Chawla et al., 2020c; Leygue et al., 2014). Researchers have proved the effectiveness of social comparison, e.g., among neighbors or similar segments of customers (Leygue et al., 2014; Mukai et al., 2022), or social communication via social media (Anda and Temmen, 2014).

6.3.4 Subsidies, rewards, and penalties

Economic instruments are policies that entail paying the customers back a monetary amount to reward savings or encourage efficiency upgrades (Cattaneo, 2019), or charging them an amount as a penalty for overconsumption (Spandagos et al., 2021). Energy taxation may be considered as such a penalty, even though it has been implemented mostly to raise revenue instead of discouraging excessive consumption (Bertoldi et al., 2013).

Joachain and Klopfert (2014) and Abrahamse et al. (2005) state that positive incentives (e.g., rewards and subsidies) or negative incentives (e.g., penalties) are widely used to lead to desired behavior changes in the short term. Both rewards and penalties belong to controlling policies that do not favor intrinsic motivation necessary to internalize regulation and maintain behaviors over time. In the contrary, subsidies, rewards, and penalties are a powerful extrinsic motivator for pro-environmental behavior. People perform a behavior because they get or lose something in return (Schweiger et al., 2020). However, this incentive frequently only persists for the duration of the rewards or penalties. As a result, motivation through rewards may be expensive and ultimately unsustainable. Furthermore, people's initial intrinsic motivation may be overshadowed and diminished by extrinsic motivation (Schweiger et al., 2020).

Since penalties are linked to unfavorable public perceptions and political cost, they are utilized less frequently in practice (Cattaneo, 2019), whereas rewards are thought to be able to enhance the good connotations connected with energy conservation. Both of these intervention types lean on the neoclassical economics approach, which highlights the tendency for self-utility satisfaction. At the same time, penalties are a part of dynamic electricity tariffs, such as critical peak pricing (CPP), when exceeding the threshold or just using electricity at more expensive times imposes an additional cost on the consumer (Belton and Lunn, 2020; Olmos et al., 2011; Duetschke and Paetz, 2013).

Finally, van der Werff and Steg (2016) argue that increasing the value of pro-environmental goals is a better **long-term strategy** than subsidizing pro-environmental behavior. Encouraging people to act sustainably is one side, while also making it simple for them and reminding them to do so is the other one.

6.3.5 Gamification

Gamification is another method for engaging people that is becoming more and more popular. In gamification, principles and elements of game-design such as achieving, exploring, competing, or connecting with other people in a behavior-change tool can stimulate people and increase engagement and motivation (Beck et al., 2019; Johnson et al., 2017; AlSkaif et al., 2018; Morganti et al., 2017).

Weiser et al. (2015) provided an overview of game design, mechanics, and elements grounded in well-established models of motivation and behavior change. Nicholson (2015) distinguished between reward-based and meaningful gamification, which influence extrinsic and intrinsic motivation, respectively. Reward-based gamification deals with provision of rewards for a desired behaviors or outcomes. Even if this type of gamification can effectively initiate participation, it is not recommended in the long term, because rewarding can harm the intristic motivation of participants. Hence reward-based gamification should be used for short-term behavior change, or if rewards can be handed out indefinitely (Nicholson, 2015; Weiser et al., 2015). In contrast, meaningful gamification can lead to enhancement of intrinsic motivation, by giving consumers the opportunity to explore a narrative, choose how to engage with the service or product, and

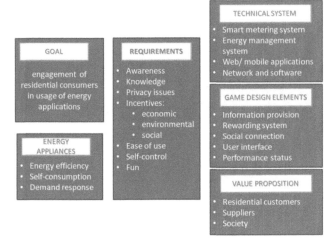

Figure 6.2. The proposed game design framework for raising engagement of residential consumers toward DSM (AlSkaif et al., 2018).

make meaningful decisions, get information (e.g., about the real-world effects of their behavior), engage with others, choose elements to develop solutions for real-world problems, and reflect—alone and with others—about what they have learned (Nicholson, 2015). If a gamification system has been well-desingned, the activated behavioral patterns becomes a habitual real-world behavior (Nicholson, 2015). AlSkaif et al. (2018) described a detailed gamification framework guiding the development of gamifica tion elements specifically for residential consumer participation in demand-side management including increase of energy efficiency, self-consumption, and demand response. After selecting the goal of the game and technical tools that can facilitate the process, a game can be designed. A typical game design, according to AlSkaif et al. (2018), includes (1) information provision, (2) rewarding system, (3) social connection, (4) user interface, and (5) performance status, as shown in Figs. 6.2 and 6.3.

Apart from including the technical system architecture enabling consumers to use energy applications, the framework identifies the value streams to different stakeholders in the energy market when using a gamification-based solution, including residential customers, energy suppliers, and society in general (AlSkaif et al., 2018). The game design is based on the theoretical framework of TTM of behavioral change (Prochaska and Diclemente, 1982).

The game must be well-designed to activate consumers. As mentioned earlier, the roll-out of smart meters does not in-

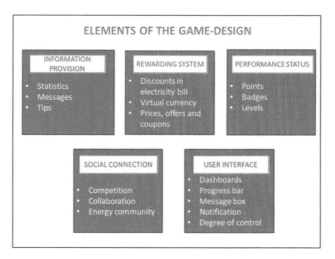

Figure 6.3. Game design elements categories for residential energy applications (AlSkaif et al., 2018).

evitably lead to energy-related behavior change (Chawla et al., 2020c,a; Chawla and Kowalska-Pyzalska, 2019; Strengers, 2013). As Strengers (2013) emphasize, the true roll-out of smart meters requires engagement of residential customers to let them take an active role in energy applications enabled by smart meters. One way to achieve this is to use gamification that can make SM applications more appealing to residential customers, by provoking them to be willing to control their energy behavior and make decisions that can lead, for instance, to cost saving and carbon footprint reduction (AlSkaif et al., 2018).

A review on gamification to facilitate pro-environmental behavior for energy efficiency by Morganti et al. (2017) found that in most cases, either web-based platforms or mobile applications are used. Another review of usage of gamified tools for domestic energy consumption by Johnson et al. (2017) observed that feedback, challenges, social sharing, rewards, and leaderboards belong to the most common elements of gamification. Empirical studies show that there is great potential in using gamification to help make smart energy system tools more effective (Johnson et al., 2017; Morganti et al., 2017; AlSkaif et al., 2018). However, in 2019 a review of gamified mobile energy apps by Beck et al. (2019) indicated that in the real world, gamification and game design elements are still heavily underutilized (Beck et al., 2019). To facilitate further the transition to a more sustainable smart energy system, companies should be aware of the potential of gamification during business model identification (Schweiger et al., 2020).

6.3.6 Retention of the effects

In addition to behavioral interventions aiming to increase consumers' awareness, knowledge, and engagement, there is a group of retention strategies that can be utilized during implementation to keep consumers engaged in the long run. In the work by Coday et al. (2005), we can find a list of retention strategies from studies targeted toward disease prevention. Surprisingly, there are some similarities in challenges in disease prevention and energy-efficient behavior. Both kinds of actions require participants' effort to start and maintain behaviors that they would not have engaged in otherwise. They also do not provide immediate gains for participants, but rather long-term effects (Coday et al., 2005).

The most common and effective retention strategies include the following:

- Sending out regular reminders and prompts if consumers fail to engage with the product or service (e.g., if they do not open their mobile app for a few days) (Frederiks et al., 2015; Schultz, 2013). Personal reminders can be effective in reacquiring consumer attention and participation (Coday et al., 2005) and in transition between the behavioral stages (Nachreiner et al., 2015). Prompts work best for simple, repetitive, and easy-to-conduct behaviors, where limited effort is needed and for people who are already motivated to engage (Schultz, 2013). All kind of visual cues and vivid descriptions should be used, as the empirical evidence shows that these are more effective in terms of influencing human behaviors that pure information (Frederiks et al., 2015).
- Offering flexibility in terms of signing a contract, or opting out of certain tasks to reduce the risk of overburdening consumers and their dropping out. Additionally, some extra level of control given to consumers to minimize their reluctance to participate in the long run (Coday et al., 2005; Weron et al., 2018; Kowalska-Pyzalska et al., 2014).
- Providing interaction with all data sources to balance the benefits and cost for consumers and other stakeholders who are involved in the process of data provision (Schweiger et al., 2020).
- Offering some level of automatization in terms of, e.g., adjusting load to the current electricity prices lowers the personal effort of consumers and decreases their discomfort regarding participation in DSM/DR programs (Kowalska-Pyzalska and Byrka, 2019; Kowalska-Pyzalska et al., 2014).

Finally, the literature emphasizes that changes in behavior can be sustained for long periods of time only if they are voluntary. Hence, rewards and penalties are strategies that can be used rather temporarily than in a long-term perspective.

6.4 Marketing of innovative energy services (IES)

Marketing generally tackles the challenge of getting more households to adopt a product, a service, or a new behavior. It is especially essential in the case of innovations launched in the energy market, which is a very specific one, in terms of both products/services and the market itself. There are several challenges that must be taken into account when preparing the marketing strategy. Firstly, the electricity is the abstract commodity which automatically lowers the interest and engagement of the potential customers. Secondly, the effects of consumer decisions tend to be delayed relative to when the decision itself occurs and the costs are incurred. Finally, the variety of IES requires different marketing methods and approaches to cope with the adoption obstacles. Some IES commercial marketing tools will be good enough, whereas for others, additional social marketing approaches should be used.

6.4.1 Definition of social marketing

The central pillar of marketing in general is to influence people to purchase a certain product or a service. However, marketing and its tools can also be used to influence people to change their behavior or engage in a completely new activity. A branch of commercial marketing that applies marketing concepts to issues that are important for societies is called **social marketing** (Sheau-Ting et al., 2013). In the case of IES, including products, services, and desired behaviors, the social marketing approach is especially important. The potential of social marketing in promoting energy transition, instead of selling goods and services, is focused on changing behavior to increase the well-being of households and communities (Kotler et al., 2016; Peattie and Peattie, 2016). For example, in the case of energy efficiency, the social marketing approach is usually associated with reducing consumption and decreasing demand for unsustainable energy sources.

Kotler et al. (2016) define social marketing as the use of marketing principles and techniques to influence a target audience to voluntarily accept, reject, modify, or abandon a behavior for the benefit of individuals, groups, or society as a whole (Kotler et al., 2016).

According to Kotler et al. (2016), a social marketing strategy consists of five major steps, as shown in Fig. 6.4:

1. selecting a given behavior that has to be changed or implemented;

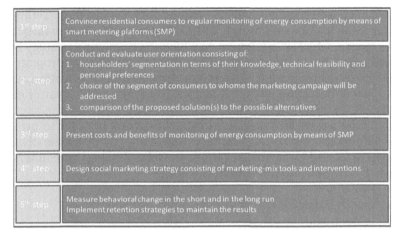

1st step	Convince residential consumers to regular monitoring of energy consumption by means of smart metering plaforms (SMP)
2nd step	Conduct and evaluate user orientation consisting of: 1. householders' segmentation in terms of their knowledge, technical feasibility and personal preferences 2. choice of the segment of consumers to whome the marketing campaign will be addressed 3. comparison of the proposed solution(s) to the possible alternatives
3rd step	Present costs and benefits of monitoring of energy consumption by means of SMP
4th step	Design social marketing strategy consisting of marketing-mix tools and interventions
5th step	Measure behavioral change in the short and in the long run Implement retention strategies to maintain the results

Figure 6.4. An example of five steps in social marketing implemented for energy monitoring behavior (based on Kotler et al., 2016; Giorgi et al., 2016; Smaliukiene and Monni, 2019).

2. evaluating users' orientation:
   - conducting users' segmentation,
   - targeting the audience,
   - positioning against competing alternatives;
3. evaluating the exchange between the costs and benefits;
4. preparing marketing mix and interventions; and
5. measuring behavioral change in the short run and long run.

Designing of social marketing should start with a **selection of behavior** that is supposed to be either introduced or changed, such as in the example provided in Fig. 6.4. In the next step, the **user orientation** must be evaluated. This is a fundamental step in social marketing design, fully based on marketing research, where all of the marketing activities are focused on the needs and wants of individuals that may relate to a selected behavior. Designing of a marketing strategy and decisions must be preceded with consumers' segmentation—that is, division of consumers based on the chosen criteria. Typically, segmentation is carried out based on the demographic characteristics, such as age, gender, or education. However, in the case of IES, psychological and environmental factors of the energy users' behavior responsible for their attitudes and lifestyles are also taken into account (Smaliukiene and Monni, 2019).

Segmentation is based on an in-depth understanding that it is impossible to be effective across all the population, as people are different. Therefore, before designing a proper marketing campaign, the population must be segmented into groups, from which chosen segments will be targeted with the social marketing mix (Smaliukiene and Monni, 2019; Thøgersen, 2017). The **target audience**, which is a segment to which the marketing strategy is dedicated, has to be large enough to make the marketing program effective. Each segment of the target audience may need different, adjusted marketing tools and actions (e.g., messages) (Bruwer et al., 2017; Kotler et al., 2016).

There are various ways to divide consumers in order to propose accurate marketing strategies for them. Following the division proposed by David Trevithick, in Delta-EE blog[2] consumers can be divided into three main categories:

- prosumers;
- energy engaged; and
- mainstream.

The first group—prosumers—is still the smallest, but constantly increasing. Consumers who belong to this group invest in energy technologies such as solar PVs, heat pumps, or home energy management systems, in order to lower their electricity bills and increase their energy independence from the energy supplier. Most prosumers are aware of the need for an energy transition and are in favor of it. Prosumers' needs are centered around self-sufficiency, energy optimization, and return on investment, but they are also willing participants in a greener energy future for all, and will collaborate as partners in these wider aims. They have also found reminders to be the key strategy in marketing energy conservation behavior.

The second segment of consumers—energy engaged—has varying degrees of understanding of their energy options and how their behavior impacts carbon emissions, but they are motivated to do more if equipped with the right knowledge and tools. This group represents the link between the early adopters and the mass market. Delivering compelling propositions to this group indicates potential to scale up as engagement levels among the mainstream increase.

Finally, the mainstream, or mass market, is characterized by having generally low levels of engagement around home energy. Some of them may have the desire to make a difference, but subconsciously they prioritize self-interest such as comfort and convenience over energy reduction or load shifting. Some are strongly motivated on some facets of climate change like recycling or meat consumption, yet do not yet have the understanding around energy consumption to take positive action. Engaging this mainstream audience is a major challenge. Data and facts, while work-

[2]https://www.delta-ee.com/blog/engaging-different-customers-in-the-energy-transition/ (accessed September 12, 2022).

ing well for more engaged consumers, are not so well suited to influence the mass market. Instead, building familiarity with social norms and acceptance of behavior change tools such as energy insights are needed using softer techniques like simplicity, visualization, and intuitiveness.

Positioning, as the next step of social marketing, deals with methods to overcome the barriers for the new behavior adjusted to different segments of customers (Ben and Steemers, 2018). Additionally, Giorgi et al. (2016) suggest that the positioning statement has to provide real examples that show how others are doing and what additional value the given behavioral change can bring. Once this statement is developed, specific strategies as to how position new demanded behavior are developed and implemented in the stage of the marketing mix.

In a further step, the pros and cons of a suggested behavior should be pointed out. The consumers must understand the value of their behavioral change. Otherwise they will refuse to introduce or change this behavior. According to exchange theory, social marketing has to offer users benefits in exchange for their behavioral change, which is usually associated with some financial or nonfinancial costs. Giorgi et al. (2016) point out that firstly users agree to change their behavior, for example, toward something more efficient or sustainable, in exchange for lower cost, greater convenience, and lifestyle choice. Secondly, within the marketing strategy other alternatives should be evaluated in order to decide how to motivate users to change their behavior and what should be offered as a value in exchange (Giorgi et al., 2016). However, it must be remembered that the meaning of value is different dependent on the segment of consumers (e.g., self-interest, social norms, or concern for the common good) (Giorgi et al., 2016).

Giorgi et al. (2016) provided a comprehensive list of proposals how to offer value to a different target audience based on their attitudes, values, and preferences. Social marketing is distinguished by its individual approach to the customers, who may have different perceptions of values of IES. For some of them, economic benefits are the most important. Thus, for this segment of customers, cutting energy bills or minimizing energy poverty is satisfactory enough to engage in a given behavior. For others, increasing energy security, acting in accordance with social norms, or fighting climate change matter most. In addition, the type of personality should be taken into account. As Giorgi et al. (2016) revealed, for environmentalists specific measures helping to incorporate changes into their lifestyles can work, while for uninterested customers, cost savings may prove to be the most effective stimuli for their behavioral change. Despite different attitudes and preferences among consumers, research results show that all segments are more willing to participate in exchange when its value is clear (Ramos et al., 2015; Korsakienė et al., 2014). Hence, a proper marketing strategy should be implemented with an integrative approach and activities should not be limited to persuasive communication only (Kotler et al., 2016). The social marketing mix will be discussed in the next section.

In the last step, the **continuous evaluation of the effectiveness of marketing strategy** is recommended in order to control the progress of the behavioral change (Smaliukiene and Monni, 2019). Since social marketing is often a continuing activity that runs over long periods of time, it is not easy to do this. At this stage, some retention strategies should be used to overcome the potential rejection of the new behavior. In particular, impact evaluation, which deals with user-specific information collected through surveys, interviews, consumer panels, opinion polls, feedback from program participants, actual evaluation, and the cost-effectiveness of the program, is important, but it is also difficult to perform. In such a case, measurable objectives as a part of social marketing activities can help to evaluate the behavioral change (Smaliukiene and Monni, 2019).

Marketing management refers to the management of the marketing mix, after analyzing opportunities, selecting target markets (that encompass the largest opportunity), and positioning (Mengaki, 2012). Marketing management additionally requires the use of market analysis (product life-cycle), market competition, distribution networks, economic evaluation, and adaptability. A marketing mix is a method that seeks to create an internally consistent action plan with cooperation between its component parts (Mengaki, 2012).

6.4.2 Traditional and social marketing mix

The marketing mix is the core concept in each marketing program explaining the summary of tools included. The commercial marketing mix consists typically of either **4P (product, price, place, and promotion)**, **5P (product, price, promotion, place, and people)**, or **7P (people, product, price, promotion, place, positioning, and packaging)** (Lovelock et al., 2015).

Traditional marketing tools for IES include first of all **product/service and its price**, on which the willingness of adoption may depend, **promotion activities** that communicate the innovation to potential customers, and place, referring to **distribution channels** via which the product/service is marketed. In the case of price, typical marketing strategies enhancing diffusion of new products include discounts (Cantono and Silverberg, 2009) and purchase bonuses (Rixen and Weigand, 2014). Sometimes giving away a limited number of products for free may also be more beneficial than if discounts or rebates are offered. This approach has proven to be particularly promising when compared to discounts (Zhang et al., 2015).

Regarding product promotion, advertising and social marketing have repeatedly been found to be successful at supporting product diffusion (Eagle et al., 2017; Sheau-Ting et al., 2013; Smaliukiene and Monni, 2019). In the case of innovations, spreading information about the product/service in a social network has a fundamental impact on the success of diffusion. The presence of the product/service in the collective consciousness raises overall awareness. Here, "opinion leaders" play a particularly important role in spreading innovations (Rogers, 2003). Opinion leaders are people who are considered to be relatively highly innovative (i.e., they adopt innovations earlier) and who also can influence a large number of their peers (Kiesling et al., 2012).

Finally, distribution channels allow the product/service to be made accessible at different places and in different ways, which can significantly influence which consumer group is exposed to it the most (Smaliukiene and Monni, 2019; Zhang et al., 2015). Several simulation studies have shown this to be a way to support product diffusion. As mentioned by Zhang et al. (2015), a variety of placement is commonly operationalized as varying the social group targeted by a marketing campaign.

Social marketing, as an approach dedicated to the marketing of the behavioral changes contains eight elements: product/service, price, place, promotion, public, partnership, policy, and purse strings (Peattie and Peattie, 2016, 2009; Sheau-Ting et al., 2013). Additionally, it includes "post-purchase maintenance," which refers to the actions aiming to keep the consumer engaged and satisfied with a given product/service or behavior (Sheau-Ting et al., 2013). Each attribute of the mix is associated with a list of strategies. Since social marketing seeks to influence social behavior and benefit the entire society, and not only the marketer, it is a useful tool for state agencies and organizations, rather than for commercial utilities which tend to use commercial marketing tools (Mengaki, 2012).

Table 6.1 presents a comparison between traditional (commercial) and social marketing mix elements.

According to Smaliukiene and Monni (2019), the social **marketing mix for energy transition** can also be presented as a group of six interrelated elements, including:

Table 6.1 A comparison between the elements of the commercial and social marketing mixes (based on Eagle et al., 2017, Mengaki, 2012, Peattie and Peattie, 2009, and Peattie and Peattie, 2016).

Element of the marketing mix	Commercial marketing 7P's	Social marketing 8P's
Product/service	Variety, quality, design, features, brand name, packaging, size, service, warranties and returns	Attributes of the selected behavior
Price	List price, discounts, allowances, payment period, credit terms	Cost of involvement in terms of time, effort, discomfort and psychological barriers
Place	Distribution channels, locations, inventory, transport	Product accessibility Communication channels to reach consumers
Promotion	Sales promotion, advertising, public relations, direct marketing, social media	Social communication to build trust and outreach via social media, local press, banners, etc.
People	Participants, staff, customers to customers co-creation	
Publics		Target & secondary audience, social networking Participation of citizens, word-of-mouth communication, endorsement of celebrities
Partnership		Engagement of local key stakeholders
Physical evidence	Service environment and evidence	
Process	Process design, self-service technologies, online service provision	
Policy		Legislation framework, access to information
Performance	Achievement of the measurable results aligned with the financial and strategic objectives	Funding from subsidies, donations

1. proposition for exchange and rewards after the behavior is established;
2. cost of changing behavior (financial and nonfinancial);
3. accessibility and the channels through which consumers are reached for information;
4. social two-way communication that includes all means for building up confidence and trust;
5. communities that are involved in cocreation, social networking, and other kinds of participation that foster behavioral changes in society at large and each household individually; and
6. public-private partnership in providing and communicating value.

The basic element of the marketing mix is **product or service** itself. IES include a broad variety of products/services that were discussed in Chapter 2. Most of them, such as dynamic electricity tariffs, are still unknown for the majority of customers, so they must be promoted with caution, like every innovation. Others, such as PV solar panels or other small-scale generators, are recently quite common among residential households, but the technology is developing rapidly and new offers will appear. Finally, the new or adjusted energy-efficient behaviors that are usually associated with IES should be introduced and promoted within the social marketing approach.

The second essential element of the marketing mix is **price**. This is the financial cost associated with the purchase of the product or the service (e.g., small-scale generator) that the consumer pays. For typical products or services, the market price corresponds to the market equilibrium between demand and supply and is associated with the cost of production. In the social marketing context, price is "the cost that the target market associates with adopting the new behavior" (Kotler et al., 2016). The product in social marketing does not entail any cost of production. It rather involves an implicit cost to perform energy conservation behavior. Price sometimes is associated with the nonfinancial cost that the consumer must bear while adopting a new product, service, or behavior. This can be discomfort of usage, change of habits, or a necessity to share private data.

Another element of the marketing mix important in the social marketing approach is **place**. This is defined as "where and when the target market will perform the desired behavior, acquire any related tangible objects, and receive any associated services" (Kotler et al., 2016). The decisions of whether to perform the behavior, where to perform it, and whether to perform it frequently or infrequently are made by the energy users (Giorgi et al., 2016).

For this element of the marketing mix, two strategies matter: provision of the right distribution channel giving the consumers access to the necessary information about energy conservation, and dissemination of information to increase awareness and knowledge about the desired behavior (Abrahamse and Steg, 2009). Convenience in obtaining information about energy conservation indicates accessibility to information, which is the point that consumers may access information easily and comfortably with little effort and time. The more easily accessible a product is, the more likely it is that a transaction will take place. To induce behavioral change, it's crucial to disseminate relevant data in the right places and create an environment that supports the adoption of energy-saving behaviors (Giorgi et al., 2016).

Promotion resembles its commercial marketing equivalent the most. Promotion is described in the context of social marketing, as "persuasive communications designed and delivered to inspire your target audience to action" (Kotler et al., 2016). In addition to being carried out through multiple communication channels, promotion may also include providing incentives, increasing the attractiveness of the desired action, and indexing incentives (Giorgi et al., 2016). Here, through a variety of communication channels, the choice of the most effective communication channels and the provision of motivation that encourages the purchase of the energy conservation behavior play the most significant roles. Numerous communication channels have been used in various social marketing interventions aimed at fostering the desired behavioral change, such as websites, printed materials, special events, and other promotional channels.

Finally, **postpurchase maintenance** is proposed as the new attribute in the social marketing mix included specifically to foster energy conservation behavior. This element of the marketing mix includes activities performed after the energy conservation behavior has been adopted. Its purpose is to maintain and retain changes that have been made by students to achieve a sustainable energy conservation behavior change. The idea of behavior "maintenance" is derived from the stages of change in the transtheoretical model by Prochaska and Diclemente (1982). A change that only lasts during the intervention period is insufficient. A sustained change is required for a sustainable energy future. Three strategies can be proposed in relation to this element: executing reinforcement, providing feedback, and providing reminders. The third point is particularly crucial because it calls for frequent reminders and memory aids in order to preserve the adoption of the desired behavior of energy conservation. Reminders help users recall to perform practices that they would otherwise forget to complete. Reminders are crucial for reminding the user of knowledge that they already have.

6.4.3 Examples of new business models

Due to rapid growth of innovative energy services that require adoption not only of new products and services but also of behaviors, key market stakeholders such as energy suppliers, energy utilities, and all market players responsible for the supply chain may design and offer new business models, adjusted to the evolving conditions. The introduction of new business models is usually provoked by the lack of certain solutions and the need to enable customers' smooth adoption. Future business models will emerge also due to the increased penetration of active customers in all sectors of the economy: on-site generation, storage, digitalization, and home automation appliances, electromobility, or zero-emission buildings. The presence of innovative energy services in the energy market provokes the appearance of additional valuable services to the electricity grids, setting the stage for the uptake of new services for energy supply and aggregation.

A good example of a new business model is the deployment of energy storage for residential households. A few new energy storage-focused business models are as follows:

- ReVolta offers companies and individuals hardware and software to give discarded batteries from electric cars a new future.
- Skoon created a battery-sharing platform on its online marketplace called "Skoon Sharing." They also launched "Skoon Suite," a rental management software tool, especially designed to manage a fleet of mobile energy assets.
- Clean Energy Global enables Business-to-Business (B2B) customers to offer Battery-as-a-Service, a white label-integrating smart energy storage in a secure cloud.

Next, the markets offer **Anything as a Service (XaaS)**; this refers to the delivery of a service without the need to buy or monitor the assets. Various XaaS models exist in the energy market, such as Energy Savings as a Service (ESaaS), Lighting as a Service (LaaS), and Heating as a Service (HaaS). Some other interesting examples of new XaaS business models are as follows:

- Signify (Philips) offers LaaS to B2B retail customers which can save up to 70% of the initial energy cost.
- Engie has been expanding its EaaS service offering commercial storage with Green Charge Networks, electric vehicle charging network EVBox, solar developer SoCore Energy, and energy services company Ecova.
- Fluvius launched the initiative "Fluvius Sustainable Buildings": a full package of energy services (prefinancing, study phase,

implementation, and energy monitoring) to promote energy efficiency in municipal housing.

- Sustainable Led Light provides cost-effective sustainable solutions for the light industry based on the LaaS principle.
- Viessman is testing HaaS, where it takes over control and maintenance of the heating systems of consumers.
- Enel X offers integrated EaaS solutions such as Power Purchase Agreements (PPAs), on- and off-site energy supply technologies, and demand response services.

Energy as a service (EaaS) is a business model in which customers pay for an energy service without having to make any upfront capital investment into solar panels, heating, or lights for example. This business model could prove to be valuable in better aligning customer incentives with operational constraints of the energy grid. The EaaS model could assist the integration of renewables, help activate demand-side management, and encourage electrification.

Some other examples of new data business models and technologies are as follows:

- ORES uses Siemens' open Internet of Things (IoT) platform MindSphere for its E-Cloud project. ORES will be able to collect and process data from local electricity needs, so the renewable energy production flows in real time.
- ENGIE has tested Vertuoz Pilot, which is a system for optimizing energy consumption that lets you balance the comfort of a building's occupants with greater energy savings.
- Elia has launched various consumer-centric test projects. For example, Flexity enables the end-consumer to contribute to the energy transition by enabling asset and valorizing flexibility.
- June Energy looks for the best market prices and switches consumers automatically between energy suppliers, based on their personal energy consumption.
- IO.Energy is a communication platform created by Elia, Lumminus, Enervalis, Fluvius, and Scholt Energy. This platform aims to demonstrate that prosumers (producers and consumers) can gain from their flexibility by optimizing it against a real-time price.

Each of these given innovation examples offers a perspective on both new opportunities and challenges on a given business level. Examples of innovative solutions adjusted to the identified challenges are shown in Fig. 6.5.

In addition to the development of new business models, the energy transition induces the deployment of new market structures and appearance of new stakeholders (Immonen et al., 2020).

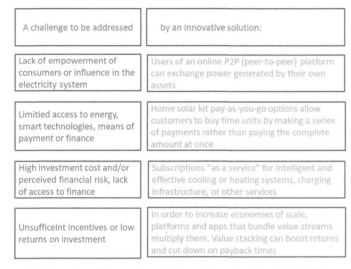

Figure 6.5. Examples of innovation solutions adjusted to identified challenges among energy end-users (from https://www.stretchinnovation.be/insight/innovative-business-models-transforming-energy-market).

First of all, it is necessary to support more real-time operation of the energy market in order to cope with high penetration of renewable energy sources. Locality will be a significant factor in the market. For instance, local markets, could be used to enhance the functioning of distribution networks, allowing distribution system operators (DSOs) to purchase flexibility to avoid overloads. Peer-to-peer (P2P) energy trading in regional energy communities or microgrids is another use for local markets. The rise of regional and decentralized markets will make the economy as a whole more complex. Thus, it will be crucial to have open communication between the various markets and sectors in order to find solutions that are globally optimal. Customers will be encouraged to avoid peak loads, for instance, through power-base network tariffing schemes. This would open up new business opportunities for companies such as retailers and energy utility providers to offer these services to consumers (Immonen et al., 2020). The energy sector's transition will also open up new economic opportunities, resulting in the creation of new stakeholders and adjustments to the responsibilities of current stakeholders. Aggregators, operators of virtual power plants, and providers of technical services, for instance, are likely to play significant roles in future energy markets (Immonen et al., 2020).

A good example of the need of creating new solutions in terms of business models and network topologies is represented by the establishment of energy communities (Coenen and Hoppe, 2022). The division of electricity market designs for active end-users and their possible business models has been proposed by Neska and Kowalska-Pyzalska (2022) as follows:

- Off-grid solutions, meaning standalone, energy self-sufficient buildings that produce, store, and consume energy autonomously. Typically, this solution is intended for prosumers who are in remote areas or can afford to be technically and economically energy independent. It is assumed that they are neither part of any energy community nor active energy market members.
- On-grid solutions applies to all possible market models, in which prosumers are connected to the power grid and can be subdivided into: (1) modern distribution electricity network, where consumers can be organized in a different way, such as energy cooperatives, community prosumerism, third-party-sponsored community, or community energy services company; (2) centralized aggregator models including community prosumerism, local energy market, and community flexibility aggregation; and (3) hybrid models that propose an approach between decentralized and centralized topology and its business models (Neska and Kowalska-Pyzalska, 2022; Reis et al., 2021; Koirala et al., 2018, 2016).

Undoubtedly, within the ongoing digitization and development of emerging technologies such as blockchain, usage of artificial intelligence, and many others, modern business models will require the management of big data. It is already anticipated that the big data analytics market specifically in the energy sector will grow at a compound annual growth rate (CAGR) of 11.28% according to Mordor Intelligence. Additionally, innovative technologies, processes, and capabilities will allow closer customer interactions, and using the available grid data or customer data drives insights to act in real time (Immonen et al., 2020). As a result, we can expect that the future will bring many new solutions based on the flexible management of demand and supply in the energy market.

6.5 Summary: how to convince residential consumers to switch to IES?

The consumer's position will become more important in the coming energy market. Nevertheless, some mechanism of directing and assisting consumers and their actions in the market is necessary because the vast majority of customers are not energy market actors and are unfamiliar with the market. Overcoming the

> How to achieve a critical mass of residential consumers necessary to boost the diffusion of IES?

> INCREASE AWARENESS & UNDERSTANDING
> • Design a proper feedback system
> • Display information in an easy and clear way to reduce confusion

> LIMIT DISTRUST AND FEAR OF CHANGE
> • Reduce perceived difficulty of adoption by emphasizing all potential benefits on societal and personal levels
> • Provide consumers with information about data protection arrangments

> PROVOKE POSITIVE WORD-OF-MOUTH
> • Convince satisfied consumers to share the information with their peers
> • Advertise in traditional and social media
> • Use tailored marketing strategies
> • Create strong social norms

Figure 6.6. Summary of the actions to be taken to overcome the current barriers to IES adoption.

consumers' **lack of knowledge** and **prior experiences**, as Immonen et al. (2020) rightly point out, would be an important role of the **aggregator** or subaggregator that represents the consumers in the market. A change in the market structure is required to enable the benefits of demand flexibility to be shared by all participating actors. Currently, delaying or otherwise moving the time of consumption is not profitable, because taxes and transmission costs are no cheaper at any other time, only the energy itself may be marginally cheaper. In order to gradually encourage consumers to become active participants in the energy market, actors in the energy sector should address these unresolved concerns, better inform consumers about demand flexibility and their own goals, and emphasize the role and benefits of consumers.

6.5.1 Policy recommendations

For now, in order to overcome the barriers of adoption and to strengthen the incentives and hence to increase the adoption rates of IES following three steps should be fulfilled: (1) increase of awareness; (2) reduction of perceived difficulty of adoption; and (3) encouragement of positive word of mouth, as presented in Fig. 6.6.

It is crucial to start by spreading information through every available means of communication (including social media, public events, and friend referral programs). Rising awareness can be achieved by the following:

• Information should be displayed in an easy and clear way to reduce confusion.

- A good feedback system for the users and suppliers is needed. Such a feedback system could play a motivational role, informing whether, e.g., after signing to a dynamic pricing program consumers' energy efficiency has increased or not or how well they are doing in comparison to their neighbors, etc.
- Energy providers must to make it possible for customers to track and analyze their own electricity usage in real time. Smart meters and smart metering information systems can be utilized as a release mechanism for self-regulatory steps to lower residential electricity use and expenses.

Secondly, designers of IES should concentrate not only on access to information and assistance, but also on convenience of usage and presenting advantages of the services, in order to lessen perceived difficulty of adoption, such as fear of change, distrust, and general uninterest:

- Since the majority of IES do not offer quick payback times, high savings rates, or significant earnings, it is crucial to stress all other potential social and individual benefits.
- Innovative service designers should be concerned with educating consumers and instructing them on how to effectively utilize modern IES. Additionally, consumers could be provided with complimentary product trials (like in-home displays).
- In the case of dynamic pricing programs, consumers may be more eager to adopt them if enabling technologies (allowing automatization and optimization of electricity consumption) are bundled with electricity services.
- It should be quick and simple to join up while choosing green or dynamic tariffs.
- To increase trust, suppliers should consider influencing customer perceptions of the appropriateness of data protection measures. Customers care about the security of private data. Suppliers of smart metering systems should take care to provide customers with information on data protection arrangements, as well as combine introduction of smart meters with dynamic pricing schemes.

Finally, positive word of mouth (e.g., recommendations from friends and neighbors who have already adopted it) and confident information from mass media would also be helpful. To boost adoption rates, creating strong social norms and critical mass, that is the minimal number of adopters for the further rate of adoption to be self-sustaining, is needed. As a whole, a thorough prior identification of the behavior causing variables and barriers, followed by the employment of a combination of the most effective strategies, boosts the intervention's effectiveness (Sopha and Kloeckner, 2016; Gans et al., 2013). Finally, interventions should be designed according to the consumers' profiles. This suggests that market segmentation is essential in proper design of interventions. Fig. 6.6 summarizes the main steps that must be taken to overcome the reluctance of residential consumers to adopt IES.

Moreover, following the observations by Immonen et al. (2020), to overcome the barriers and obstacles to the smoother diffusion of IES, various rationalization and management issues should be raised, such as:

- better transparency between energy utilities, aggregators, and other energy market players;
- the market structure should enable competition wherever it is possible to disrupt the monopolistic practices among DSOs. In particular, competition between different electricity sellers and transparency of electricity pricing is required to allow customers to choose the best possible seller that represents their values;
- a regulated system is required for selling self-produced solar power to neighbors, and to make the acquisition of solar PV panels profitable, thus also supporting the fight against climate change;
- new charging model is needed as charging according to peak power should be rationalized so that it has minimal impact on the daily life of the consumer. In addition, it should be equal for all consumers;
- to ensure customers' safety and privacy, data management and trade should be a certified procedure, and consumer privacy should be regulated in terms of data collecting via various types of smart devices; and
- consumer participation efforts to rationalize their electricity consumption should be supported by the government in the form of tax reliefs, for example.

6.5.2 IES as a cure for the global crisis

A global crisis, including the COVID-19 pandemic and the outbreak of war in Ukraine, has occurred simultaneously with opportunities (Jiang et al., 2021). It reshapes the original, prepandemic business models, education systems, and lifestyles, accelerating the growth of digitalization in all these areas (Schwarz et al., 2020), as well as the need to increase energy independence and replace fossil fuels with renewable energy.

In the case of the pandemic, empirical evidence has revealed that COVID-19 had an impact on shifting electricity consumption, but the final outcome was rather ambiguous and highly dependent on user behaviors as well as energy efficiency at a place (home or office). Jiang et al. (2021) pointed out that there is still a lack of studies including social factors in the assessment to prove that teleworking and e-learning are better than centralized office and schools in terms of energy efficiency. On the other hand, it is clear that the lockdowns and remote ways of working and learning have led to reductions of energy consumption in commuting and transportation. However, there is still some uncertainty regarding whether the potential increase in nonwork travel and home energy use outweighs the gains from reduced commuting or not (Hook et al., 2020; Jiang et al., 2021). There are authors, such as O'Brien and Aliabadi (2020), who suggest that the rebound effect of tele-work actually tends to offset and even exceed energy savings significantly. As a result, the overall effect on energy consumption due to changes in lifestyles and daily routines of the residential consumers depends on several factors, such as: (1) the difference in energy efficiency of lighting, cooling, and heating system of home versus office; (2) occupancy level (how many people occupies a room while tele-working or e-learning); (3) duration of usage of the electronic devices, e.g., computers; and (4) commuting distances—if it is a so-called "15 min city," the energy consumption is less significant (Jiang et al., 2021).

Even though it is still difficult to predict with certainty how the recent geopolitical changes will impact electricity consumers' behavior, at least some IES have significant potential to develop due to the turmoil in the energy market. For example, as Bielecki et al. (2021) emphasized, the pressure to work and educate remotely should contribute to an increase in the digital competence of society, which may result in an increased interest in new forms of activity and cooperation based on demand-response and prosumption mechanisms, with digital settlements for energy and service exchanges. In the case of consumers' readiness to become prosumers, the literature states that this depends on a variety of factors, including government policies and consumer attitudes. However, there are a few reasons why some residential consumers may now, in the postpandemic period, be more willing to become prosumers in the aftermath of the military conflict. The most significant reasons include the following:

- Energy security: The conflict in Ukraine has highlighted the importance of energy security, particularly for countries that rely heavily on imports of natural gas. Becoming a prosumer, such as by installing solar panels or other renewable energy sources, can help to reduce a household's reliance on external sources of energy. In other words, consumers become more aware of the benefits of reducing their reliance on external sources of energy.

- Environmental concerns: The war may increase awareness of the importance of reducing greenhouse gas emissions and promoting renewable energy. Some consumers may be motivated to become prosumers in order to reduce their carbon footprint and contribute to a more sustainable energy system.
- Government incentives: Some governments may introduce incentives to encourage consumers to become prosumers, such as tax breaks or subsidies for renewable energy installations. The military conflict in Eastern Europe may increase governments' focus on energy security and sustainability, which could lead to more favorable policies for prosumers.
- Cost savings: Becoming a prosumer can also help to reduce energy costs over the long term, particularly as the cost of renewable energy technologies continues to decrease. This may be particularly appealing to consumers who are concerned about the economic impact of the war in Ukraine.

Next, it is probable that the observed rising tendency of electricity prices can have a significant impact on demand-side management (DSM) and demand response (DR) programs. As mentioned in Chapter 2, DSM refers to efforts to manage electricity demand by shifting consumption to off-peak periods, reducing overall consumption, and increasing the efficiency of energy use. DR programs, on the other hand, involve incentivizing consumers to reduce their electricity usage during periods of high demand or grid instability.

When electricity prices increase, consumers are likely to become more conscious of their energy usage and seek ways to reduce their consumption. Higher electricity prices can lead to greater investment in energy-efficient technologies and renewable energy sources. This is because consumers and businesses may be more motivated to reduce their reliance on expensive, non-renewable energy sources and shift towards more cost-effective and sustainable alternatives. In result, we can observe the increase in participation in DSM/DR programs, as consumers may be more willing to change their energy consumption habits in order to avoid high electricity bills. In addition, higher electricity prices can also increase the financial benefits of participating in DSM/DR programs. For example, if the price of electricity during peak periods is significantly higher than during off-peak periods, consumers may be more motivated to shift their energy usage to off-peak hours or reduce overall consumption during peak periods in order to save money.

However, it is important to note that the impact of electricity prices on DSM/DR programs will depend on a variety of factors, including the design of the programs, the level of consumer education and awareness, and the availability of alternative energy sources. Additionally, some consumers may not have the ability to shift their energy usage or reduce consumption due to the nature of their jobs or other factors, which could limit the effectiveness of DSM/DR programs.

6.5.3 Companies and innovative energy services

Overall, the energy market presents a number of challenges, but there are a variety of marketing strategies and business models that can be used to overcome these challenges and offer consumers sustainable and cost-effective energy solutions. We will first discuss the possible business models that make usage of IES, such as the following:

- Energy efficiency solutions offered to consumers and businesses: This can include energy audits, insulation and weatherization services, and energy-efficient appliances and lighting. Businesses can also offer energy management services that use data analytics to help consumers identify opportunities for energy savings.
- Renewable energy solutions, such as solar or wind power offered to individual residential consumers: This can include the installation and maintenance of renewable energy systems, as well as the sale of renewable energy credits to businesses and individuals.
- Demand response and energy storage: Businesses can also offer demand response and energy storage services to help consumers manage their energy usage and reduce peak demand. This can include the installation of smart home systems and the sale of battery storage solutions.
- Green marketing techniques: These can be used to appeal to environmentally-conscious consumers. This can include promoting the use of renewable energy sources, reducing carbon emissions, and offering sustainable products and services.
- Finally, some businesses are moving toward subscription-based models, where consumers pay a monthly fee for access to renewable energy or energy-efficient products and services. This can provide consumers with predictable costs and encourage them to adopt more sustainable energy practices.

As discussed earlier, there are also several marketing tools that can be used to encourage consumers to become more active in the energy market, including the following:

- Education and awareness campaigns belong to the most important tools for encouraging consumer participation in the energy market. Businesses can offer information and resources to help consumers better understand the energy market and their options for participating in it.

- Personalized messaging can help to make energy-related information more relevant and engaging to individual consumers. By tailoring marketing messages to consumers' specific needs and preferences, businesses can increase the likelihood that they will take action.
- Providing incentives, such as discounts or rebates, can be a powerful motivator for consumer behavior. For example, businesses can offer discounts on energy-efficient products or services to encourage consumers to adopt more sustainable energy practices.
- Gamification can be used to make energy-related activities more fun and engaging for consumers. For example, businesses can develop apps or online games that encourage users to reduce their energy usage or switch to renewable energy sources.
- Social media can be a powerful tool for raising awareness and engaging consumers in the energy market. Businesses can use social media platforms to share information about energy-related events, news, and initiatives, as well as to communicate directly with consumers, and many others.

By using a combination of education, personalized messaging, incentives, gamification, and social media, businesses can encourage consumers to become more active in the energy market and adopt more sustainable energy practices.

At the same time, marketing of innovative products and services allows enterprises to keep up with changes in the market, and even to overtake them and create them. It is also an important tool for building a competitive advantage and the company's image on the outside. From the point of view of the welfare economics, innovations in the energy market can contribute to the growth of social well-being by improving the functioning of the power system, improving the security and reliability of energy supply, increasing technical, economic, and environmental efficiency. Introducing innovative products and services on the energy market is therefore a driving force for the development of both enterprises and the entire economy.

6.5.4 Take-home messages and final remarks

In this book, the following innovations in the energy market have been included:

- small generation installations based on renewable energy sources (RES), popular among households and in the sector of small and medium-sized enterprises (SMEs), e.g., photovoltaic panels, small wind farms, and heat pumps. By installing such devices, the owner becomes a prosumer or an entity that simultaneously produces and consumes electricity;

- green electricity tariffs and programs offered by energy sellers/suppliers, characterized in that part or all of the energy offered comes from RES;
- demand-side management and demand response (DSM/DR) tools, in particular the so-called dynamic electricity tariffs, for which the price of electricity varies depending on its price on the wholesale market (on the energy exchange) or in specific, predetermined time intervals, and incentive programs, at which companies from the SME sector may decide, for example, on participation in power reduction programs on demand of the transmission system operator; and
- information systems related to smart energy meters (SM platforms), including various types of smart plugs, devices and applications for easier and/or automated monitoring and management of end-user energy consumption.

These innovations represent examples of innovative products, processes, and marketing strategies, as well as innovative systems of energy management. In addition, by leveraging IoT technologies, it is possible to create more sustainable and cost-effective energy systems that benefit both consumers and the environment. In other words, IoT has the potential to revolutionize the energy industry by enabling more efficient and effective delivery of innovative energy services. The most significant IoT technologies that can influence the diffusion of IES include the following:

- Smart grids, which use sensors and monitoring devices to detect faults and adjust energy flows in real-time. This helps to reduce the occurrence of blackouts and other disruptions, and also enables the integration of renewable energy sources into the grid.
- Energy management systems (EMS), where IoT can be used to optimize the use of energy in homes and businesses, to monitor energy consumption, control heating and cooling systems, and adjust lighting levels. By using IoT technologies, EMS can be automatically adjusted based on real-time data, making them more efficient and reducing energy waste.
- Smart appliances and smart devices make usage of IoT. For example, a smart refrigerator can adjust its temperature based on the amount of food inside, reducing energy consumption when the fridge is not full. Similarly, smart thermostats can learn the preferences of homeowners and adjust heating and cooling settings accordingly.

- Energy storage systems, such as batteries, use IoT to optimize their consumption of energy. By using IoT technologies, these systems can be automatically charged and discharged based on energy demand, reducing the need for expensive peak power generation.

Looking optimistically into the future, we can expect further rapid development of technologies and digitization, and thus (1) improvement of current IES solutions and (2) the emergence of new ones that will be even better suited to the needs of consumers; at the same time, this will enable energy market operators to manage demand effectively and follow the lead of distributed renewable energy sources. In the future, the user-centric approach, involving the identification of consumers' needs and a focus on putting users at the center of a product or a service design and its development, will probably also be applied in the energy market. Hence, the usage of design thinking approach while creating new IES or adjusting the existing ones may prove to be the solution of the future, commonly used by businesses.

6.6 References and proposed additional readings

Behavioral interventions:
- Abrahamse and Steg (2013) Social influence approaches to encourage resource conservation: a meta-analysis. Global Environ Change 23, 1773–1785 (Abrahamse and Steg, 2013)
- Buchanan et al. (2014) Feeding back about eco-feedback: how do consumers use and respond to energy monitors? Energy Policy 73, 138–146 (Buchanan et al., 2014)
- Foulds et al. (2017) Energy monitoring as a practice: investigating use of the iMeasure online energy feedback tool. Energy Policy 104, 194–402 (Foulds et al., 2017)
- Hobman and Frederiks (2014) Barriers to green electricity subscription in Australia: "love the environment, love renewable energy... but why should I pay more?" Energy Research and Social Science 3, 78–88 (Hobman and Frederiks, 2014)
- Iweka et al. (2019) Energy and behaviour at home: a review of intervention methods and practices. Research and Social Science 57, 101238 (Iweka et al., 2019)
- Kowalska-Pyzalska (2018) What makes consumers adopt to innovative energy services in the energy market? A review of incentives and barriers. Renewable and Sustainable Energy Reviews 82, 3, 3570–3581 (Kowalska-Pyzalska, 2018b)

- Lopes et al. (2012) Energy behaviors as promoters of energy efficiency: a 21st century review. Renewable and Sustainable Energy Reviews 16, 4095–4104 (Lopes et al., 2012)
- Słupik et al. (2021) How to encourage energy savings behaviours? The most effective incentives from the perspective of European consumers. Energies 14, 8009 (Słupik et al., 2021)
- Spandagos et al. (2021) Social influence and economic intervention policies to save energy at home: critical questions for the new decade and evidence from air-condition use. Renewable and Sustainable Energy Reviews 143, 11091 (Spandagos et al., 2021)
- Zhou and Yang (2016) Understanding household energy consumption behavior: the contribution of energy big data analytics. Renewable and Sustainable Energy Reviews 56, 810–819 (Zhou and Yang, 2016)

Social marketing and marketing mix:
- Ben and Steemers (2018) Household archetypes and behavioural patterns in UK domestic energy use. Energy Efficiency 11, 3, 761–771 (Ben and Steemers, 2018)
- Bruwer et al. (2017) Domain-specific market segmentation: a wine-related lifestyle (WRL) approach. Pacific Journal of Marketing and Logistics 29(1) 4–26 (Bruwer et al., 2017)
- Eagle et al. (2017) Social marketing strategies for renewable energy transitions. Australasian Marketing Journal 25(2) 141–148 (Eagle et al., 2017)
- Giorgi et al. (2016) Public Understanding of the Links between Climate Change and (i) Food and (ii) Energy Use (EV0402): Final report. A report to the Department for Environment, Food and Rural Affairs. Brook Lyndhurst. Defra, London (Giorgi et al., 2016)
- Korsakiene et al. (2014) Impact of energy prices on industrial sector development and export: Lithuania in the context of Baltic states. Procedia—Social and Behavioral Sciences, 110, 461–469 (Korsakienė et al., 2014)
- Kotler et al. (2016) Social Marketing: Improving the Quality of Life, SAGE Publications, Inc. 5th Edition (Kotler et al., 2016)
- Lovelock et al. (2015) Services Marketing: An Asia-Pacific and Australian Perspective. Frenchs Forest, N.S.W. Pearson Australia, 6th edition (Lovelock et al., 2015)
- Mengagki (2012) Social marketing mix for renewable energy in Europe based on consumer stated preferences surveys. Renewable Energy 39, 30–39 (Mengaki, 2012)
- Peattie and Peattie (2009) Social marketing: a pathway to consumption reduction? Journal of Business Research 62, 2, 260–268 (Peattie and Peattie, 2009)

- Peattie and Peattie (2016) Ready to fly solo? Reducing social marketing's dependence on commercial marketing theory. Marketing Theory 3, 3, 365–385 (Peattie and Peattie, 2016)
- Ramos et al. (2015) The role of information for energy efficiency in the residential sector. Energy Economics 52, S17–S29 (Ramos et al., 2015)
- Sheau-Ting et al. (2013) What is the optimum social marketing mix to market energy conservation behaviour: an empirical study. Journal of Environmental Management 15, 196–205 (Sheau-Ting et al., 2013)
- Smaliukiene and Monni (2019) A step-by-step approach to social marketing in energy transition. Insights into Regional Development 1, 1, 19–32 (Smaliukiene and Monni, 2019)
- Thøgersen (2017) Housing-related lifestyle and energy saving: A multi-level approach. Energy Policy 102, 73–87 (Thøgersen, 2017)
- Zhang et al. (2015) Data-driven agent-based modeling, with application to rooftop solar adoption. In Proceedings of the International Joint Conference on Autonomous Agents and Multiagent Systems, AAMAS, 513–521 (Zhang et al., 2015)

Marketing strategies:
- AlSkaif et al. (2018) Gamification based framework for engagement of residential customers in energy applications. Energy Research & Social Science 44, 187–195 (AlSkaif et al., 2018)
- Anda and Temmen (2014) Smart metering for residential energy efficiency: the use of community based social marketing for behavioural change and smart grid introduction. Renewable Energy 67, 119–127. (Anda and Temmen, 2014)
- Backhaus et al. (2011) Key Findings and Policy Recommendations to Improve Effectiveness of Energy Performance Certificates & the Energy Performance of Buildings Directive. ECN-O-11-083, 2011, Petten (Backhaus et al., 2011)
- Beck et al. (2019) Not so gameful: a critical review of gamification in mobile energy applications. Energy Research & Social Science 51, 32–39 (Beck et al., 2019)
- Brucal and Roberts (2019) Do energy efficiency standards hurt consumers? Evidence from household appliance sales. J. Environ. Econ. Manag. 96, 88–107 (Brucal and Roberts, 2019)
- Caballero and Ploner (2022) Boosting or nudging energy consumption? The importance of cognitive aspects when adopting non-monetary interventions. Energy Research & Social Science 91, 102734 (Caballero and Ploner, 2022)
- Coday et al. (2005) Strategies for retaining study participants in behavioral intervention trials: retention experiences of the NIH

Behavior Change Consortium. Ann. Behav. Med. 29(2), 55–65 (Coday et al., 2005)

- Gangale et al. (2013) Consumer engagement: an insight from smart grid projects in Europe. Energy Policy 60, 621–628 (Gangale et al., 2013)
- Gaspari et al. (2021) Energy transition at home: a survey on the data and practices that lead to a change in household energy behavior. Sustainability 13, 9 (Gaspari et al., 2021)
- Girod et al. (2017) How do policies for efficient energy use in the household sector induce energy-efficiency innovation? An evaluation of European countries. Energy Policy 103, 223–237 (Girod et al., 2017b)
- Goeltz and Hahnel (2016) What motivates people to use energy feedback systems? A multiple goal approach to predict long-term usage behaviour in daily life. Energy Research and Social Science 21, 155–166 (Gölz and Hahnel, 2016)
- Gonzalez et al. (2020) Barriers and challenges of the recommendation list of measures under the EPBD scheme: a critical review. Energy and Buildings 223, 110065 (Gonzalez-Caceres et al., 2020)
- Graffeo et al. (2015) To make people save energy tell them what others do but also who they are: a preliminary study. Frontiers in Psychology 6 (Graffeo et al., 2015)
- Gumz et al. (2022) Social influence as a major factor in smart meters' acceptance: findings from Brazil. Results in Engineering 15, 100510 (Gumz et al., 2022)
- Iwasaki (2019) Using Eco-Home Diagnosis to reduce household energy consumption: a case study on behavioral changes in Fukuoka Prefecture, Japan. Energy Policy 132, 893–900 (Iwasaki, 2019)
- Kowalska-Pyzalska and Byrka (2019) Determinants of the willingness to energy monitoring by residential consumers: a case study in the city of Wroclaw in Poland. Energies 12, 907 (Kowalska-Pyzalska and Byrka, 2019)
- Mankoff et al. (2010) StepGreen.org: increasing energy saving behaviors via social networks. Proceedings of the International AAAI Conference on Web and Social Media 106–113 (Mankoff et al., 2010)
- Martin (2020) Making sense of renewable energy: practical knowledge, sensory feedback and household understandings in a Scottish island microgrid. Energy Research and Social Science 66, 101501 (Martin, 2020)
- McMichael and Shipworth (2013) The value of social networks in the diffusion of energy-efficiency innovations in UK house-

holds. Energy Policy 53, 159–168 (McMichael and Shipworth, 2013)
- Morganti et al. (2017) Gaming for Earth: serious games and gamification to engage consumers in pro-environmental behaviours for energy efficiency. Energy Research & Social Science 29, 95–102 (Morganti et al., 2017)
- Mukai et al. (2022) What effect does feedback have on energy conservation? Comparing previous household usage, neighbourhood usage, and social norms in Japan. Energy Research & Social Science 86, 10243 (Mukai et al., 2022)
- Nolan et al. (2008) Normative social influence is underdetected. Personality and Social Psychology Bulletin 34, 913–923 (Nolan et al., 2008)
- Ozawa et al. (2017) Tailor-made feedback to reduce residential electricity consumption: the effect of information on household lifestyle in Japan. Sustainability 9, 4 (Ozawa et al., 2017)
- Rathi and Chunekar (2015) Not to buy or can be "nudged" to buy? Exploring behavioral interventions for energy policy in India. Energy Research & Social Science 7, 78–83 (Rathi and Chunekar, 2015)
- Schweiger et al. (2020) Active consumer participation in smart energy systems. Energy and Buildings 227, 110359 (Schweiger et al., 2020)
- Taylor et al. (2014) Targeting utility customers to improve energy savings from conservation and efficiency program. Appl. Energy 115, 25–36 (Taylor et al., 2014)
- Voelker et al. (2021) Watt's up at home? Smart meter data analytics from a consumer-centric perspective. Energies 14, 719 (Voelker et al., 2021)

Business models:
- Coenen and Hoppe (2022) Renewable Energy Communities and the Low Carbon Energy Transition in Europe. Palgrae MacMillian (Coenen and Hoppe, 2022)
- Immonen et al. (2021) Consumer viewpoint on a new kind of energy market. Electric Power Systems Research 180, 106153 (Immonen et al., 2020)
- Koirala et al. (2016) Energetic communities for community energy: a review of key issues and trends shaping integrated community energy systems. Renewable and Sustainable Energy Reviews 56, 722–744 (Koirala et al., 2016)
- Köppl et al. (2022) Enabling Business Models and Grid Stability: Case Studies from Germany, Energy Communities. Academic Press 229–243 (Köppl et al., 2022)
- Neska and Kowalska-Pyzalska (2022) Conceptual design of energy market topologies for communities and their practical ap-

plications in EU: a comparison of three case studies. Renewable and Sustainable Energy Reviews 169, 112921 (Neska and Kowalska-Pyzalska, 2022)

- Reis et al. (2021) Business models for energy communities: a review of key issues and trends. Renewable and Sustainable Energy Reviews 144, 111013 (Reis et al., 2021).

Bibliography

Abrahamse, W., Steg, L., 2009. How do socio-demographic and psychological factors relate to households' direct and indirect energy use and savings? Journal of Economic Psychology 30, 711–720.

Abrahamse, W., Steg, L., 2011. Factors related to household energy use and intention to reduce it: the role of psychological and socio-demographic variables. Research in Human Ecology 18, 30–40.

Abrahamse, W., Steg, L., 2013. Social influence approaches to encourage resource conservation: a meta-analysis. Global Environmental Change 23, 1773–1785. https://doi.org/10.1016/j.gloenvcha.2013.07.029.

Abrahamse, W., Steg, L., Vlek, C., Rothengatter, T., 2005. A review of intervention studies aimed at household energy conservation. Journal of Environmental Psychology 25, 273–291. https://doi.org/10.1016/j.jenvp.2005.08.002.

Acharjee, P., 2013. Strategy and implementation of smart grids in India. Energy Strategy Reviews 1, 193–204.

Adjei, A., Hamilton, L., Roys, M., 2011. A study of homeowners' energy efficiency improvements and the impact of the energy performance certificate. BRE (Building Research Establishment).

Agarwal, J., DeSarbo, W.S., Malhotra, N.K., Rao, V.R., 2015. An interdisciplinary review of research in conjoint analysis: recent developments and directions for future research. Customer Needs and Solutions 2, 19–40. https://doi.org/10.1007/s40547-014-0029-5.

Aghaei, J., Alizadeh, M., 2013. Demand response in smart electricity grids equipped with renewable energy sources: a review. Renewable and Sustainable Energy Reviews 18, 64–72.

Agora Energiewende and Ember 2021. The European Power Sector in 2020: Up-to-Date Analysis on the Electricity Transition.

Ai He, H., Greenberg, S., Huang, E., 2010. One size does not fit all: applying the transtheoretical model to energy feedback technology design. In: Conference on Human Factors in Computing Systems, CHI'10.

Ajzen, I., 1985. From intentions to actions: a theory of planned behavior. In: Kuhl, J., Beckmann, J. (Eds.), Action Control. In: SSSP Springer Series in Social Psychology. Springer, Berlin, Heidelberg.

Ajzen, I., 1991. The theory of planned behavior. Organizational Behavior and Human Decision Processes 50, 179–211.

Ajzen, I., Fishbein, M., 2005. The influence of attitudes on behavior. In: Albarracin, D., Johnson, B.T., Zanna, M.P. (Eds.), The Handbook of Attitudes. Erlbaum, Mahwah, N.J., pp. 173–221.

Alberini, A., Gans, W., Towe, C., 2016. Free riding, upsizing, and energy efficiency incentives in Maryland homes. Energy Journal 37, 259–290. https://www.iaee.org/en/publications/ejarticle.aspx?id=2685.

Ali, S., Poulova, P., Akbar, A., Javed, H., Danish, M., 2020. Determining the influencing factors in the adoption of solar photovoltaic technology in Pakistan: a decomposed technology acceptance model approach. Economies 8. https://doi.org/10.3390/economies8040108.

Alkawsi, G., Ali, N., Baashar, Y., 2020. An empirical study of the acceptance of iot-based smart meter in Malaysia: the effect of electricity-saving knowledge and environmental awareness. IEEE Access 8, 42794–42804. https://doi.org/10.1109/ACCESS.2020.2977060.

Allcott, H., 2011. Social norms and energy conservation. Journal of Public Economics 95, 1082–1095.

Alotaibi, I., Abido, M., Khalid, M., Savkin, A., 2020. A comprehensive review of recent advances in smart grids: a sustainable future with renewable energy resources. Energies 13. https://doi.org/10.3390/en13236269.

AlSkaif, T., Lampropoulos, I., van den Broek, M., van Sark, W., 2018. Gamification based framework for engagement of residential customers in energy applications. Energy Research & Social Science 44, 187–195. https://doi.org/10.1016/J.ERSS.2018.04.043.

Anda, M., Temmen, J., 2014. Smart metering for residential energy efficiency: the use of community based social marketing for behavioural change and smart grid introduction. Renewable Energy 67, 119–127.

Arts, J., Frambach, R., Bijmolt, T., 2011. Generalizations on consumer innovation adoption: a meta-analysis on drivers of intention and behavior. International Journal of Research in Marketing 28, 134–144. https://doi.org/10.1016/j.ijresmar.2010.11.002.

ATKearney, 2012. HAN within Smart Grids. Report (in Polish).

Avancini, D., Rodrigues, J., Martins, S., Rabelo, R., Al-Muhtadi, J., Solic, P., 2019. Energy meters evolution in smart grids: a review. Journal of Cleaner Production 217, 702–715.

Ayers, I., Raseman, S., Shih, A., 2013. Evidence from two large field experiments that peer comparison feedback can reduce residential energy usage. The Journal of Law, Economics and Organization 29, 992–1022.

Ayres, I., Raseman, S., Shih, A., 2013. Evidence from two large field experiments that peer comparison feedback can reduce residential energy usage. The Journal of Law, Economics and Organization Advance Access. https://doi.org/10.1093/jleo/ews020.

Backhaus, J., Tigchelaar, C., Best-Waldhober, M.D., 2011. Key findings and policy recommendations to improve effectiveness of energy performance certificates & the energy performance of buildings directive, Petten, ECN-O-11-083, 2011.

Bamberg, S., 2013a. Applying the stage model of self-regulated behavioral change in a car use reduction intervention. Journal of Environmental Psychology 33, 68–75.

Bamberg, S., 2013b. Changing environmentally harmful behaviors: a stage model of self-regulated behavioral change. Journal of Environmental Psychology 34, 151–159.

Bartczak, A., Chilton, S., Czajkowski, M., Meyerhoff, J., 2017. Gain and losses of money in a choice experiment. the impact of financial loss aversion and risk preferences on willingness to pay to avoid renewable energy externalities. Energy Economics 65, 326–334.

Bass, F.M., 1969. A new product growth for model consumer durables. Management Science 15, 215–227.

Batalla-Bejerano, J., Trujillo-Baute, E., Villa-Arrieta, M., 2020. Smart meters and consumer behaviour: insights from the empirical literature. Energy Policy 144.

Bator, R., Phelps, K., Tabanico, J., Schultz, P., Walton, M., 2019. When it is not about the money: social comparison and energy conservation among residents who do not pay for electricity. Energy Research & Social Science 56. https://doi.org/10.1016/j.erss.2019.05.008.

Beck, A., Chitalia, S., Rai, V., 2019. Not so gameful: a critical review of gamification in mobile energy applications. Energy Research & Social Science 51, 32–39. https://doi.org/10.1016/J.ERSS.2019.01.006.

Bellido, M., Rosa, L., Pereida, A., Falcoa, D., Ribeiro, S., 2018. Barriers, challenges and opportunities for microgrid implementation: the case of federal university of Rio de Janeiro. Journal of Cleaner Production 180, 203–216.

Belton, C., Lunn, P., 2020. Smart choices? An experimental study of smart meters and time-of-use tariffs in Ireland. Energy Policy 140.

Belyaev, L., 2010. Electricity Market Reforms: Economics and Policy Challenges. Springer-Verlag, New York.

Ben, H., Steemers, K., 2018. Household archetypes and behavioural patterns in UK domestic energy use. Energy Efficiency 11, 761–771. https://doi.org/10.1007/s12053-017-9609-1.

Bertoldi, P., Rezessy, S., Oikonomou, V., 2013. Rewarding energy savings rather than energy efficiency: exploring the concept of a feed-in tariff for energy savings. Energy Policy 56, 526–535. https://doi.org/10.1016/j.enpol.2013.01.019.

Bertoldo, R., Poumadère, M., Rodrigues Jr., L.C., 2015. When meters start to talk: the public's encounter with smart meters in France. Energy Research & Social Science 9, 146–156. https://doi.org/10.1016/j.erss.2015.08.014.

Biegel, B., Westenholz, M., Hansen, L., Stoustrup, J., Andersen, P., Harbo, S., 2014. Integration of flexible consumers in the ancillary service markets. Energy, 479–489.

Bielecki, S., Skoczkowski, T., Sobczak, L., Buchoski, J., Maciag, Ł., Dukat, P., 2021. Impact of the lockdown during the Covid-19 pandemic on electricity use by residential users. Energies 14. https://doi.org/10.3390/en14040980.

Billanes, J., Enevoldsen, P., 2021. A critical analysis of ten influential factors to energy technology acceptance and adoption. Energy Reports 7, 6899–6907.

Bird, L., Wüstenhagen, R., Aabakken, J., 2002. A review of international green power markets: recent experience, trends, and market drivers. Renewable & Sustainable Energy Reviews 6, 513–536.

Biresselioglu, M., Nilsen, M., Demir, M., Royrvik, J., Koksvik, G., 2018. Examining the barriers and motivators affecting European decision makers in the development of smart and green energy technologies. Journal of Cleaner Production 198, 417–429.

Bollinger, B., Gillingham, K., 2012. Peer effects in the diffusion of solar photovoltaic panels. Marketing Science 31, 900–912.

Bolton, R., 2022. Making Energy Markets. Springer Nature, Switzerland AG.

Borchers, A.M., Duke, J.M., Parsons, G.R., 2007. Does willingness to pay for green energy differ by source? Energy Policy 5, 3327–3334.

Brucal, A., Roberts, M., 2019. Do energy efficiency standards hurt consumers? Evidence from household appliance sales. Journal of Environmental Economics and Management 96, 88–107.

Bruwer, J., Roediger, B., Herbst, F., 2017. Domain-specific market segmentation: a wine-related lifestyle (wrl) approach. Asia Pacific Journal of Marketing and Logistics 29. https://www.emeraldinsight.com/doi/abs/10.1108/APJML-10-2015-0161.

Buchanan, K., Banks, N., Preston, I., Russo, R., 2016. The British public's perception of the UK smart metering initiative: threats and opportunities. Energy Policy 91, 87–97.

Buchanan, K., Russo, R., Anderson, B., 2014. Feeding back about eco-feedback: how do consumers use and respond to energy monitors? Energy Policy 73, 138–146.

Bugden, D., Stedman, R., 2019. A synthetic view of acceptance and engagement with smart meters in the United States. Energy Research and Social Science 47, 137–145.

Bukarica, V., Tomšić, Z., 2017. Energy efficiency policy evaluation by moving from techno-economic towards whole society perspective on energy efficiency market. Renewable and Sustainable Energy Reviews 70, 968–975. https://doi.org/10.1016/j.rser.2016.12.002.

Burchell, K., Rettie, R., Roberts, T., 2016. Householder engagement with energy consumption feedback: the role of community action and communications. Energy Policy 88, 178–186.

Burgess, J., Nye, M., 2008. Re-materialising energy use through transparent monitoring systems. Energy Policy 36, 4454–4459.

Buryk, S., Mead, D., Mourato, S., Torriti, J., 2015. Investigating preferences for dynamic electricity tariffs: the effect of environmental and system benefit disclosure. Energy Policy 80, 190–195.

Byrka, K., Jędrzejewski, A., Sznajd-Weron, K., Weron, R., 2016. Difficulty is critical: the importance of social factors in modeling diffusion of green products and practices. Renewable and Sustainable Energy Reviews 62, 723–735.

Caballero, N., Ploner, M., 2022. Boosting or nudging energy consumption? The importance of cognitive aspects when adopting non-monetary interventions. Energy Research & Social Science 91. https://doi.org/10.1016/j.erss.2022.102734.

Cambell, A., 2013. Word of mouth and percolation in social networks. American Economic Review 103, 2466–2498.

Cantono, S., Silverberg, G., 2009. A percolation model of eco-innovation diffusion: the relationship between diffusion, learning economies and subsidies. Technological Forecasting & Social Change 76, 487–496.

Cattaneo, C., 2019. Internal and external barriers to energy efficiency: which role for policy interventions? Energy Efficiency 12, 1293–1311. https://doi.org/10.1007/s12053-019-09775-1.

Chadwick, K., Russell-Bennett, R., Biddle, N., 2022. The role of human influences on adoption and rejection of energy technology: a systematised critical review of the literature on household energy transitions. Energy Research & Social Science 89. https://doi.org/10.1016/j.erss.2022.102528.

Chandrasekaran, D., Tellis, G.J., 2007. A critical review of marketing research on diffusion of new products. In: Malhotra, N.K. (Ed.), Review of Marketing Research, vol. 3. Emerald Group Publishing Ltd., pp. 39–80.

Chawla, Y., Kowalska-Pyzalska, A., 2019. Public awareness and consumer acceptance of smart meters among Polish social media users. Energies 12, 2759.

Chawla, Y., Kowalska-Pyzalska, A., Oralhan, B., 2020a. Attitudes and opinions of social media users towards smart meters' rollout in Turkey. Energies 13. https://doi.org/10.3390/en13030732.

Chawla, Y., Kowalska-Pyzalska, A., Silveira, P.D., 2020b. Marketing and communications channels for diffusion of electricity smart meters in Portugal. Telematics and Informatics 50, 101385.

Chawla, Y., Kowalska-Pyzalska, A., Skowronska-Szmer, A., 2020c. Perspectives of smart meters' roll-out in India: an empirical analysis of consumers' awareness and preferences. Energy Policy 146, 111798. https://doi.org/10.1016/j.enpol.2020.111798.

Chawla, Y., Kowalska-Pyzalska, A., Widayat, W., 2019. Consumer willingness and acceptance of smart meters in Indonesia. Resources 8, 177. https://doi.org/10.3390/resources8040177.

Chen, C., Xu, X., Arpan, L., 2017. Between the technology acceptance model and sustainable energy technology acceptance model: investigating smart meter acceptance in the United States. Energy Research and Social Science 25, 93–104.

Chen, H., Long, R., Niu, W., Feng, Q., Yang, R., 2014. How does individual low-carbon consumption behavior occur? An analysis based on attitude process. Applied Energy 116, 376–386.

Chen, M.F., 2016. Extending the theory of planned behavior model to explain people's energy savings and carbon reduction behavioral intentions to mitigate climate change in Taiwan–moral obligation matters. Journal of Cleaner Production 112, 1746–1753. https://doi.org/10.1016/j.jclepro.2015.07.043.

Chen, Y., Zhang, L., Xu, P., Di Gangi, A., 2021. Electricity demand response schemes in China: pilot study and future outlook. Energy 224. https://doi.org/10.1016/j.energy.2021.120042.

Cheshmehzgani, A., 2020. Covid-19 and household energy implications: what are the main impacts on energy use? Heliyon 6, 05202.

Chou, J., Kim, C., Ung, T., Yutami, I., Lin, G., Son, H., 2015. Cross-country review of smart grid adoption in residential buildings. Renewable & Sustainable Energy Reviews 48, 192–213.

Chou, J.S., Yutami, I., 2014. Smart meter adoption and deployment strategy for residential buildings in Indonesia. Applied Energy 128, 336–349. https://doi.org/10.1016/j.apenergy.2014.04.083.

Clark, C., Kotchen, M., Moore, M., 2003. Internal and external influences on pro-environmental behavior: participation in a green electricity program. Journal of Environmental Psychology 23, 237–246.

Claudy, M., Garcia, R., O'Driscoll, A., 2015. Consumer resistance to innovation—a behavioral reasoning perspective. Journal of the Academy of Marketing Science 43, 528–544. https://doi.org/10.1007/s11747-014-0399-0.

Claudy, M.C., Michelsen, C., O'Driscoll, A., Mullen, M.R., 2010. Consumer awareness in the adoption of microgeneration technologies. an empirical investigation in the republic of Ireland. Renewable and Sustainable Energy Reviews 14, 2154–2160.

Coday, M., Boutin-Foster, C., Sher, T., Tennant, J., Greaney, M., Saunders, S., 2005. Strategies for retaining study participants in behavioral intervention trials: retention experiences of the NIH behavior change consortium. Annals of Behavioral Medicine 29, 55–65.

Coenen, F., Hoppe, T., 2022. Renewable Energy Communities and the Low Carbon Energy Transition in Europe. Palgrae MacMillian.

Colasante, A., D'Adamo, I., Morone, P., 2021. Nudging for the increased adoption of solar energy? Evidence from a survey in Italy. Energy Research & Social Science 74. https://doi.org/10.1016/j.erss.2021.101978.

Connor, P., Baker, P., Xenias, D., Balta-Ozkan, N., Axon, C., Cipcigan, L., 2014. Policy and regulation for smart grids in the United Kingdom. Renewable and Sustainable Energy Reviews, 269–286. https://doi.org/10.1016/j.rser.2014.07.065.

Coy, D., Malekpour, S., Saeri, A., Dargaville, R., 2021. Rethinking community empowerment in the energy transformation: a critical review of the definitions, drivers and outcomes. Energy Research & Social Science 72.

Crispim, J., Braz, J., Castro, R., Esteves, J., 2014. Smart grids in the EU with smart regulation: experiences from the UK, Italy and Portugal. Utilities Policy 31, 85–93.

Dall-Orsoletta, A., Cunha, J., Araújo, M., Ferreira, P., 2022. A systematic review of social innovation and community energy transitions. Energy Research & Social Science 88. https://doi.org/10.1016/j.erss.2022.102625.

Danne, M., Meier-Sauthoff, S., Musshoff, O., 2021. Analyzing German consumers' willingness to pay for green electricity tariff attributes: a discrete choice experiment. Energy, Sustainability and Society 11. https://doi.org/10.1186/s13705-021-00291-8.

Darby, S., McKenna, E., 2012. Social implications of residential demand response in cool temperature climates. Energy Policy 49, 759–769.

Davis, F., 1989. Perceived usefulness, perceived ease of use, and user acceptance of information technology. Management Information Systems Quarterly 13, 319–340.

Davis, F., Bagozzi, R., Warshaw, P., 1989. User acceptance of computer technology: a comparison of two theoretical models. Management Science 35, 982–1003.

Deffuant, G., Huet, S., Amblar, F., 2005. An individual-based model of innovation diffusion mixing social value and individual benefit. American Journal of Sociology 110, 1041–1069.

Delmas, M., Fischlein, M., Asensio, O., 2013. Information strategies and energy conservation behavior: a meta-analysis of experimental studies from 1975 to 2012. Energy Policy 61, 729–739. https://doi.org/10.1016/j.enpol.2013.05.109.

Diaz-Rainey, I., Ashton, J., 2011. Profiling potential green electricity tariff adopters: green consumerism as an environmental policy tool? Business Strategy and The Environment 20, 456–470.

Diaz-Rainey, I., Tzavara, D., 2012. Financing the decarbonized energy system through green electricity tariffs: a diffusion model of an induced consumer environmental market. Technological Forecasting & Social Change 79, 1693–1704.

Diaz-Rainey, I., Tzavara, D., 2015. Investment inefficiency and the adoption of eco-innovations: the case of household energy efficiency technologies. Energy Policy 82, 105–117.

Dogaru, L., 2020. The main goals of 4th industrial revolution. RES perspective. Procedia Manufacturing 46, 397–401.

Duetschke, E., Paetz, A., 2013. Dynamic electricity pricing – which programs do consumers prefer? Energy Policy 59, 226–234.

Dunlap, R., 2008. The new environmental paradigm scale: from marginality to worldwide use. The Journal of Environmental Education 40, 3–18.

Dunlap, R., Liere, K., Mertig, A., Jones, R., 2000. New trends in measuring environmental attitudes:

measuring endorsement of the new ecological paradigm: a revised NEP scale. Journal of Social Issues 56, 425–442.

D'hulst, R., Labeeuw, W., Beusen, B., Claessens, S., Deconinck, G., Vanthournout, K., 2015. Demand response flexibility and flexibility potential of residential smart appliances: experiences from large pilot test in Belgium. Applied Energy 155, 79–90. https://doi.org/10.1016/j.apenergy.2015.05.101.

Eagle, L., Osmond, A., McCarthy, B., Low, D., Lesbirel, H., 2017. Social marketing strategies for renewable energy transitions. Australasian Marketing Journal 25, 141–148. https://doi.org/10.1016/j.ausmj.2017.04.006.

East, R., Hammond, K., Lomax, W., 2008. Measuring the impact of positive and negative word of mouth on brand purchase probability. International Journal of Research in Marketing 25, 215–224.

Ek, K., 2005. Psychological determinants of attitude towards "green" electricity: the case of Swedish wind power. Energy Policy 33, 1677–1689.

Ek, K., Soederholm, P., 2008. Norms and economic motivation in the Swedish green electricity market. Ecological Economics 68, 169–182.

Ellabban, O., Abu-Rub, H., 2016. Smart grid customers' acceptance and engagement: an overview. Renewable and Sustainable Energy Reviews 65, 1285–1298.

Elsharkawy, H., Rutherford, P., 2015. Retrofitting social housing in the UK: home energy use and performance in a pre-community energy saving programme (cesp). Energy and Buildings 88, 25–33.

EMI, A., 2014. Turkey smart grid 2023 vision and strategy roadmap summary report. Available online www.smartgridturkey.org. (Accessed 10 November 2019).

Engelken, M., Roemer, B., Drescher, M., Welpe, I., Picot, A., 2016. Comparing drivers, barriers and opportunities of business models for renewable energy: a review. Renewable & Sustainable Energy Reviews 60, 795–809.

European Commission, 2009. Directive 2009/72/ec of the European Parliament and of the council of 13 July 2009 concerning common rules for the internal market in electricity and repealing directive 2003/54/e. https://eur-lex.europa.eu/legal-content/EN/ALL/?uri=CELEX:32009L0072.

European Commission, 2012. Directive 2012/27/EU of the European Parliament and of the council of 25 October 2012 on energy efficiency, amending directives 2009/125/EC and 2010/30/EC and repealing directives 2004/8/EC and 2006/32/EC. Official Journal of the European Union L 315, 1–56.

European Commission, 2016. European Commission: Accelerating Clean Energy Innovation: COM(2016) 763 Final: Winter Package. European Commission, Brussels. Access from http://ec.europa.eu/energy/en/news/commission-process-new-rules-consumer-centered-clean-energy-transition.

European Commission, 2018. European Smart Metering Benchmark. Benchmarking Smart Metering Deployment in the EU-28. Revised final report, European Commission, DG Energy, 27 June 2019.

European Commission, 2019. Clean Energy for All Europeans. European Commission, Directorate-General for Energy, Publications Office. https://data.europa.eu/doi/10.2833/9937.

European Commission, 2020. Climate Target Plan – Stepping up Europe's 2030 Climate Ambition: Impact Assessment Part 2. European Commission, Brussels.

European Commission, 2022. Communication from the Commission to the European Parliament, the European Council, the Council, the European Economic and Social Committee and the Committee of the Regions "REPowerEU Plan". (COM(2022) 230 final of 18 May 2022).

Faires, A., Cook, M., Neame, C., 2007. Towards a contemporary approach for understanding consumer behavior in the context of domestic energy use. Energy Policy 35, 4381–4390.

Faruqui, A., Sergici, S., 2010. Household response to dynamic pricing of electricity – a survey of the experimental evidence. Journal of Regulatory Economics 38, 193–220.

Flambard, V., Kpoviessi, J., Romaniuc, R., 2021. Encouraging energy efficiency among residents of smart and green buildings. In: Magnaghi, E., Flambard, V., Mancini, D., Jacques, J., Gouvy, N. (Eds.), Organizing Smart Buildings and Cities. In: Lecture Notes in Information Systems and Organization. Springer, pp. 141–157.

Fogg, B., 2009. A behavior model for persuasive design. In: Proceedings of the 4th International Conference on Persuasive Technology – Persuasive'09. ACM Press, New York, USA.

Fornara, F., Pattitoni, P., Mura, M., Strazzera, E., 2016. Predicting intention to improve household energy efficiency: the role of value-belief-norm theory, normative and informational influence, and specific attitude. Journal of Environmental Psychology 45, 1–10. https://doi.org/10.1016/j.jenvp.2015.11.001.

Fouad, M., Kanarachos, S., Allam, M., 2022. Perceptions of consumers towards smart and sustainable energy market services: the role of early adopters. Renewable Energy 187, 14–33.

Foulds, C., Robison, R., Macrorie, R., 2017. Energy monitoring as a practice: investigating use of the iMeasure online energy feedback tool. Energy Policy 104, 194–202.

Frank, B., Enkawa, T., Schvaneveldt, S., Torrico, B., 2015. Antecedents and consequences of innate willingness to pay for innovations: understanding motivations and consumer preferences of prospective early adopters. Technological Forecasting & Social Change 99, 252–266.

Franz, H.-W., Hochgerner, J., Howaldt, J., 2012. Final observations. In: Challenge Social Innovation. Springer, Berlin, Germany.

Frederiks, E., Stenner, K., Hobman, E., 2014. Household energy use. applying behavioral economics to understand consumer decision making and behavior. Renewable and Sustainable Energy Reviews 41, 1385–1394.

Frederiks, E., Stenner, K., Hobman, E., 2015. Household energy use: applying behavioural economics to understand consumer decision-making and behaviour. Renewable and Sustainable Energy Reviews 41, 1385–1394.

Freier, J., von Loessl, V., 2022. Dynamic electricity tariffs: designing reasonable pricing schemes for private households. Energy Economics 112.

Gadenne, D., Sharma, B., Kerr, D., Smith, T., 2011. The influence of consumers' environmental beliefs and attitudes on energy saving behaviors. Energy Policy 39, 7684–7694.

Gamel, J., Bauer, A., Decker, T., Menrad, K., 2021. Financing wind energy projects: an extended theory of planned behavior approach to explain private households' wind energy investment intentions in Germany. Renewable Energy 182, 592–601. https://doi.org/10.1016/j.renene.2021.09.108.

Gangale, F., Mengolini, A., Onyeji, I., 2013. Consumer engagement: an insight from smart grid projects in Europe. Energy Policy 60, 621–628.

Gans, W., Alberini, A., Longo, A., 2013. Smart meter devices and the effect of feedback on residential electricity consumption: evidence from a natural experiment in northern Ireland. Energy Economics 36, 729–743.

Gao, L., Wang, S., Li, J., Haidong, L., 2017. Application of the extended theory of planned behavior to understand individual's energy saving behavior in workplaces. Resources, Conservation and Recycling 127, 107–113.

Gaspari, J., Antonini, E., Marchi, L., Vodola, V., 2021. Energy transition at home: a survey on the data and practices that lead to a change in household energy behavior. Sustainability 13.

Geelen, D., Reinders, A., Keyson, D., 2013. Empowering the end-user in smart grids: recommendations for the design of products and services. Energy Policy 61, 151–161.

Geroski, P.A., 2000. Models of technology diffusion. Research Policy 29, 603–625.

Gerpott, T., Mahmudova, I., 2010. Determinants of green electricity adoption among residential customers in Germany. International Journal of Consumers Studies 34, 464–473.

Gerpott, T., Paukert, M., 2013. Determinnants of willingness to pay for smart meters: an empirical analysis of household customers in Germany. Energy Policy 61, 483–495.

Giorgi, S., Fell, D., Austin, A., Wilkins, C., 2016. Public understanding of the links between climate change and (i) food and (ii) energy use (ev0402): Final report. Department for Environment, Food and Rural Affairs, Brook Lyndhurst, Defra, London.

Girod, B., Mayer, S., Nägele, F., 2017a. Economic versus belief-based models: shedding light on the adoption of novel green technologies. Energy Policy 101, 415–426. https://doi.org/10.1016/j.enpol.2016.09.065.

Girod, B., Stucki, T., Woerter, M., 2017b. How do policies for efficient energy use in the household sector induce energy-efficiency innovation? An evaluation of European countries. Energy Policy 103, 223–237.

Goldenberg, J., Libai, B., Muller, E., 2001. Talk of the network: a complex system look at underlying process of word-of-mouth. Marketing Letters 12, 211–223.

Gollwitzer, P.M., Heckhausen, H., Ratajczak, H., 1990. From weighing to willing: approaching a change decision through pre- or postdecisional mentation. Organizational Behaviour and Human Decision Processes 45, 41–65.

Gonzalez-Caceres, A., Lassen, A., Nielsen, T., 2020. Barriers and challenges of the recommendation list of measures under the EPBD scheme: a critical review. Energy and Buildings 223.

Good, N., Ellis, K., Mancarella, P., 2017. Review and classification of barriers and enablers of demand response in the smart grid. Renewable and Sustainable Energy Review 16, 57–72.

Gosnell, G., McCoy, D., 2021. Market failures and willingness to accept the smart energy transition: Experimental evidence from the UK. Centre for Climate Change Economics and Policy Working Paper No. 369 ISSN 2515-5709 (Online).

Gouws, T., Van Rheede van Oudtshoorn, G., 2011. Correlation between brand longevity and the diffusion of innovations theory. Journal of Public Affairs 11, 236–242.

Graffeo, M., Ritov, I., Bonini, N., Hadjichristidis, C., 2015. To make people save energy tell them what others do but also who they are: a preliminary study. Frontiers in Psychology 6. https://doi.org/10.3389/fpsyg.2015.01287.

Gruber, H., Verboven, F., 2001. The diffusion of mobile telecommunications services in the European Union. European Economic Review 45, 577–588.

Guenther, M., Stummer, C., Wakolbiner, L., Wildpaner, M., 2011. An agent-based simulation approach for the new product diffusion of a novel biomass fuel. Journal of the Operational Research Society 62, 12–20.

Guerreiro, S., Batel, S., Lima, M., 2015. Making energy visible: sociopsychological aspects associated with the use of smart meters. Energy Efficiency 8, 1149–1167. https://doi.org/10.1007/s12053-015-9344-4.

Gumz, J., Fettermann, D., Sant' Anna, A., Tortorella, G., 2022. Social influence as a major factor in smart meters' acceptance: findings from Brazil. Results in Engineering 15.

Gupta, R., Jain, K., 2012. Diffusion of mobile telephony in India: an empirical study. Technological Forecasting and Social Change 79, 709–715. https://doi.org/10.1016/j.techfore.2011.08.003.

Gyamfi, S., Krumdieck, S., Urmee, T., 2013. Residential peak electricity demand response – highlights of some behavioral alissues. Renewable and Sustainable Energy Reviews 25, 71–77.

Gölz, S., Hahnel, U., 2016. What motivates people to use energy feedback systems? A multiple goal approach to predict long-term usage behaviour in daily life. Energy Research and Social Science 21, 155–166. https://doi.org/10.1016/j.erss.2016.07.006.

Hall, S., Brown, D., Davis, M., Ehrtmann, M., Holstenkamp, L., 2019. Prosumers for the energy union: mainstreaming active participation of citizens in the energy transition. Business models for prosumers in Europe, Deliverable 4.1 of the Horizon. 2020 PROSEU project (H2020-LCE-2017) Grant Agreement N°764056.

Hansen, P., Liu, X., Morrison, G., 2019. Agent-based modelling and socio-technical energy transitions: a systematic literature review. Energy Research & Social Science 49. https://doi.org/10.1016/j.erss.2018.10.021.

Hansla, A., Gamble, A., Juliusson, A., Gaerling, T., 2008. Psychological determinants of attitude towards and willingness to pay for green electricity. Energy Policy 36, 768–774.

Hargreaves, T., Nye, M., Burgess, J., 2010. Making energy visible: a qualitative field study of how householders interact with feedback from smart energy monitors. Energy Policy 38, 6111–6119. https://doi.org/10.1016/j.enpol.2010.05.068.

Hargreeaves, T., Nye, M., Burgess, J., 2013. Keeping energy visible? Exploring how households interact with feedback from smart energy monitors in the longer term. Energy Policy 52, 126–134.

Hasheem, M., Wang, S., Ye, N., Farooq, M., Shahid, H., 2022. Factors influencing purchase intention of solar photovoltaic technology: an extended perspective of technology readiness index and theory of planned behaviour. Cleaner and Responsible Consumption 7. https://doi.org/10.1016/j.clrc.2022.100079.

Hast, A., Syri, S., Jokiniemi, J., Huuskonen, M., Cross, S., 2015. Review of green electricity products in the United Kingdom, Germany and Finland. Renewable & Sustainable Energy Reviews 42, 1370–1384.

Heckhausen, H., Gollwitzer, P., 1987. Thought contents and cognitive functioning in motivational versus volitional states of mind. Motivation and Emotion 11, 101–120.

Henn, L., Taube, O., Kaiser, F., 2019. The role of environmental attitude in the efficacy of smart-meter-based feedback interventions. Journal of Environmental Psychology 63, 74–81. https://doi.org/10.1016/j.jenvp.2019.04.007.

Herrmann, M., Brumby, D., Cheng, L., Gilbert, X., Oreszczyn, T., 2021. An empirical investigation of domestic energy data visualizations. International Journal of Human Computer Studies 152.

Hess, D., 2014. Smart meters and public acceptance: comparative analysis and governance implications. Health, Risk & Society 16, 243–258.

Higgins, A., Paevere, P., Gardner, J., Quezada, G., 2012. Combining choice modelling and multi-criteria analysis for technology diffusion: an application to the uptake of electric vehicles. Technological Forecasting and Social Change 79, 1399–1412.

Hinson, S., Bolton, P., Barber, S., 2019. Energy smart meters. Commons Library Briefing. No. 8119.

Hmielowski, J., Boyd, A., Harvey, G., Joo, J., 2019. The social dimensions of smart meters in the United States: demographics, privacy, and technology readiness. Energy Research & Social Science 55, 189–197.

Hobman, E., Frederiks, E., 2014. Barriers to green electricity subscription in Australia: "love the environment, love renewable energy...but why should I pay more? Energy Research and Social Science 3, 78–88.

Hobman, E., Frederiks, E., Stenner, K., Meikle, S., 2016. Uptake and usage of cost-reflective electricity pricing: insights from psychology and behavioral economics. Renewable & Sustainable Energy Reviews 57, 455–467.

Hochgerner, J., 2012. New combinations of social practices in the knowledge society. In: Franz, H.-W.,

Hochgerner, J., Howaldt, J. (Eds.), Challenge Social Innovation. Springer, Berlin, Germany.

Hohnisch, M., Pittnauer, S., Stauffer, D., 2008. A percolation-based model explaining delayed takeoff in new-product diffusion. Industrial and Corporate Change 17, 1001–1017.

Hook, A., Sovacool, B., Sorrell, S., 2020. A systematic review of the energy and climate impacts of teleworking. Environmental Research Letters 15.

Horstink, L., Wittmayer, J., Ng, K., Luz, G., Marín-González, E., Gährs, S., Brown, D., 2020. Collective renewable energy prosumers and the promises of the energy union: taking stock. Energies 13, 421. https:// doi.org/10.3390/en13020421.

Houde, S., Aldy, J., 2017. Consumers' response to state energy efficient appliance rebate programs. American Economic Journal: Economic Policy 9, 227–255. https:// www.aeaweb.org/articles?id=10.1257/pol.20140383.

Hu, Z., Kim, J.H., Wang, J.H., Byrne, J., 2015. Review of dynamic pricing programs in the U.S. and Europe: status quo and policy recommendations. Renewable and Sustainable Energy Reviews 42, 743–751.

Hua, W., Chen, Y., Qadrdan, M., Jiang, J., Sun, H., Wu, J., 2022. Applications of blockchain and artificial intelligence technologies for enabling prosumers in smart grids: a review. Renewable and Sustainable Energy Reviews 161, 112308.

Huang, Y., Ahmad, M., Ali, S., Kirikkaleli, D., 2022. Does eco-innovation promote cleaner energy? Analyzing the role of energy price and human capital. Energy 239. https:// doi.org/10.1016/j.energy.2021.122268.

Hubert, A., 2011. Empowering People, Driving Change: Social Innovation in the European Union. BEPA (Bureau of European Policy Advisers), Brussels, Belgium.

Hyysalo, S., Johnson, M., Juntunen, J., 2017. The diffusion of consumer innovation in sustainable energy technologies. Journal of Cleaner Production 162, S70–S82. https:// doi.org/10.1016/j.jclepro.2016.09.045.

Immonen, A., Kiljander, J., Aro, M., 2020. Consumer viewpoint on a new kind of energy market. Electric Power Systems Research 180. https:// doi.org/10.1016/j.epsr.2019.106153.

Iwasaki, S., 2019. Using eco-home diagnosis to reduce household energy consumption: A case study on behavioral changes in Fukuoka Prefecture Japan. Energy Policy 132, 893–900.

Iweka, O., Liu, S., Shukla, A., Yan, D., 2019. Energy and behaviour at home: a review of intervention methods and practices. Energy Research and Social Science 57. https:// doi.org/10.1016/j.erss.2019.101238.

Jabir, H., Teh, J., Ishak, D., Abunima, H., 2018. Impacts of demand-side management on electrical power systems: a review. Energies 11. https:// doi.org/10.3390/en11051050.

Jager, W., 2006. Stimulating the diffusion of photovoltaic systems: a behavioral perspective. Energy Policy 34, 1935–1943.

Jee, Y., Lee, E., Baek, K., Ko, W., Kim, J., 2022. Data-analytic assessment for flexumers under demand diversification in power system. IEEE Access 10, 33313–33319. https:// doi.org/10.1109/ACCESS.2022.3162077.

Jiang, P., Fan, Y., Klemeš, J., 2021. Impacts of Covid-19 on energy demand and consumption: challenges, lessons and emerging opportunities. Applied Energy 285. https:// doi.org/10.1016/j.apenergy.2021.116441.

Joachain, H., Klopfert, F., 2014. Smarter than metering? Coupling smart meters and complementary currencies to reinforce the motivation of households for energy savings. Ecological Economics 105, 89–96.

Johnson, D., Horton, E., Mulcahy, R., Foth, M., 2017. Gamification and serious games within the domain of domestic energy consumption: a systematic review. Renewable & Sustainable Energy Reviews 73, 249–264. https:// doi.org/10.1016/J.RSER.2017.01.134.

Joseph, A., 2015. Smart grid and retail competition in India: a review on technological and managerial initiatives and challenges. Procedia Technology 21, 155–162.

Kahma, N., Matschoss, K., 2017. The rejection of innovations? Rethinking technology diffusion and the non-use of smart energy services in Finland. Energy Resources & Social Science 34, 27–36.

Karakaya, E., Hidalgo, A., Nuur, C., 2014. Diffusion of eco-innovations: a review. Renewable and Sustainable Energy Reviews 33, 1935–1943.

Kardooni, R., Yusoff, S., Kari, F., 2016. Renewable energy technology acceptance in Peninsular Malaysia. Energy Policy 88, 1–10. https:// doi.org/10.1016/j.enpol.2015.10.005.

Kashintseva, V., Strielkowski, W., Streimikis, J., Veynbender, T., 2018. Consumer attitudes towards industrial co_2 capture and storage products and technologies. Energies 11.

Kaufmann, S., Kuenzel, K., Loock, M., 2013. Customer value of smart metering: explorative evidence from a choice-based conjoint study in Switzerland. Energy Policy 53, 229–239.

Keller, A., Eisen, C., Hanss, D., 2019. Lessons learned from applications of the stage model of self-regulated behavioral change: a review. Frontiers in Psychology 10. https://doi.org/10.3389/fpsyg.2019.01091.

Khachatryan, H., Joireman, J., Casavant, K., 2013. Relating values and consideration of future and immediate consequences to consumer preference for biofuels: a threedimensional social dilemma analysis. Journal of Environmental Psychology 34, 97–108.

Kiesling, E., Güntherand, M., Stummer, C., Wakolbinger, L.M., 2012. Agent-based simulation of innovation diffusion: a review. Central European Journal of Operations Research 20, 183–230.

Knapp, L., Ladenburg, J., 2015. How spatial relationships influence economic preferences for wind power – a review. Energies 8, 6177–6201.

Koirala, B., Araghi, Y., Kroesen, M., Ghorbani, A., Hakvoort, R., Herder, P., 2018. Trust, awareness, and independence: insights from a socio-psychological factor analysis of citizen knowledge and participation in community energy systems. Energy Research & Social Science 38, 33–40.

Koirala, B., Koliou, E., Friege, J., Hakvoort, R., Herder, P., 2016. Energetic communities for community energy: a review of key issues and trends shaping integrated community energy systems. Renewable & Sustainable Energy Reviews 56, 722–744.

Korsakienė, R., Tvaronavičienė, M., Smaliukienė, R., 2014. Impact of energy prices on industrial sector development and export: Lithuania in the context of Baltic states. Procedia – Social and Behavioral Sciences 110, 461–469. https://doi.org/10.1016/j.sbspro.2013.12.890.

Kotler, P., Roberto, N., Lee, N., 2016. Social Marketing: Improving the Quality of Life, 5th edition. SAGE Publications, Inc. ISBN 978-0761924340.

Kowalska-Pyzalska, A., 2015. Social acceptance of green energy and dynamic electricity tariffs – a short review. In: International Conference on Modern Electronic Power Systems (MEPS). 6-9 July, 2015, Wroclaw, Poland.

Kowalska-Pyzalska, A., 2016. An analysis of factors enhancing adoption of smart metering platforms: an agent-based modeling approach. In: 13th European Energy Market (EEM) Conference. Porto, Portugal, 6–9 June 2016.

Kowalska-Pyzalska, A., 2017. Willingness to Pay for Green Energy. an Agent-Based Model in Netlogo Platform. International Conference on the European Energy Market. EEM, Dresden, Germany.

Kowalska-Pyzalska, A., 2018a. An empirical analysis of green electricity adoption among residential consumers in Poland. Sustainability 10, 2281.

Kowalska-Pyzalska, A., 2018b. What makes consumers adopt to innovative energy services in the energy market? A review of incentives and barriers. Renewable and Sustainable Energy Reviews 82, 3570–3581.

Kowalska-Pyzalska, A., 2019. Do consumers want to pay for green electricity? A case study from Poland. Sustainability 11.

Kowalska-Pyzalska, A., Byrka, K., 2019. Determinants of the willingness to energy monitoring by residential consumers: a case study in the city of Wroclaw in Poland. Energies 12, 907.

Kowalska-Pyzalska, A., Maciejowska, K., Suszczyński, K., Sznajd-Weron, K., Weron, R., 2014. Turning green: agent-based modeling of the adoption of dynamic electricity tariffs. Energy Policy 71, 164–174.

Kowalska-Pyzalska, A., Ćwik, K., Jędrzejewski, A., Sznajd-Weron, K., 2016. Linking consumer opinions with reservation prices in an agent-based model of innovation diffusion. Acta Physica Polonica A 129, 1055–1059.

Kowalska-Pyzalska, A., Byrka, K., Serek, J., 2020a. How to Foster the adoption of electricity smart meters? A longitudinal field study of residential consumers. Energies 13. https://doi.org/10.3390/en13184737.

Kowalska-Pyzalska, A., Kott, J., Kott, M., 2020b. Why Polish market of alternative fuel vehicles (AFVs) is the smallest in Europe? SWOT analysis of opportunities and threats. Renewable and Sustainable Energy Reviews 133, 110076.

Kowalska-Pyzalska, A., Michalski, R., Kott, M.A., Skowrońska-Szmer, A., Kott, J., 2022. Consumer preferences towards alternative fuel vehicles. results from the conjoint analysis. Renewable and Sustainable Energy Reviews 155, 1–28.

Kowalska-Styczeń, A., Sznajd-Weron, K., 2012. Access to information in word of mouth marketing within a cellular automata model. Advances in Complex Systems 15, 1250080.

Krantz, D., Tversky, A., 1971. Conjoint-measurement analysis of composition rules in psychology. Psychological Review 78, 151–169. https://doi.org/10.1037/h0030637.

Krishnamurthy, C., Kriström, B., 2014. Determinants of the price-premium for green energy: evidence from an OECD cross-section. Environmental & Resource Economics, 1–32.

Krishnamutri, T., Schwartz, D., Davis, A., Fischoff, B., de Bruin, W.B., Lave, L., Wang, J., 2012. Preparing for smart grid technologies: a behavioral decision research approach to understanding consumer expectations about smart meters. Energy Policy 41, 790–797.

Krishnan, T.V., Bass, F.M., Jain, D.C., 1999. Optimal pricing strategy for new products. Management Science 45, 1650–1663.

Kumar, A., 2019. Beyond technical smartness: rethinking the development and implementation of sociotechnical smart grids in India. Energy Research & Social Science 49, 158–168.

Kumar, A., Sah, B., Singh, A., Deng, Y., He, X., 2017. A review of multi criteria decision making (mcdm) towards sustainable renewable energy development. Renewable and Sustainable Energy Reviews 69, 596–609.

Köppl, S., Springmann, E., Regener, V., Weigand, A., 2022. Enabling Business Models and Grid Stability: Case Studies from Germany, Energy Communities. Academic Press.

Laciana, C., Rovere, S., Podesta, G., 2013. Exploring associations between micro-level models of innovation diffusion and emerging macro-level adoption patterns. Physica A: Statistical Mechanics and Its Applications 392, 1873–1884.

Lammers, I., Hoppe, T., 2019. Watt rules? Assessing decision-making practices on smart energy systems in Dutch city districts. Energy Research & Social Science 47, 233–246.

Lamnatou, C., Chemisana, D., Cristofari, C., 2022. Smart grids and smart technologies in relation to photovoltaics, storage systems, buildings and the environment. Renewable Energy, 1376–1391.

Larsen, F., 2013. A cross-market study of consumers' attitudes to green electricity. International Journal of Business and Social Science 4.

Lee, E., Kang, M., Song, J., Kang, M., 2020. From intention to action: habits, feedback and optimizing energy consumption in South Korea. Energy Research and Social Science 64.

Lennon, B., Dunphy, N., Sanvicente, E., 2019. Community acceptability and the energy transition: a citizens' perspective. Energy, Sustainability and Society 9, 35.

Leonhardt, R., Noble, B., Poelzer, G., Fitzpatrick, P., Belcher, K., Holdmann, G., 2022. Advancing local energy transitions: a global review of government instruments supporting community energy. Energy Research & Social Science 83.

Leygue, C., Ferguson, E., Skatova, A., Spence, A., 2014. Energy sharing and energy feedback: affective and behavioral reactions to communal energy displays. Frontiers in Energy Research 2, 1–12.

Li, C., Dragicevic, T., Diaz, N., Luna Hernandez, A., Guan, Y., Rasmussen, T., Beheshtaein, S., 2017. Grid architecture for future distribution system — a cyber-physical system perspective. In: Conference:

IECON 2017–43rd Annual Conference of the IEEE Industrial Electronics Society.

Li, Z., Ye, H., Liao, N., Wang, R., Qiu, Y., Wang, Y., 2022. Impact of Covid-19 on electricity energy consumption: a quantitative analysis on electricity. International Journal of Electrical Power & Energy Systems 140. https://doi.org/10.1016/j.ijepes.2022.108084.

Liao, F., Molin, E., van Wee, B., 2017. Consumer preferences for electric vehicles: a literature review. Transport Reviews 37, 252–275.

Lim, S.Y., Kim, H.J., Yoo, S.H., 2017. South Korean houshehold's willingness to pay for replacing coal with natural gas. A view from CO2 emissions reduction. Energies 10.

Lineweber, D., 2011. Understanding residential customer support for and opposition to smart grid investments. The Electricity Journal 24, 92–100.

Liobikienė, G., Dagiliūtė, R., Juknys, R., 2021. The determinants of renewable energy usage intentions using theory of planned behaviour approach. Renewable Energy 170, 587–594. https://doi.org/10.1016/j.renene.2021.01.152.

Liu, W., Wang, C., Mol, A., 2013. Rural public acceptance for renewable energy deployment: the case of Shandong in China. Applied Energy 102, 1187–1196.

Liu, X., Wang, X.C., Yi Jian, I., Chi, H.L., Yang, D., Hon-Wan Chan, E., 2021. Are you an energy saver at home? The personality insights of household energy conservation behaviors based on theory of planned behavior. Resources, Conservation and Recycling 174. https://doi.org/10.1016/j.resconrec.2021.105823.

Lobaccaro, G., Carlucci, S., Löfström, E., 2016. A review of systems and technologies for smart homes and smart grids. Energies 9, 1–33.

Lopes, M., Antunes, C., Janda, K., Peixoto, P., Martins, N., 2016. The potential of energy behaviors in a smart(er) grid: policy implications from a Portuguese exploratory study. Energy Policy 90, 233–245.

Lopes, M., Antunes, C., Martins, N., 2012. Energy behaviors as promoters of energy efficiency: a 21st century review. Renewable and Sustainable Energy Reviews 16, 4095–4104.

Lovelock, C.H., Patterson, P., Wirtz, J., 2015. Services Marketing: An Asia-Pacific and Australian Perspective. Frenchs Forest, N.S.W., Pearson Australia. 6th edition.

Lowitzsch, J., 2019. Energy Transition — Financing Consumer Coownership in Renewables. Palgrave Macmillan, Cham, Switzerland.

Lutzenhiser, L., 1991. A cultural model of households energy consumption. Energy 17, 47–60.

Ma, C., Rogers, A., Kragt, M., Zhang, F., Polyakov, M.e.A., 2015. Consumers' willingness to pay for renewable energy: a meta-regression analysis. Resource and Energy Economics 42, 93–109.

Ma, G., Lin, J., Li, N., 2018. Longitudinal assessment of the behavior-changing effect of app-based eco-feedback in residential buildings. Energy and Buildings 159, 486–494.

MacDonald, S., Eyre, N., 2018. An international review of markets for voluntary green electricity tariffs. Renewable and Sustainable Energy Reviews 91, 180–192.

Maciejowska, K., Jędrzejewski, A., Kowalska-Pyzalska, A., Weron, R., 2016. Impact of social interactions on demand curves for innovative products. Acta Physica Polonica A 129, 1045–1049.

Mack, B., Tampe-Mai, K., 2016. An action theory-based electricity saving web portal for households with an interface to smart meters. Utilities Policy, 51–63. https://doi.org/10.1016/j.jup.2016.05.003.

Mack, B., Tampe-Mai, K., Kouros, J., Roth, F., Diesch, E., 2019. Bridging the electricity saving intention-behavior gap: a German field experiment with a smart meter website. Energy Research & Social Science 53, 34–46.

MacPherson, R., Lange, I., 2013. Determinants of green electricity tariff uptake in the UK. Energy Policy 62, 920–933.

Mahmood, N., Zhao, Y., Lou, Q., Geng, J., 2022. Role of environmental regulations and eco-innovation in energy structure transition for green growth: evidence from OECD. Technological Forecasting and Social Change 183. https://doi.org/10.1016/j.techfore.2022.121890.

Mankoff, J., Fussell, S., Dillahunt, T., Glaves, R., Grevet, C., Johnson, M., 2010. StepGreen.org: increasing energy saving behaviors via social networks. In: Proceedings of the International AAAI Conference on Web and Social Media. https://ojs.aaai.org/index.php/ICWSM/article/view/14011.

Marikyan, D., Papagiannidis, S., Alamanos, E., 2019. A systematic review of the smart home literature: a user perspective. Technological Forecasting & Social Change 138, 139–154. https://doi.org/10.1016/j.techfore.2018.08.015.

Martin, M., 2020. Making sense of renewable energy: practical knowledge, sensory feedback and household understandings in a Scottish island microgrid. Energy Research and Social Science 66.

Masini, A., Menichetti, E., 2012. The impact of behavioral factors in the renewable energy investment decision making process: conceptual framework and empirical findings. Energy Policy 40, 23–38.

Matschoss, K., Mikkonen, I., Gynther, L., Koukoufikis, G., Uihlein, A., Murauskaite-Bull, I., 2021. Drawing policy insights from social innovation cases in the energy field. Energy Policy 161. https://doi.org/10.1016/j.enpol.2021.112728.

McKenna, E., Richardson, I., Thomson, M., 2012. Smart meter data: balancing consumer privacy concerns with legitimate applications. Energy Policy 41, 807–814.

McMichael, M., Shipworth, D., 2013. The value of social networks in the diffusion of energy-efficiency innovations in UK households. Energy Policy 53, 159–168.

Meijer, F., Straub, A., Mlecnik, E., 2018. Impact of Home Energy Monitoring and Management Systems (hems): Triple-a: Stimulating the adoption of low-carbon technologies by homeowners through increased awareness and easy access. Report on Impact of HEMS. Interreg, Lille, France.

Mendonca, M., Jacobs, D., Sovacool, B., 2009. Powering the Green Economy: The Feed-in Tariff Handbook. Routledge.

Mengaki, A., 2012. Social marketing mix for renewable energy in Europe based on consumer stated preferences surveys. Renewable Energy 39, 30–39.

Mengolini, A., Vasiljevska, J., Covrig, C., Gangale, F., 2017. Smart Grid Projects Outlook 2017: Facts, Figures and Trends in Europe. European Commission, Joint Research Centre, Publications Office. https://data.europa.eu/doi/10.2760/701587, 2017.

Michie, S., Atkins, L., West, R., 2014. The behaviour change wheel. A guide to designing interventions. Silverback Publishing.

Milciuviene, S., Kiršiene, J., Doheijo, E., Urbonas, R., Milcius, D., 2019. The role of renewable energy prosumers in implementing energy justice theory. Sustainability 11, 5286.

Mittal, A., Krejci, C., Dorneich, M., 2019. An agent-based approach to designing residential renewable energy systems. Renewable and Sustainable Energy Reviews 112, 1008–1020. https://doi.org/10.1016/j.rser.2019.06.034.

Moglia, M., Cook, S., McGregor, J., 2017. A review of agent-based modelling of technology diffusion with special reference to residential energy efficiency. Sustainable Cities and Society 31, 173–182. https://doi.org/10.1016/j.scs.2017.03.006.

Moreno-Munoz, A., Bellido-Outeirino, F., Siano, P., Gomez-Nieto, M., 2016. Mobile social media for smart grids customer engagement: emerging trends and challenges. Renewable & Sustainable Energy Reviews 53, 1611–1616. https://doi.org/10.1016/J.RSER.2015.09.077.

Morganti, L., Pallavicini, F., Cadel, E., Candelieri, A., Archetti, F., Mantovani, F., 2017. Gaming for Earth: serious games and gamification to engage consumers in pro-environmental behaviours for energy efficiency. Energy Research & Social Science 29, 95–102. https://doi.org/10.1016/j.erss.2017.05.001.

Mukai, T., Niskio, K.I., Komatsu, H., Sasaki, M., 2022. What effect does feedback have on energy conservation? Comparing previous household usage, neighbourhood usage, and social norms in Japan. Energy Research & Social Science 86.

Murakami, K., Ida, T., Tanaka, M., Friedman, L., 2015. Consumers' willingness to pay for renewable and nuclear energy: a comparative analysis between the US and Japan. Energy Economics 50, 178–189.

Nachreiner, M., Mack, B., Matthies, E., Tampe-Mai, K., 2015. An analysis of smart metering information systems: a psychological model of self-regulated behavioral change. Energy Research & Social Science 9, 85–97.

Nakamura, E., 2016. Electricity saving behavior of households by making efforts, replacing appliances, and renovations: empirical analysis using a multivariate ordered probit model. International Journal of Consumer Studies 40, 675–684.

Navon, A., Machlev, R., Carmon, D., Onile, A., Belikov, J., Levron, Y., 2021. Effects of the Covid-19 pandemic on energy systems and electric power grids—a review of the challenges ahead. Energies 14 (4), 1056. https://doi.org/10.3390/en14041056.

Negro, S., Alkemade, F., Hekkert, M., 2012. Why does renewable energy diffuse so slowly? A review of innovation system problems. Renewable and Sustainable Energy Reviews 16, 3836–3846.

Neska, E., Kowalska-Pyzalska, A., 2022. Conceptual design of energy market topologies for communities and their practical applications in EU: a comparison of three case studies. Renewable and Sustainable Energy Reviews 169. https://doi.org/10.1016/j.rser.2022.112921.

Nicholson, S., 2015. Recipe for meaningful gamification. In: Gamification in Education and Business. Springer International Publishing, Cham.

Nicolson, M., Huebner, G., Shipworth, D., 2017. Are consumers willing to switch to smart time of use electricity tariffs?: The importance of loss-aversion and electric vehicle ownership. Energy Research & Social Science 23, 82–96.

Nolan, J., Schultz, P., Cialdini, R., Goldstein, N., Griskevicius, V., 2008. Normative social influence is underdetected. Personality and Social Psychology Bulletin 34, 913–923.

Nomura, N., Akai, M., 2004. Willingness to pay for green electricity in Japan as estimated through contingent valuation method. Applied Energy 78, 453–463.

Noonan, D., Hsieh, L., Matisoff, D., 2013. Spatial effects in energy-efficient residential hvac technology adoption. Environment and Behavior 45, 476–503.

Ntanos, S., Kyriakopoulos, G., Chalikias, M., Arabatzis, G., Skordoulis, M., 2018. Public perceptions and willingness to pay for renewable energy: a case study from Greece. Sustainability 10, 687.

Ntanos, S., Kyriakopoulos, G., Skordoulis, M., Chalikias, M., Arabatzis, G., 2019. An application of the new environmental paradigm (NEP) scale in a Greek context. Energies 12. https://doi.org/10.3390/en12020239.

Nyczka, P., Sznajd-Weron, K., 2013. Anticonformity or independence? Insights from statistical physics. Journal of Statistical Physics 151, 174–202.

Nygren, A., Kontio, P., Lyytimaki, J., Varho, V., Tapio, P., 2015. Early adopters boosting the diffusion of sustainable small-scale energy solutions. Renewable and Sustainable Energy Reviews 46, 79–87.

O'Brien, W., Aliabadi, F., 2020. Does telecommuting save energy? A critical review of quantitative studies and their research methods. Energy and Buildings.

O'Connell, N., Pinson, P., Madsen, H., O'Malley, M., 2014. Benefits and challenges of electricity demand response: a critical review. Renewable and Sustainable Energy Reviews 39, 686–699.

OECD 2009. Eco-innovation in industry: enabling green growth. OECD, Paris, ISBN: 978-92-64-07721-8.

Oerlemans, L., Chan, K.Y., Voschenk, J., 2016. Willingness to pay for green electricity: a review of the contingent valuation literature and its source of error. Renewable and Sustainable Energy Reviews 66, 875–885.

Ofgem, 2011. Energy Demand Research Project Final Analysis. London, UK.

Ohnmacht, T., Schaffner, D., Weibel, C., Schad, H., 2017. Rethinking social psychology and intervention design: a model of energy savings and human behavior. Energy Research & Social Science 26, 40–53.

Olmos, L., Ruester, S., Liong, S.J., Glachant, J.M., 2011. Energy efficiency actions related to the rollout of smart meters for small consumers: application to the Austrian system. Energy 36, 4396–4409.

Ozaki, R., 2011. Adopting sustainable innovation: what makes consumers sign up to green electricity? Business Strategy and the Environment 20, 1–17.

Ozawa, A., Furusato, R., Yoshida, Y., 2017. Tailor-made feedback to reduce residential electricity consumption: the effect of information on household lifestyle in Japan. Sustainability 9, 528.

Ozbafli, A., Jenkins, G., 2016. Estimating the willingness to pay for reliable electricity supply: a choice experiment study. Energy Economics 56, 443–452.

Paetz, A.G., Duetschke, E., Fichtner, W., 2012. Smart homes as a means to sustainable energy consumption: a study of consumer perceptions. Journal of Consumer Policy 35, 23–41.

Pagani, G., Aiello, M., 2016. From the grid to the smart grid, topologically. Physica A: Statistical Mechanics and its Applications 449, 160–175.

Pagliuca, M., Panarello, D., Punzo, G., 2022. Values, concern, beliefs, and preference for solar energy: a comparative analysis of three European countries. Environmental Impact Assessment Review. https://doi.org/10.1016/j.eiar.2021.106722.

Palm, A., 2022. Innovation systems for technology diffusion: an analytical framework and two case studies. Technological Forecasting and Social Change 182. https://doi.org/10.1016/j.techfore.2022.121821.

Palmer, J., Sorda, G., Madlener, R., 2015. Modeling the diffusion of residential photovoltaic systems in Italy: an agent-based simulations. Technological Forecasting & Social Change 99, 106–131.

Papachristos, G., 2017. Diversity in technology competition: the link between platforms and sociotechnical transitions. Renewable and Sustainable Energy Reviews 73, 291–306.

Paravantis, J., Stigka, E., Mihalakakou, G., Michalena, E., Hills, J., Dourmas, V., 2018. Social acceptance of renewable energy projects: a contingent valuation investigation in Western Greece. Renewable Energy 123, 639–651.

Peattie, K., Peattie, S., 2009. Social marketing: a pathway to consumption reduction? Journal of Business Research 62, 260–268. https://doi.org/10.1016/j.jbusres.2008.01.033.

Peattie, S., Peattie, K., 2016. Ready to fly solo? Reducing social marketing's dependence on commercial marketing theory. Marketing Theory 3, 365–385. https://doi.org/10.1177/147059310333006.

Peres, R., Muller, E., Mahajan, V., 2010. Innovation diffusion and new product growth models: a critical review and research directions. International Journal of Research in Marketing 27, 91–106.

Perlaviciute, G., Steg, L., 2014. Climate change and individual decision making: an examination of knowledge, risk-perception, self-interest and their interplay. Renewable and Sustainable Energy Review 35, 361–381.

Peters, D., Axsen, J., Mallett, A., 2018. The role of environmental framing in socio-political acceptance of smart grid: the case of British Columbia, Canada.

Renewable and Sustainable Energy Reviews 82, 1939–1951.

Petri, I., Barati, M., Rezgui, Y., Rana, O., 2020. Blockchain for energy sharing and trading in distributed prosumer communities. Computers in Industry 123.

Podgornik, A., Sucic, B., Blazic, B., 2016. Effects of customized consumption feedback on energy efficient behavior in low-income households. Journal of Cleaner Production 130, 25–34.

Pol, E., Ville, S., 2009. Social innovation: Buzz word or enduring term? The Journal of Socio-Economics 38, 878–885.

Ponce-Jara, M., Ruiz, E., Sancristobal, E., Perez-Molina, C., Castro, M., 2017. Smart grid: assessment of the past and present in developed and developing countries. Energy Strategy Reviews 18, 38–52.

Pongiglione, F., 2011. Contextual and psychological factors shaping evaluations and acceptability of energy alternatives: Integrated review and research agenda. FEEM Working Paper, Fondazione Eni Enrico Mattei, 1–27.

Poortinga, W., Steg, L., Vlek, C., Wiersma, G., 2003. Household preferences for energy-saving measures: a conjoint analysis. Journal of Economic Psychology 24, 49–64.

Pratt, B., Erickson, J., 2020. Defeat the peak: behavioral insights for electricity demand response program design. Energy Research & Social Science 61. https://doi.org/10.1016/j.erss.2019.101352.

Primc, K., Ogorevc, M., Slabe-Erker, R., Bartolj, T., Murovec, N., 2021. How does Schwartz's theory of human values affect the proenvironmental behavior model? Baltic Journal of Management 16, 276–297. https://doi.org/10.1108/BJM-08-2020-0276.

Prochaska, J., Diclemente, C., 1982. Transtheoretical therapy: toward a more integrative model of change. Psychotherapy: Theory, Research & Practice 19, 276–288. https://doi.org/10.1037/h008843.

Procter, R.J., 2013. Integrating time-differentiated rates, demand response, and smart grids to manage power system costs. The Electricity Journal 26, 50–59.

Przybyła, P., Sznajd-Weron, K., Weron, R., 2014. Diffusion of innovation within an agent-based model: spinsons, independence and advertising. Advances in Complex Systems 17, 1450004.

Qin, Q., Liang, F., Li, L., Wei, Y., 2017. Selection of energy performance contracting business models: a behavioral decision-making approach. Renewable & Sustainable Energy Reviews 72, 422–433.

Radl, J., Fleischhacker, A., Huglen Revheim, F., Lettner, G., Auer, H., 2020. Comparison of profitability of PV electricity sharing in renewable energy communities in selected European countries. Energies 13.

Raimi, K., Carrico, A., 2016. Understanding and beliefs about smart energy technology. Energy Research & Social Science 12, 68–74.

Ramos, A., Gago, A., Labandeira, X., Linares, P., 2015. The role of information for energy efficiency in the residential sector. Energy Economics 52, S17–S29. https://doi.org/10.1016/j.eneco.2015.08.022.

Rathi, S., Chunekar, A., 2015. Not to buy or can be 'nudged' to buy? Exploring behavioral interventions for energy policy in India. Energy Research & Social Science 7, 78–83.

Razavi, R., Gharipour, A., 2018. Rethinking the privacy of the smart grid: what your smart meter data can reveal about your household in Ireland. Energy Research & Social Science 44, 312–323.

Reis, I., Goncalves, I., Lopes, M., Antunes, C., 2021. Business models for energy communities: a review of key issues and trends. Renewable & Sustainable Energy Reviews 144.

REN21, 2021. Renewables 2021 Global Status Report. Renewable Energy Policy Network for the 21st Century. Paris, France, ISBN 978-3-948393-03-8.

Report, 2022. Meter market outlook, 2027. In: Bonafiede Research, Global Smart. https://www.bonafideresearch.com/product/220349941/global-smart-meter-market. (Accessed 19 January 2023).

Ringler, P., Keles, D., Fichtner, W., 2016. Agent-based modelling and simulation of smart electricity grids and markets – a literature review. Renewable and Sustainable Energy Reviews 57, 205–215.

Rixen, M., Weigand, J., 2014. Agent-based simulation of policy induced diffusion of smart meters. Technological Forecasting and Social Change 85, 153–167.

Robert, J., 2019. What energy communities need from regulation? European Energy & Climate Journal 8, 13–27.

Rodriques-Barreiro, L., Fernandez-Manzanal, R., Serra, L., Carrasquer, J., et al., 2013. Approach to a casual model between attitudes and environmental behavior. A graduate case study. Journal of Cleaner Production 48, 116–125.

Roe, B., Teisl, M., Levy, A., Russell, M., 2001. US consumers' willingness to pay for green electricity. Energy Policy 29, 917–925.

Rogers, E., 2003. Diffusion of Innovations, 5th ed. Free Press, New York.

Ropuszyńska-Surma, E., Weglarz, M., 2016. The pro-economical behavior of households and their knowledge about changes in the energy market. Energy and Fuels 35. E3S Web of Conferences 14, 01006.

Saviotti, P.P., Pyka, A., 2017. Innovation, structural change and demand evolution: does demand saturate? Journal of Evolutionary Economics 27, 337–358. https://doi.org/10.1007/s00191-015-0428-2.

Schleich, J., Faure, C., Klobasa, M., 2017. Persistence of the effects of providing feedback alongside smart metering devices on household electricity demand. Energy Policy 107, 225–233.

Schleich, J., Schuler, J., Pfaff, M., Frank, R., 2022. Do green electricity tariffs increase household electricity consumption? Applied Economics. https://doi.org/10.1080/00036846.2022.2102574.

Schot, J., Kanger, L., Verbong, G., 2016. The roles of users in shaping transitions to new energy systems. Nature Energy 1, 1–7. https://doi.org/10.1038/nenergy.2016.54.

Schuitema, G., Ryan, L., Aravena, C., 2017. The consumer's role in flexible energy systems: an interdisciplinary approach to changing consumers' behavior. IEEE Power & Energy Magazine 15, 53–60. https://doi.org/10.1109/MPE.2016.2620658.

Schultz, P., 2013. Strategies for promoting proenvironmental behavior: lots of tools but few instructions. European Psychologist 23, 1–11.

Schultz, W., Nolan, J., Cialdini, R., Goldstein, N., Griskevicius, V., 2007. The constructive, destructive and reconstructive power of social norms. Psychological Science 18, 429–434.

Schwartz, S., 2012. An overview of the Schwartz theory of basic values. Online Readings in Psychology and Culture 2. https://doi.org/10.9707/2307-0919.1116.

Schwarz, M., Scherrer, A., Hohmann, C., Heiberg, J., Brugger, A., Nuñez-Jimenez, A., 2020. Covid-19 and the academy: it is time for going digital. Energy Research & Social Science 68.

Schweiger, G., Eckerstorfer, L., Hafner, I., Fleischhacker, A., Radl, J., Glock, B., Wastian, M., Rößler, M., Lettner, G., Popper, N., Corcoran, K., 2020. Active consumer participation in smart energy systems. Energy and Buildings 227. https://doi.org/10.1016/j.enbuild.2020.110359.

Shaukat, N., Ali, S., Mehmood., C., 2018. A survey on consumers empowerment, communication technologies, and renewable generation penetration within smart grid. Renewable and Sustainable Energy Reviews 81, 1453–1475.

Sheau-Ting, L., Mohammed, A.H., Weng-Wai, C., 2013. What is the optimum social marketing mix to market energy conservation behaviour: an empirical study. Journal of Environmental Management 15, 196–205. https://doi.org/10.1016/j.jenvman.2013.10.001.

Shen, C., Alberini, A., Timilsina, G., 2022. The impact of Covid-19 on electricity generation: an empirical investigation policy. Research Working Paper, 10116.

© Washington, DC: World Bank. http://localhost:4000//entities/publication/24105fd5-ac0c-528d-8fd0-2406c51e246b.

Sheth, J., 2020. Impact of Covid-19 on consumer behavior: will the old habits return or die? Journal of Business Research 117, 280–283.

Siano, P., 2014. Demand response and smart grids – a survey. Renewable and Sustainable Energy Reviews 30, 461–478.

Sidiras, D., Koukios, E., 2004. Solar systems diffusion in local markets. Energy Policy 32, 2007–2018.

Smaliukiene, R., Monni, S., 2019. A step-by-step approach to social marketing in energy transition. Insights into Regional Development. https://doi.org/10.9770/ird.2019.1.1(2)hal-02115288.

Smith, D., 2006. Exploring Innovation. The McGrew-Hill Companies. New York.

Sohn, K., Kwon, O., 2020. Technology acceptance theories and factors influencing artificial intelligence-based intelligent products. Telematics and Informatics 47. https://doi.org/10.1016/j.tele.2019.101324.

Soon, J., Ahmad, S.A., 2015. Willingly or grudgingly? A meta-analysis on the willingness-to-pay for renewable energy use. Renewable and Sustainable Energy Reviews 44, 877–887. https://doi.org/10.1016/j.rser.2015.01.041.

Sopha, B., Kloeckner, C., 2016. Psychological factors in the diffusion of sustainable technology: a study of Norwegian household's adoption of wood pellet heating. Renewable and Sustainable Energy Review 15, 2756–2765.

Sopha, B., Kloeckner, C., Febrianti, D., 2017. Using agent-based modeling to explore policy options supporting adoption of natural vehicles in Indonesia. Journal of Environmental Policy 52, 149–165.

Sorrell, S., 2015. Reducing energy demand: a review of issues, challenges and approaches. Renewable & Sustainable Energy Reviews 47, 74–82.

Sovacool, B., Furszyfer Der Rio, D., 2020. Smart home technologies in Europe: a critical review of concepts, benefits, risks and policies. Renewable and Sustainable Energy Reviews 120, 109663.

Sovacool, B., Kivimaa, P., Hielscher, S., Jenkins, K., 2017. Vulnerability and resistance in the United Kingdom's smart meter transition. Energy Policy 109, 767–781.

Spandagos, C., Baark, E., Ng, T., Yarime, M., 2021. Social influence and economic intervention policies to save energy at home: critical questions for the new decade and evidence from air-condition use. Renewable & Sustainable Energy Reviews 143.

Star, A., Isaacson, M., Haeg, D., Kotewa, L., 2010. The dynamic pricing mousetrap: why isn't the world beating down our door?. In: ACEEE Summer Study

on Energy Efficiency in Buildings 2010, Proceedings 2, pp. 257–268.

Steg, L., Dreijerink, L., Abrahamse, W., 2005. Factors influencing the acceptability of energy policies: a test of vbn theory. Journal of Environmental Psychology 25, 415–425.

Steg, L., Shwom, R., Dietz, T., 2018. What drives energy consumers?: engaging people in a sustainable energy transition. IEEE Power & Energy Magazine 16, 20–28. https://doi.org/10.1109/MPE.2017.2762379.

Stenner, K., Frederiks, E., Hobman, E., Cook, S., 2017. Willingness to participate in direct load control: the role of consumer distrust. Applied Energy 189, 76–88.

Stern, P., 2000. Towards a coherent theory of significant environmental behavior. Journal of Social Issues 56, 407–424.

Stern, P., 2014. Individual and household interactions with energy systems: toward integrated understanding. Energy Research and Social Science 1, 41–48.

Stigka, E., Paravantis, J., Mihalakakou, G., 2014. Social acceptance of renewable energy sources: a review of contingent valuation applications. Renewable and Sustainable Energy Reviews 32, 100–106.

Strantzali, E., Aravossis, K., 2015. Decision making in renewable energy investments: a review. Renewable & Sustainable Energy Reviews 55, 885–898.

Strbac, G., 2008. Demand-side management: benefits and challenges. Energy Policy 36, 4419–4426.

Strengers, S., 2013. Smart energy technologies in everyday life: smart utopia? Palgrave Macmillan, London https://doi.org/10.1057/9781137267054.

Stummer, C., Kiesling, E., Günther, M., Vetschera, R., 2015. Innovation diffusion of repeat purchase products in a competitive market: an agent-based simulation approach. European Journal of Operational Research 245, 157–167.

Su, W., Liu, M., Zeng, S., Streimikiene, D., Balezenti s, T., Alisauskaite-Seskiene, I., 2018. Valuating renewable microgeneration technologies in Lithuanian households: a study on willingness to pay. Journal of Cleaner Production 191, 318–329.

Summeren, L.V., Wieczorek, A., Verbong, G., 2021. The merits of becoming smart: how Flemish and Dutch energy communities mobilise digital technology to enhance their agency in the energy transition. Energy Research & Social Science 79.

Sundt, S., Rehdanz, K., 2015. Consumers' willingness to pay for green electricity: a meta-analysis of the literature. Energy Economics 51, 1–8.

Sundt, S., Rehdanz, K., Meyerhoff, J., 2020. Consumers' willingness to accept time-of-use tariffs for shifting electricity demand. Energies 13.

Sung, B., Park, S.D., 2018. Who drives the transition to a renewable-energy economy? Multi-actor perspective on social innovation. Sustainability 10, 448–480.

Sznajd-Weron, K., Szwabiński, J., Weron, R., 2014a. Is the person-situation debate important for agent-based modeling and vice-versa? PLoS ONE 9 (11), e112203.

Sznajd-Weron, K., Szwabiński, J., Weron, R., Weron, T., 2014b. Rewiring the network. What helps an innovation to diffuse? Journal of Statistical Mechanics: Theory and Experiment, P03007.

Słupik, S., Kos-Łabędowicz, J., Trzęsiok, J., 2021. How to encourage energy savings behaviours? The most effective incentives from the perspective of European consumers. Energies 14. https://doi.org/10.3390/en14238009.

Tabi, A., Hille, S., Wüstenhagen, R., 2014. What makes people seal the green power deal? — Customer segmentation based on choice experiment in Germany. Ecological Economics 107, 206–215.

Tahir, M., Chen, H., Khan, A., Javed, M., Cheema, K., Laraik, N., 2020. Significance of demand response in light of current pilot projects in China and devising a problem solution for future advancements. Technology in Society 63. https://doi.org/10.1016/j.techsoc.2020.101374.

Taylor, N., Jones, P., Kipp, M., 2014. Targeting utility customers to improve energy savings from conservation and efficiency program. Applied Energy 115, 25–36.

Thakur, J., Chakraborty, B., 2019. Impact of compensation mechanisms for pv generation on residential consumers and shared net metering model for developing nations: a case study of India. Journal of Cleaner Production 218, 696–707.

Thorsens, P., Williams, J., Lawson, R., 2012. Consumer responses to time varying prices for electricity. Energy Policy 49, 552–561.

Thøgersen, J., 2017. Housing-related lifestyle and energy saving: a multi-level approach. Energy Policy 102, 73–87. https://doi.org/10.1016/j.enpol.2016.12.015.

Tiefenbeck, V., Staake, T., Roth, K., Sachs, O., 2013. For better or for worse? Empirical evidence of moral licensing in a behavioral energy conservation campaign. Energy Policy 57, 160–171.

Trotta, G., 2020. Electricity awareness and consumer demand for information. https://doi.org/10.1111/ijcs.12603.

Turner, M., Kitchenham, B., Brereton, P., Charters, S., Budgen, D., 2010. Does the technology acceptance model predict actual use? A systematic literature review. Information and Software Technology 52, 463–479.

Umpfenbach, K., Esparrago, J., Tomescu, M., Kampman, B., Vendrik, J., Naber, N., George, J., Winkler, J.,

Breitschopf, B., 2022. Energy prosumers in Europe citizen participation in the energy transition. European Environment Agency (ed.), EEA Report No 01/2022. Publications Office of the European Union, Luxembourg. https://doi.org/10.2800/030218.

Valor, C., Antonetti, P., Crisafulli, B., 2022. Emotions and consumers' adoption of innovations: an integrative review and research agenda. Technological Forecasting and Social Change 179. https://doi.org/10.1016/j.techfore.2022.121609.

Venkatesh, V., Thong, J., Xu, X., 2012. Consumer acceptance and use of information technology: extending the unified theory of acceptance and use of technology. Management Information Systems Quarterly 36, 157–178. https://doi.org/10.2307/41410412.

Verbong, G., Beemsterboer, S., Sengers, F., 2013. Smart grids or smart users? Involving users in developing a low carbon electricity economy. Energy Policy 52, 117–125.

Vitiello, S., Andreadou, N., Ardelean, M., Fulli, G., 2022. Smart metering roll-out in Europe: where do we stand? Cost benefit analyses in the clean energy package and research trends in the green deal. Energies 15. https://doi.org/10.3390/en15072340.

Voelker, B., Reinhardt, A., Faustine, A., Pereira, L., 2021. Watt's up at home? Smart meter data analytics from a consumer-centric perspective. Energies 14, 719.

de Vries, G., Boon, W., Peine, A., 2016. User-led innovation in civic energy communities. Environmental Innovation and Societal Transitions 19, 51–65. https://doi.org/10.1016/j.eist.2015.09.001.

Vázquez-Canteli, J., Nagy, Z., 2019. Reinforcement learning for demand response: a review of algorithms and modeling techniques. Applied Energy 235, 1072–1089. https://doi.org/10.1016/J.APENERGY.2018.11.002.

Wallenborn, G., Orsini, M., Vanhaverbeke, J., 2011. Household appropriation of electricity monitors. International Journal of Consumer Studies 35, 146–152.

Wang, S., Fan, J., Zhao, D., Yang, S., Fu, Y., 2016. Predicting consumers' intention to adopt hybrid electric vehicles: using an extended version of the theory of planned behavior model. Transportation 43, 123–143.

Warkentin, M., Goel, S., Menard, P., 2017. Shared benefits and information privacy: what determines smart meter technology adoption? Journal of the Association for Information Systems 18. https://doi.org/10.17705/1jais.00474.

Webb, D., Soutar, G., Mazzarol, T., Saldaris, P., 2013. Self-determination theory and consumer behavioral change: evidence from a household energy-saving behavior study. Journal of Environmental Psychology 35, 59–66.

Weiser, P., Bucher, D., Cellina, F., Luca, V., 2015. A taxonomy of motivational affordances for meaningful gamified and persuasive technologies. In: Proceedings of EnviroInfo and ICT for Sustainability 2015. Atlantis Press.

Weiss, T., Diesing, M., Krause, M., Heinrich, K., Hilbert, A., 2016. Effective Visualizations of Energy Consumption in a Feedback System – a Conjoint Measurement Study. International Conference on Business Information Systems, Business Information System. Springer International Publishing.

van der Werff, E., Steg, L., 2016. The psychology of participation and interest in smart energy systems: comparing the value-belief-norm theory and the value-identity-personal norm model. Energy Research & Social Science 22, 107–114.

Weron, T., Kowalska-Pyzalska, A., Weron, R., 2018. The role of educational trainings in the diffusion of smart metering platforms: an agent-based modeling approach. Physica A, Statistical Mechanics and its Applications 505, 591–600.

Wicki, L., Pietrzykowski, R., Kusz, D., 2022. Factors determining the development of prosumer photovoltaic installations in Poland. Energies 15. https://doi.org/10.3390/en1516589.

Wilson, C., Downlatabadi, H., 2007. Models of decision making and residential energy use. Annual Review of Environment and Resources 32, 169–203. https://doi.org/10.1146/annurev.energy.32.053006.141137.

Wiser, R., 2007. Using contingent valuation to explore willingness to pay for renewable energy: a comparison of collective and voluntary payment vehicles. Ecological Economics 62, 419–432.

Wittmayer, J., Hielscher, S., Fraaije, M., Avelino, F., Rogge, K., 2022. A typology for unpacking the diversity of social innovation in energy transitions. Energy Research & Social Science 88. https://doi.org/10.1016/j.erss.2022.102513.

Wolsink, M., 2014. Distributed generation of sustainable energy as a common pool resource: social acceptance in rural setting of smart (micro-) grid configurations. In: Frantál, B., Martinát, S. (Eds.), New Rural Spaces: Towards Renewable Energies, Multifunctional Farming, and Sustainable Tourism. University of Amsterdam, Amsterdam, the Netherlands.

Wolsink, M., 2020. Distributed energy systems as common goods: socio-political acceptance of renewables in intelligent microgrids. Renewable & Sustainable Energy Reviews 127, 109841.

Wood, G., Day, R., Creamer, E., van der Horst, D., Hussain, A., Liu, S., Shukla, A., Iweka, O., Gaterell, M., Petridis, P., Adams, N., Brown, V., 2019. Sensors, sense-making and sensitivities: UK household experiences with a feedback display on energy consumption and indoor environmental conditions. Energy Research and Social Science 55, 93–105.

Wuestenhagen, R., Bilharz, M., 2006. Green energy market development in Germany: effective public policy and emerging customer demand. Energy Policy 34, 1681–1696.

Wuestenhagen, R., Wolsink, M., Buerer, M., 2007. Social acceptance of renewable energy innovation: an introduction to the concept. Energy Policy 35, 2683–2691.

Xie, B., Zhao, W., 2018. Willingness to pay for green electricity in Tianjin, China: based on the contingent valuation method. Energy Policy 114, 98–107.

Yadav, R., Pathak, G., 2016. Young consumers' intention towards buying green products in a developing nation: extending the theory of planned behavior. Journal of Cleaner Production 135, 732–739.

Yavuz, L., Önen, A., Muyeen, S., Kamwa, I., 2019. Transformation of microgrid to virtual power plant – a comprehensive review. IET Generation, Transmission & Distribution 13, 1994–2005.

Yoo, S.H., Kwak, S.Y., 2009. Willingness to pay for green electricity in Korea: a contingent valuation study. Energy Policy 37, 5408–5416.

Yue, T., Long, R., Chen, H., 2013. Factors influencing energy-saving behavior of urban households in Jiangsu Province. Energy Policy 62, 665–675.

Zabkowski, T., Gajowniczek, K., 2013. Smart metering and data privacy issues. Information Systems in Management 2, 239–249.

Zarnikau, J., 2003. Consumer demand for green power and energy efficiency. Energy Policy 31, 1661–1672.

Zeng, L., Yu, Y., Li, J., 2014. China's promoting energy-efficient products for the benefit of the people program in 2012: results and analysis of the consumer impact study. Applied Energy 133, 22–32.

Zeppini, P., Frenken, K., Izquierdo, L.R., 2013. Innovation diffusion in networks: the microeconomics of percolation. Working paper 13.02. Eindhoven Center for Innovative Studies.

Zhang, H., Vorobeychik, Y., Letchford, J., Lakkaraju, K., 2015. Data-driven agent-based modeling, with application to rooftop solar adoption. In: Proceedings of the International Joint Conference on Autonomous Agents and Multiagent Systems, AAMAS, pp. 513–521.

Zhang, L., Wu, Y., 2012. Market segmentation and willingness to pay for green electricity among urban residents in China: the case of Jiangsu Province. Energy Policy 51, 514–523.

Zhang, T., Nuttall, W.J., 2011. Evaluating government's policies on promoting smart metering diffusion in retail electricity markets via agent-based simulation. Journal of Product Innovation Management 28, 169–186.

Zheng, M., Meinrenken, C., Lackener, K., 2014. Agent-based model for electricity consumption and storage to evaluate economic viability of tariff arbitrage for residential sector demand response. Applied Energy 126, 297–306.

Zhong, H., Tan, Z., He, Y., Xie, L., Kang, C., 2020. Implications of Covid-19 for the electricity industry: a comprehensive review. CSEE Journal of Power and Energy Systems 6.

Zhou, K., Yang, S., 2016. Understanding household energy consumption behavior: the contribution of energy big data analytics. Renewable and Sustainable Energy Reviews 56, 810–819.

Zhou, S., Brown, M., 2017. Smart meter deployment in Europe: a comparative case study on the impacts of national policy schemes. Journal of Cleaner Production 144, 22–32.

Zhou, Y., Chen, H., Xu, S., Wu, L., 2018. How cognitive bias and information disclosure affect the willingness of urban residents to pay for green power? Journal of Cleaner Production 189, 552–562.

Zoric, J., Hrovatin, N., 2012. Household willingness to pay for green electricity in Slovenia. Energy Policy 47, 180–187.

Index

A
Acceptance, 79, 89, 90, 107, 112, 114, 165, 169, 170
  community, 115
  consumers, 115, 117
  customers, 115
  IES, 153
  innovation, 114, 136
  market, 115
  smart metering, 115
  social, 107, 114, 115, 129, 153, 161
Adoptable energy conservation, 170
Adoption, 38, 39, 41, 57, 58, 63, 78, 79, 86, 108, 122, 124, 125, 127, 128, 167, 188, 189
  barriers, 193
  behavior, 58, 82, 96, 121
  decisions, 57
  energy behaviors, 95
  households, 110
  IES, 81, 117, 151
  innovation, 55, 57–59, 64, 165
  market, 37
  obstacles, 180
  outweigh, 154
  perceived difficulty, 121, 150, 193, 194
  process, 28, 55, 57, 58, 60, 87, 96
  rates, 69, 70, 115, 143, 144, 151, 193
  willingness, 184
Advanced metering infrastructure (AMI), 13
Agent-based model, 149
Agent-based modeling, 64
Aggressive renewable energy, 15
Annual energy savings obligations, 9
Annual household energy consumption, 40

Artificial intelligence (AI), 13, 126
Attitudes environmental, 121

B
Barriers, 28, 32, 107–109, 183, 194, 195
  adoption, 193
  environmental, 152
  market, 110
Battery electric vehicles (BEV), 3
Behavior
  adoption, 58, 82, 96, 121
  change, 79, 83, 85, 86, 176
  change acceptance, 183
  consumers, 77, 114, 149, 166, 172, 199
  environmental, 95, 122–124, 128, 140
  intention, 82
Behavior change wheel (BCW), 83, 85
Behavioral
  change, 24, 27, 45, 78, 83, 85, 86, 138, 140, 143, 156, 169, 173, 177, 183
  innovation, 77
  intention, 81, 90, 91
Business models, 107, 113, 189–192, 198, 205
Business models for
  prosumers, 31
  renewable energy, 110

C
Cheap renewables, 36
Clean energy, 25
Clean Energy Packaging (CEP) framework, 25
Clean energy transition, 25
Cognitive barriers, 155
Collective prosumers, 31
Community
  acceptance, 115

energy, 31, 146, 192
  prosumerism, 192
Compact fluorescent lamps (CFL), 171
Companies supplying electricity, 136
Compound annual growth rate (CAGR), 40, 192
Conjoint analysis (CA), 109
Conserving energy, 122
Consumers, 1–3, 21, 22, 55–57, 77, 78, 107, 109, 165–167
  acceptance, 115, 117, 120, 121
  access, 47, 188
  adoption rates, 57
  attitudes, 137, 149, 153, 196
  awareness, 59, 142
  behavior, 77, 114, 149, 166, 172, 199
  behavior change, 172
  benefit, 66
  better control, 25
  choice, 80, 129
  confidence, 148
  decisions, 180
  demographics, 58
  durable goods, 62
  education, 198
  electricity, 1, 2, 5, 10, 16, 17, 21, 24, 37, 47, 114
  electricity consumption, 126
  energy, 87
  energy demand, 21
  energy usage, 174
  engagement, 28, 128, 145
  engagement in energy conservation, 143
  expresses, 142
  feel responsible, 95
  groups, 174
  inattention, 169
  indifference, 69, 147
  insignificant, 144
  interact, 38